Home-Based
Services
for Troubled
Children

Child, Youth, and Family Services

Edited by
Ira M. Schwartz and
Philip AuClaire

Home-Based
Services
for Troubled
Children

University of Nebraska Press

Lincoln and London

© 1995 by the University of Nebraska Press
All rights reserved
Manufactured in the United States of America
⊗ The paper in this book meets
the minimum requirements of American National
Standard for Information Sciences –
Permanence of Paper for Printed Library Materials,
ANSI Z39.48-1984.
Library of Congress Cataloging in Publication Data
Home-based services for
troubled children / edited by Ira M. Schwartz and
Philip AuClaire. p. cm. –
(Child, youth, and family services) Includes biblio-
graphical references and index.
ISBN 0-8032-4217-4   1. Problem children –
Services for – United States.
2. Juvenile delinquents – Services for – United States.
3. Home-based family services – United States.
4. Child welfare – Government policy – United States.
I. Schwartz, Ira M.   II. AuClaire,
Philip.   III. Series.   HV881.H66   1995
362.7′4–dc20   94-45167 CIP

To Elaine

A Great Teacher

Contents

Foreword

Much has been written about the crisis in child welfare in the United States. However, the most accurate description of the state of child welfare services was made by the National Commission on Children (1991) when the commission observed, "If the nation had deliberately designed a system that would frustrate the professionals who staff it, anger the public who finance it, and abandon the children who depend on it, it could not have done a better job than the present child welfare system" (p. 293).

Child welfare professionals, federal, state, and local elected public officials, private foundations, child advocacy groups, professional associations, and public interest organizations are desperately searching for effective strategies to reform child welfare. While little progress has been made in this area to date, there is growing support for family preservation services as a primary tool for preventing the out-of-home placement of children. This book brings together some of the best thinking about family preservation and family support services. It should be helpful to those interested in strengthening services to children and families.

In Chapter 1, Kathleen Wells examines the origins, history, and contemporary issues pertaining to family-based services. Her chapter documents the fact that family-based services is not a particularly new concept. She also explores some of the critical ethical dilemmas and issues that such services present.

Chapter 2, by Jill Kinney and Kelly Dittmar, describes the nationally recognized Homebuilders model of family preservation services and some of the research about that method of intervention.

In Chapter 3, Elizabeth Tracy, James Whittaker, Francis Boylan, Paul Neitman, and Edward Overstreet discuss the value of social support network interventions, drawing upon their research at Boysville of Michigan. They report that social support network interventions must be individualized to each family; they also note that such interventions, though promising, are not a panacea and must be offered in collaboration with other vital services to families. The authors also introduce the notion that social support services may need to be provided to families at different points along the service delivery continuum.

Robert Halpern, in Chapter 4, discusses some of the benefits from more general family support services. Halpern explores the family support services research, the implications that the research has for policy, and the role that such services might play in the service delivery continuum.

Chapters 5 and 6 examine the role of family-based services with delinquent youth, a topic of growing interest. Scott Henggeler and Charles Borduin report on their groundbreaking work using a multisystemic treatment approach with serious juvenile offenders. Jeffrey Butts and William Barton describe the results from an experiment testing intensive home-based probation services as an alternative to commitment to a state youth corrections agency. In each instance, the researchers report that intensive home-based services appear to be an effective approach to working with seriously delinquent youth without compromising public safety.

Chapter 7 explores some of the policy and systemic issues that need to be considered when trying to assess the impact of family preservation strategies. Ira M. Schwartz uses child welfare data and experiences from the state of Michigan to highlight the policy, administrative, political, and social variables that can affect a child welfare system. His main point is that the impact of family preservation interventions must be examined in a broader context; otherwise, the probabilities are high that outcome findings will be incomplete or misleading.

Chapter 8 examines some of the critical fiscal issues pertaining to home-based services. Sandra O'Donnell and Ronald D. Davidson explore such issues as government contracting for services, financing strategies, and ways to maximize federal and state resources. This chapter should be particularly helpful to policymakers and administrators in the public and private sectors.

Reference

National Commission on Children. (1991). *Beyond rhetoric: A new American agenda for children and families (Final Report).* Washington DC: Author.

Acknowledgments

This book would not have been possible were it not for the cooperation and hard work of many people. We are grateful to the authors who met deadlines and never complained, and to Marti Smith, who typed and coordinated the development of the manuscript. Her prior experience in managing similar projects made the process flow smoothly and efficiently. Geza Hrazdina, an outstanding graduate student, critiqued the chapters, offered valuable suggestions about how they could be strengthened, and assisted with the editing process. Danielle Hogston, the administrator of the Center for the Study of Youth Policy, generated the index and assumed responsibility for assembling the final document. More importantly, she and Marti Smith provided the moral support we needed to complete this task.

Home-Based
Services
for Troubled
Children

Family Preservation Services in Context: Origins, Practices, and Current Issues

Kathleen Wells

This chapter is an overview of family preservation services: their origins and practices as well as some of the policy, ethical, and research issues they raise. The focus here is upon *intensive family preservation services,* as opposed to family-based services in general or other services designed to preserve or to reunify families. This restriction allows the discussion to be tied to one treatment model; it is not intended to equate family preservation efforts with one approach.

As employed here, family preservation services refer to services designed to prevent the out-of-home placement of children—that is, the placement of children in foster care, group homes, residential treatment centers, psychiatric hospitals, and correctional institutions. Although prevention of child placement is a primary goal of these services, the focus of treatment is the child's family. Relying upon a wide range of interventions, services are delivered in families' homes, for as many hours as are needed, over a relatively brief period of time.

The earliest family preservation services programs were launched in the early 1970s (Bryce, 1988) in part due to concern over the high number of children in out-of-home placement (Shyne & Schroeder, 1978), the negative effects of placement on children and families, and the high cost of out-of-home care. These concerns, coupled with the presumed success of early family preservation services programs (Kinney, Madsen, Fleming, & Haapala, 1977), spurred the development of family preservation services. In addition, the federal government and many state governments passed legislation during this time to allow public monies to pay for such services. Thus, it is not surprising that the number of family preservation services programs has increased over the last 15 years. Although the current number of such programs is unknown, their expansion has no doubt mirrored that of family-based programs in general: For example, the National Resource Center on Family-Based Services listed 20 programs in their 1982 program directory and 269 in their 1988 directory, the most recent available directory (National Resource Center on Family-Based Services, 1988).

This expansion has been due to several factors, including the following: (1) Family preservation services are grounded in unassailable values—the importance of having children grow up with their own parents and of child and family self-sufficiency; (2) providers have actively promoted the use of these services; (3) the family preservation concept has been aided and developed by prominent American foundations, most notably the Edna McConnell Clark Foundation (Nelson, 1988b); and (4) preservation services are compatible with the emergent emphasis in public policy upon permanency planning, treatment of children in the least restrictive environment possible, and provision of community-based treatment programs in the child welfare, mental health, and juvenile justice systems, respectively.

Therefore, it is not surprising that there is widespread agreement that family preservation services have an important role to play in systems serving children. However, at this point of service expansion and empirical knowledge, a critical evaluation of the issues relevant to their implementation and further expansion is clearly needed. Their expansion poses serious policy dilemmas, and their implementation raises ethical issues. Also, the accumulating evidence that family preservation services are not equally effective or appropriate for all families with children at risk of out-of-home placement suggests programmatic and research questions. My assumption here is not that family preservation services should be eliminated but rather that they should not be expanded without attention to some of the dilemmas, issues, and questions raised in this chapter.

This chapter begins this evaluation by first defining family preservation services and then tracing their historical antecedents, theoretical underpinnings, and the impetus for their development. Then, based upon all of the above, some of the salient issues raised by this analysis are delineated.

Definition of Family Preservation Services

There is no consensus as to the exact nature of family preservation services (Whittaker & Tracy, 1988). However, two service models are well known and have been replicated widely: the learning theory–based Homebuilders model and the family systems theory–based Iowa model (Nelson, 1988a). Chapter 2 presents a description of the Homebuilders model and clarifies the kinds of services under discussion.

Not all programs adhere to the Homebuilders model or, for that matter, to the Iowa model, which emphasizes a family systems approach to treatment. Indeed, family preservation services vary with respect to their goals, organization and structure, and role in a community. Nelson (1988a) has identified a set of dimensions, drawn from the program evaluation literature, that could be used to describe this variability. These include: the developmental stage of the program (e.g., the number of years the program has been in operation), the organizational structure of the program (e.g., its location in a public or private agency), the duration of the program (e.g., the average length of time families spend in the program), the staffing pattern of the program (e.g., the number of workers assigned to a family), and the mechanisms in place for assessment and case planning.

In spite of the diversity in programs, family preservation services share some underlying assumptions: that enhanced family functioning is the vehicle through which individual problems and needs should be addressed; that services provided at home and as needed enhance workers' understanding of families and increase the likelihood that they can help families change; that an integrated response to both the concrete (e.g., housing) and social-psychological (e.g., marital difficulty) problems of families is necessary to family preservation; and that a time-limited service conveys to families a belief in their own capabilities (Nelson, 1988b).

Additionally, family preservation services share some common features. Pecora and his colleagues (Pecora, Fraser, Haapala, & Barlome, 1987) have identified a set of 14 attributes of these services. The most central of these features are that services last no more than 90 days; services are provided two to three times a week for one to four hours at a time; services are routinely provided in the home; workers are available 24 hours a day for emergency visits or calls; families are provided with "concrete" services; and service providers encourage family empowerment and believe that most children are better off in their own homes.

3

These shared assumptions and common features of family preservation services render them a unique and new service delivery model. Yet several key concepts pertinent to family preservation services were anticipated by child welfare practices and trends emerging at the turn of the century (McGowan, 1988).

Historical Antecedents of Family Preservation Services

The earliest and most direct precursor of family preservation services was the use of "friendly visitors" by charity organizations in the last century (McGowan, 1988). The Charity Organization Movement, begun in 1869 in London, sought to rationalize philanthropy. The purpose of the charity organization societies—which soon sprang up in American cities—was to coordinate philanthropic resources so that worthy cases would be provided with relief. Originally, the intent was to promote more efficient administration of private charities; however, they eventually came to provide relief with their own funds. In this effort, they used volunteers "to visit, counsel, and instruct the poor; . . . [these] friendly visitors were expected to be combination detectives and moral influences. They were to ascertain the reason for the applicants' need and to help them overcome it" (Bremner, 1971, p. 52). Anticipating contemporary reactions to family preservation services, Boston's Irish-American poet John Boyle O'Reilly "wrote scathingly of 'The organized charity scrimped and iced / In the name of a cautious, statistical Christ'" (Bremner, 1971, p. 53).

In the early part of the century, some methods employed by friendly visitors became part of the newly developing social work practice. Frankel (1988) noted that "The first generation of professional caseworkers, like their voluntary predecessors, operated almost exclusively through home visits. They were primarily concerned with the provision of concrete services and recognized the advantages of home visits for both accurate observation and putting the family at ease. Considerable time and energy were also spent in mobilizing natural helping networks and coordinating services" (p. 139). Thus some of the features of family preservation services have been a part of social work practice for a long time.

About the same time that social work was emerging as a profession, several broad concepts pertinent to the development of family preservation services were emerging as well (McGowan, 1988). For example, the development of Societies for the Prevention of Cruelty to Children in the 1870s

4

helped establish the concepts of "state intervention in family life" and "minimal acceptable standards of parenting." Other pertinent concepts included the establishment of the juvenile court in 1899, the concept of differential treatment of child and adult offenders, the Child Guidance Clinic Movement, which started around 1910, and the concept of treating children within the context of their "natural environments" (Glasscote, Fishman, & Sonis, 1972).

However, it was not until the Family Centered Project of St. Paul (Geismar, 1957; Stinson & Associates, 1955), which was launched in the early 1950s, that the basic approach taken by family preservation services providers today emerged. This project was one of several in the United States at that time concerned with treatment of multiproblem families—families who were "overwhelmed by multiple problems, and . . . were unlikely to respond favorably to requests for introspection," the technique required for psychodynamic treatment approaches in use at the time (Wood & Ludwig, 1989, p. 65).

This project developed in St. Paul partly in response to a community survey that revealed that 6% of St. Paul's recipients of social welfare services used about half of such services in the community. Community leaders believed that an effort had to be made to reduce the disproportionate use of services by such families. The project that evolved focused upon families with children who were in clear and present danger and depended upon what was called a family-centered approach. In this approach, the focus of treatment was the family, considered as a unit, and services were delivered at home. Workers took responsibility for all of a family's psychosocial needs. Although this approach was conceptualized as long-term treatment, grounded in the traditional casework principles of the time, project staff used a range of intervention techniques distinguished by their directness (e.g., "expressing to the families matters of community concern" and "sharing diagnostic impressions with clients"), experimental nature (e.g., "we realized we did not know enough about . . . what goes on in the total family interaction"), and emphasis upon the families as partners in the helping process. The project also attempted to develop mechanisms to coordinate the community resources available for such families.

The results of the St. Paul project were encouraging (Geismar, 1957); Bryce (1988) observed that the project's in-house evaluations revealed that about two thirds of their families improved. Bryce further noted that "These rather impressive results encouraged the public sector to field several projects with multi-problem families in ensuing years. However, these programs differed significantly from the St. Paul project and therefore the results were not encouraging" (p. 183).

It is not clear why the St. Paul project was not widely replicated with precision, though the staff's own characterization of the project hints at one reason: "We are trying to narrow down the numbers of families we cannot successfully treat. Maybe the essential newness [of the project] is in the optimism. Maybe the essential opposition to saying there's anything new comes from a sense of not having arrived anywhere" (Stinson & Associates, 1955, p. 15).

Indeed, the project and the interventions tried were not only new but were rather radical within the context of the child welfare system of the time and the individually oriented treatment approaches that dominated agency practice in the 1950s. Their effort was also bold, for in the absence of well-developed models of family treatment and behavioral change, they groped to develop concepts pertaining to family systems and parent-child relationships that are taken for granted today. It is probably not an accident that family preservation services did not emerge until the 1970s, after such models had been developed.

Theoretical Underpinnings of Family Preservation Services

In fact, family preservation services draw upon several theoretical perspectives that gained prominence between 1950 and 1970. Barth (1988) identified social learning theory, family systems theory, crisis intervention theory, and ecological perspectives on child development as providing the major theoretical underpinnings of family preservation services. The following section relies upon his analysis.

Prior to elucidating how each of these perspectives is reflected in family preservation services, it is important to note that even well-articulated family preservation services models such as Homebuilders are not developed fully so that the connections made between theory and practice are an evolving rather than to a finished practice approach. Programs also vary in the extent to which they draw upon each theory.

SOCIAL LEARNING THEORY

Social learning theory (e.g., Bandura, 1977) treats behavior as a function

6

of the reciprocal interaction between individual and environmental determinants. These determinants are not considered fixed but rather are viewed as potentials. An individual's behavior will partly determine which environmental potential will be activated and vice versa. In this theory, "symbolic, vicarious, and self-regulatory processes assume a prominent role" (Bandura, 1977, p. 12) as codeterminants of behavior. A common method for understanding behavior is the analysis of dyadic exchanges. This approach allows one to identify the ways in which the behavior of one member triggers a particular behavioral response in the other that, in turn, offers a counteraction "that mutually shapes the social milieu in a predictable direction" (Bandura, 1977, p. 198).

Barth (1988) identifies the two major contributions of social learning to practice as the rejection of "the belief that changes in thinking and feeling necessarily antecede changes in behavior . . . [and] their grasp of the way that family members learn from each other" (p. 97). Working within this perspective, practitioners have devised a number of strategies (e.g., use of "time-out," development of contracts, practicing cognitive restructuring, training in self-management skills) (Barth, 1988) that have been applied to families in conflict by family preservation services providers (Kinney et al., 1977).

FAMILY SYSTEMS THEORY

Family systems theory (e.g., Satir, 1967) is linked to various forms of family therapy and cannot be considered apart from therapeutic approaches that have developed within this tradition (Barth, 1988). Structural family therapy (Minuchin, 1974) is an approach widely used by providers of family preservation services. In this approach, the individual is understood within his or her social context, particularly the context of the family. Minuchin identified the underlying assumptions of this treatment: An individual's psychic life is not entirely an internal process; changes in family structure (i.e., position) contribute to changes in the behavior and the inner psychic processes of the members of the family system; and when a therapist works with a family, he or she enters the family system.

Interventions focus upon ways of altering the interactions of family members. The focus of intervention is the family system. The goal is to modify family functioning through altering the positions of family members. The therapist "joins" the system in order to change how it functions. To effect this change, the therapist relies on properties of the system that are conceptualized in terms of such variables as boundaries, alignment, and power. It is hypothesized that the family has self-regulating mechanisms so that once a change occurs, it will be perpetuated.

The emphasis of family systems theory upon improving family functioning through altering the position of family members is compatible with the perspective of many family preservation services providers, although it is social learning theory that has provided much technology for the clinical interventions employed.

CRISIS THEORY

According to most crisis theorists (e.g., Caplan, 1964), individuals who are not experiencing a crisis handle day-to-day stress with the resources they have available. A crisis occurs when there is an "imbalance between the perceived difficulty and significance of a threatening situation and the coping resources available to an individual" (Cohen & Nelson, 1983, p. 14). Although failure to resolve a crisis can lead to psychopathology, a crisis is considered a normal response to a threatening external event—a response that is expected to last four to six weeks. A variety of variables, such as an individual's coping skills and social support, are believed to mediate an individual's capacity to respond effectively to a crisis. Individuals in crisis are believed to be highly motivated to obtain help and highly susceptible to change.

Crisis intervention techniques follow from these assumptions. There is no effort to diagnose an individual's problem; rather, the effort is to understand the characteristics of the precipitating event, the individual's efforts at mastery and coping skills, and the social support available. Treatment is brief, typically no more than twelve sessions, and is directed at reducing symptoms and returning the individual to his or her precrisis state. Therapists are often paraprofessionals; they attempt to establish a collegial relationship with their clients and work to connect individuals to other sources of support in their communities.

The underlying assumptions of family preservation services—that the threat of placing a child outside the home constitutes a crisis, that during this crisis the child's family is more open to change than in other periods, that a speedy response to a family's request for help is critical, and that the goal of

8

intervention is not to cure psychopathology but rather to return families to their precrisis state—are all compatible with crisis theory.

ECOLOGICAL "THEORY"

Ecological theory (e.g., Bronfenbrenner, 1979) is less a theory and more a perspective. Its "principal use has been as a framework for organizing knowledge, generating research questions and evaluating social policy" (Garbarino, 1982, p. 13). Taking ecology as its guiding metaphor, this perspective emphasizes the interdependence of individuals and events in the social world. In this view, the social world is composed of systems that provide the multiple contexts in which a child develops. The child is construed as an active organism who shapes and responds to not only the family system but also those of the peer group, the school, the neighborhood, and the church. These "microsystems" are, in turn, affected by larger systems, such as cultural belief systems, and the relationships among them. The strength of the links between systems (e.g., between the child's home and school) affect child development, with weak links putting a child's development at risk. Inadequate social resources and cultural impoverishment are conditions reflecting weak links within and across systems and have been identified by Garbarino (1982) as major risks to a child's development. He believes they undermine the values and beliefs upon which child competence is built.

Germain and Gitterman (1980) have also applied this perspective to the relationship between practitioners and their clients. They stressed the importance of evaluating the impact of agency structure and functions, professional attitudes toward clients, and social definitions of status and role upon the help provided to families in need.

The emphasis upon evaluating the impact of the environment on a family's functioning, providing advocacy services to make the systems of which a family is a part more responsive to its needs, and taking on advocacy efforts for classes of families in the larger society is compatible with an ecological perspective. Family preservation services programs, however, vary widely in the extent to which these features play a prominent role in the services they provide (Barth, 1988).

The grounding of family preservation services in contemporary social science contributes to the enthusiasm with which these services have been met and helps explain why a number of family preservation–like programs

9

emerged at about the same time. For example, the Home and Community Treatment program, designed to prevent re-placement of children discharged from residential treatment, began in 1969. The Lower East Side Family Union program, developed to provide services to very poor, minority families with children at risk of placement in foster care, began in 1972. The Families, Inc., program to prevent placement of children in juvenile justice system institutions began in 1974 (Bryce, 1988).

Impetus for the Development of Family Preservation Services

The impetus for the development of family preservation services extended beyond the availability of practical knowledge needed to implement a new approach. Such services emerged out of concern over the placement problem bolstered by critiques of a wide range of existing societal values, institutions, and practices that were all part of the social ferment of the 1960s and 1970s.

THE PLACEMENT PROBLEM

Between 1900 and the late 1950s, the child welfare system was a relatively small, independent, and reactive system oriented to providing services to children outside their own homes.

The first major critique of this system was presented with the publication of *Children in Need of Parents* (Maas & Engler, 1959), a study of children in foster care (McGowan, 1988). This study documented that few efforts were made to keep children in their own homes and that three quarters of the children who entered foster care were unlikely to return home. In spite of the consensus among child welfare professionals reached early in the century (*Proceedings of the Conference on the Care of Dependent Children*, 1909) and in spite of federal policies (most notably Titles IV and V of the Social Security Act of 1935) intended to keep children at home (McGowan, 1983), the foster care system was providing long-term care rather than temporary placements for children of families who could not function as a unit (McGowan, 1988).

The findings from the Maas and Engler study were confirmed in studies conducted in the 1960s and 1970s (Stein, 1987), and during this same time other investigations were conducted. These studies revealed that half of the foster care children had no services prior to their placement (Vasaly, 1976, cited in Bryce, 1988) and many faced the same problems that led to their placement after they returned home (Turner, 1984).

These lines of research converged to highlight the importance of working with the families of children at risk of placement in foster care and to support emerging conceptualizations of permanency planning (Maluccio, Fein, & Olmstead, 1986), which emphasized not only discharging children in foster care either to their own parents or to adoptive parents but also preventing out-of-home placement. Family preservation services were both supported by the permanency planning movement and perceived as an integral part of services needed to achieve its goals.

The impetus for the development of family preservation services within the child mental health system grew out of a concern over the quality of institutionally based treatment for children and the necessity of treatment for all children who were placed, rather than the placement of children in residential and inpatient services per se. Concern over treatment of disturbed children was expressed as early as 1909 when the White House Conference on Children that year called attention to their needs (U.S. Congress, 1986). However, it was not until the Report of the 1969 Joint Commission on the Mental Health of Children, *Crisis in Child Mental Health,* that attention was focused upon the quality of care hospitalized children received. The commission report (Joint Commission on Mental Health of Children, 1969) noted: "There are a few superb institutions in the country, many are marginal; however, most are disgraceful and intolerable" (p. 42). It went on to state that the nation had neither the trained personnel nor the funds to provide the residential care needed. Not surprisingly, the 1978 President's Commission on Mental Health called for, among other things, an increase in high-quality residential services.

The publication of *Children Without Homes* (Knitzer, Allen, & McGowan, 1978), an evaluation of the conditions of children who were in foster care, treatment institutions, and correctional facilities, raised not only the issue of the quality of treatment but also the appropriateness of hospital treatment for some children. The study authors concluded that as many as 40% of hospital placements were unsuitable, that few alternatives to such treatment existed for severely disturbed children, and that the available services were poorly coordinated.

The lack of community-based mental health services and the fragmentation of services for emotionally disturbed children had been of longstanding concern to mental health professionals (Glasscote, Fishman, & Sonis, 1972). After the initial success of such services in averting foster care placement in the child welfare system, family preservation services came to be viewed as an integral part of the continuum of services that should be available to severely emotionally disturbed children (Stroul & Friedman, 1986).

In the 1960s and 1970s, concerns were also raised regarding the effectiveness and fairness of the juvenile justice system. The issue of effectiveness centered on the ability of the system to prevent recidivism. The issue of fairness centered on its ability to apply appropriate and standardized penalties to juveniles, especially those who committed nonserious crimes and status offenses (Hawkins & Doueck, 1987). There was also a growing consensus as to the importance of avoiding labeling youth as "delinquent" and of preventing their movement into the adult prison system.

These concerns contributed to the passage of the 1974 Juvenile Justice and Delinquency Prevention Act, one provision of which authorized the use of federal funds to divert some juvenile offenders from juvenile justice system institutions to alternative community-based treatment programs. Alternatives, within the context of juvenile justice system reforms, were defined generally as residential treatment centers, group or foster homes, halfway houses, and adolescent units in psychiatric hospitals.

The influential 1975 National Assessment of Juvenile Corrections Study (Vinter, Downs, & Hall, 1975) contributed to this movement. Study authors concluded: "Nothing we learned in this study challenges the criticisms leveled against traditional institutions for the handling of juvenile offenders or the argument that community-based corrections are more economical and probably at least as effective" (p. 79).

Anticipating later criticisms of the deinstitutionalization movement, they also noted "we are troubled with the evidence that community modes of corrections can so readily result in expansion of the system rather than serving primarily as substitutes for institutions" (p. 79). It was not until the mid-1980s (Hawkins, 1984), however, that family preservation services were considered as one type of community-based treatment program for youth in the juvenile justice system.

SOCIETAL TRENDS AND SUPPORTIVE LEGISLATION

In addition to concern over the drift of children in foster care, the placement of children in inadequate and overly restrictive residential and inpatient treatment, and the movement of status offenders into the youth prison system, there were a variety of societal trends that facilitated the development of family preservation services. These included: the deinstitutionalization movement and its emphasis upon treatment of children in community-based programs; the child advocacy movement and the establishment of various groups concerned with the interests of children; the initiation of class action lawsuits to obtain rights of and to protect benefits for various client groups; and the development of adoptive and foster care parent groups devoted to providing adoption opportunities for children considered hard to place (McGowan, 1988).

The social ferment of the 1960s and 1970s that the above movements imply contributed to the passage of a variety of federal laws that supported concepts such as "community-based treatment" (e.g., the 1963 Community Mental Health Centers Act, the Juvenile Justice and Delinquency Prevention Act of 1974), "continuum of care" (e.g., the 1980 Mental Health Systems Act), "treatment in the least restrictive environment" (e.g., the 1975 Education for All Handicapped Children Act), and children as an "underserved group" (e.g., the 1981 Alcohol and Drug Abuse and Mental Health Services Block Grant) that indirectly furthered the development of family preservation services. In the early 1980s, legislation was passed that authorized the creation of the 1983 Child and Adolescent Service System Program at the National Institute of Mental Health, which broadened the concept of what constitutes a mental health treatment.

By 1992, the only federal legislation that directly supported the development of these services was the Adoption Assistance and Child Welfare Act of 1980. This act was intended "to insure that reasonable efforts are made to prevent placement, to arrange placement in the most appropriate setting, and to discharge children to permanent homes in a timely manner" (McGowan, 1988, p. 77). This act "created incentives for more widespread development of the various types of preventive or family preservation services that had started to evolve in different localities" (p. 77).[1]

Issues Raised by Family Preservation Services

In part, due to the moral mandate expressed in the 1980 child welfare legislation and the fiscal incentives for family preservation services created by this legislation, by 1990 family preservation services had been implemented, albeit spottily, in three of the major systems serving children and families—child welfare, mental health, and juvenile justice—and were operating in about half the states (Ooms & Beck, 1990). Yet, the first wave of enthusiasm for family preservation services had also ebbed by 1990, and some of the difficult questions were being raised pertaining to their significance. Although there is considerable overlap among the policy, ethical, and research questions and issues raised by family preservation services, for ease of presentation, they are presented separately below.

Central to the debate that should occur pertaining to family preservation services are three broad ethical issues that such services raise. First is the issue of what risks to child safety should one be willing to take in order to keep a child's family intact. Current policies are contradictory. For example, the Child Abuse Prevention and Treatment Act of 1974 mandates reporting of child abuse, and the 1980 Adoption Assistance and Child Welfare Act mandates family autonomy (McGowan, 1988). While there is no single answer to the dilemma posed, the success at resolution may depend ultimately upon the efficiency with which children in genuine danger can be protected by the state. In fact, McGowan (1988) has noted that in order to maintain the integrity of family preservation services, child protection laws must be strengthened.

The second ethical issue is the extent to which family preservation services should be a mandated treatment. This is a particularly salient issue for services provided within the context of the juvenile justice system. In this context, juvenile offenders are held to be both "accountable and redeemable," and family preservation services are ordered by a court as an alternative to placement of a child in an institution.

Traditionally, psychological treatment in this country has been conceptualized as occurring within the context of a relationship between a healer and a patient that has been established with the full and informed consent of both parties. The expectation is that the healer will guide the patient through a process that will alleviate the patient's suffering. However, the process is considered valuable in its own right, offering support and the potential for enhanced self-awareness; it is also assumed that the healer does not have a vested interest in the client's adherence to specific goals and, indeed, that the patient may develop personal goals that could not have been anticipated at the beginning of treatment.

Although many families in the child welfare, child mental health, and juvenile justice systems are, by definition, subject to social control, the impact of mandating treatment upon its effectiveness is unclear. What happens to the nature of the therapeutic relationship between service providers and their clients or, for that matter, to service effectiveness when treatment is ordered by a court is not well delineated. At least one concern raised by such practice is that the mandated treatment will force the adoption of values and goals, within the context of a coerced treatment, that are not those of clients, and that a family's right to privacy will be violated. Indeed, the very intrusiveness (and limited evidence with respect to effectiveness) of family preservation services makes this issue particularly important for consideration by the field.

The third ethical issue raised by family preservation services is their role in what should be a larger effort to address the plight of an increasing number of American families in need of food, a home, and medical care. Since 1980, there has been an increase in the percentage of children and youth living in poverty, an increase in the percentage of children and youth living in female-headed single-parent families, and a decline in the types of basic services available in the public and private domain (Burt & Pittman, 1985). The Children's Defense Fund (1988) reported that in 1988 one in four children was poor, one in five was at risk of becoming a teen parent, one in six had no health insurance, one in seven was at risk of dropping out of school, and one in two had a working mother, but few had high-quality child care. McGowan (1988) has aptly observed that "there seems to be a cruel irony in the fact that those who have long argued the need to provide services designed to maintain children in their own homes are being given the opportunity to demonstrate the viability of this approach at the very time when obstacles to family preservation are mounting" (p. 78).

It goes without saying that family preservation services can neither solve the problems of poverty and cultural impoverishment nor serve as substitutes for the long-term care and treatment some children need. At some level, the question becomes: What kind of resources are we willing to commit toward ensuring constructive and developmentally appropriate environments for all American children and their families?

Indeed, the type and distribution of all services to children and families will involve increasingly difficult choices because of the deteriorating state of the American economy. For example, in 1988, after accounting for federal expenditures for defense, Social Security, Medicare, and interest payments on the federal debt, there were fewer funds, relative to the GNP (Gross National Product), for all other federally funded activities (e.g., transportation, education, social services) than at any time since the early 1960s (Minarik, 1988). Minarik notes: "[B]ecause of the defense buildup and the growth of net interest, the continued expansion of Social Security and Medicare necessarily squeezed other domestic spending. Yet there was virtually no discussion or debate of the merits of this path relative to any conceivable alternative" (p. 10). This debate should include an evaluation of the requirements for healthy families, considered in the broadest possible context, and the role of public and private sectors in promoting the well-being of families.

RESEARCH ISSUES

Determining the recipients of family preservation services involves ethical, programmatic, and research issues. This section focuses on some of the research issues, specifically the nature of extant evidence regarding the target population for, and the effectiveness of, preservation services.

Family preservation services have been offered primarily as an alternative to out-of-home placement for those families who meet criteria for entrance into programs (see Kinney et al., 1977). In order to document that these services are functioning in this capacity, one would need evidence that they have been offered to children who would have been placed without these services, and that the placement prevention rates found are due to involvement in these programs.

The evidence pertaining to both of these issues is limited, as is often the case for social-psychological services. Indeed, the empirical base for intensive and restrictive services for children is very limited. The intent here is not to hold family preservation services accountable to a higher research standard than other services but to argue for a more cautious approach to the interpretation of data than has sometimes been taken.

A complete review of the literature is beyond the scope of this chapter. Instead, the discussion relies upon a review of a dozen widely cited investigations in this area, illustrating some of the limitations of the family preservation services research literature.[2]

FAMILIES SELECTED FOR SERVICES

Criteria for entrance into family preservation services programs vary. However, the six criteria developed for the Homebuilders program (Kinney et al., 1977) are illustrative: At least one family member must express the desire to keep the family together; no key family member can refuse the option that the family stay together; the family must be in a crisis state; the child must be at risk of imminent placement out of his or her home; parents must sign a consent form; and the family must not pose a danger to the Homebuilders staff. (In a later article, Kinney and her colleagues (Kinney, Haapala, Booth, & Leavitt, 1988) indicated that noninvolvement in a drug culture on the part of the parents might be another criterion for entrance into Homebuilders programs.)

While it is clear that not all of the children approved for placement would qualify for family preservation programs, we do not have any information as to what portion of the population of children approved for placement would meet entrance criteria. This limits our ability to estimate the potential impact of these programs.

In addition, in order to demonstrate that family preservation services are working as alternatives to placement for the families served, it is necessary to demonstrate that families had children who would have been placed without these programs. The evidence with respect to this point is inadequate and suffers from several limitations. First, as Tracy's (1991) review of approaches taken to the definition of "at risk of imminent placement" suggests, the definitions employed vary widely, and they could even be considered bureaucratic as opposed to clinical designations. Second, even within the context of a single program, in the articles reviewed there was no evaluation that attempted to establish the reliability of judgments of "at risk of imminent placement." And third, some studies indicate that not all children who are identified as needing placement, according to any criteria, will, in fact, be placed. For example, in one study 28% of the children who were referred to, but not served by, the Homebuilders program (because the program was full) were not placed (Kinney et al., 1988). Changing definitions of "at risk of imminent placement" and consequences of this designation make interpretation of placement prevention rates for those who are served difficult.

A final issue remains to be cast as a research question: Is it always in the child's best interest to remain at home? In the articles reviewed, there was no investigation that attempted to assess whether remaining at home was in the child's best interest, or whether the child needed long-term treatment and/or treatment provided in a residential or inpatient setting. Therefore, the presumption that all children who meet the criteria for participation in family preservation services should remain at home and be treated with family preservation services has not yet been tested. While this presumption is consistent with American values regarding families and findings from child development research regarding the ideal context for child development, the presumption may not be valid for some few children. The point here is not that the presumption should be abandoned but that the exceptions to this "rule" must not be overlooked.

EFFECTIVENESS OF FAMILY PRESERVATION SERVICES

The effectiveness of family preservation services has primarily been discussed in terms of the percentage of children who remain at home at the end of a program (or some months posttreatment), the difference in the percentage of family preservation children and children receiving traditional services who remain at home after service termination, and the cost of providing a family with family preservation services relative to the cost of out-of-home care. A thorough cost analysis of family preservation services has not yet been done (Whittaker & Tracy, 1988) and would be difficult to do (Magura, 1981). Major limitations of this literature are its failure to acknowledge differences in the costs of differing types of out-of-home placements that children may use and its failure to take into account the auxiliary and support services that families may need after service termination.

A literature is accumulating with respect to the effectiveness issue, and it, too, is inadequate. Two sets of investigations of service effectiveness will illustrate some of the limitations of this literature. Since 1982, the Homebuilders program staff has tracked all their clients up to one year after intake; they report that 88% of children served were not placed out of the home for two or more weeks during that time (Kinney et al., 1988). However, without a control group, without assessments of the reliability of judgments of "at risk of imminent placement," and without information pertaining to the policy context in which programs were operating, especially the number of placements that were available in communities and their stability over time, these studies do not demonstrate that 88% of the children who remained at home would have been placed without the intervention *or* that the program is responsible for the placement rates found. Moreover, these studies, as reported in the 1988 report, do not address well the issue of how children and their families are actually functioning posttreatment, as the studies do not employ multiple indicators of success, multiple informants, or data analysis techniques that take into account regression effects.

Information on how children and their families are functioning is particularly important for family preservation services research because longitudinal research (see Barth & Berry, 1987) based on programs that share some features of family preservation services has called attention to the possibility that neglected and abused children who remain at home may be subject to higher rates of abuse than similar children who are placed in foster care. It is not clear if such findings will be replicated for family preservation services and for other populations, but they underscore the need for the inclusion of comprehensive developmental assessments of at-risk children who remain at home as well as children who are in placement.

Studies that have included more rigorous controls (AuClaire & Schwartz, 1986, 1987; Feldman, 1991; Yuan, 1990) suggest that family preservation services may reduce child placement in the short run but that their effectiveness diminishes over time. AuClaire and Schwartz (1986, 1987) found that 56% of children who entered family preservation services were placed during the study period (12 months postintake), compared to 59% of children in the nontreatment comparison group. However, there were statistically significant differences between the two groups in terms of the type of placements used and the number of days spent in placement. Children in family preservation services used more emergency shelter placements and spent fewer days in placement than did comparison children. Feldman (1991) found that 13% of children receiving these services were placed outside the home at the end of service, compared to 26% of comparison children. However, at 12 months postdischarge, 46% of family preservation services children were placed, compared to 58% of comparison children. Yuan (1990) found that within eight months from the date of referral, 25% of family preservation families experienced a placement, compared to 20% of comparison group families.

It is difficult to interpret differences found among studies because it is likely that characteristics of the families, the programs in which they were involved, the service system context in which programs were operating, and different approaches to the definition of placement all affected placement outcomes. Indeed, studies of the correlates of placement (see Fraser, Pecora, & Haapala, 1988) suggest some child-related variables (e.g., prior inpatient psychiatric placement and age of the child) that might account for differences in placement rates. In addition, the overall rate of children entering placement in a community may not be affected by even highly successful family preservation programs because some of the factors affecting placement (e.g., poverty) are unaffected by these programs.

In sum, as the high percentages of children who remain at home after service provision suggest, family preservation services hold real promise for preventing the out-of-home placement of children. Yet it is also true that many questions remain regarding the proportion of the population at risk of out-of-home placement that can be served and the long-term consequences of service provision. Therefore, we need to exercise caution when describing the scope and effectiveness of services. Moreover, the effectiveness of services should be considered in light of criteria for entrance into the programs, the clinical and other characteristics of families served, hypothesized limitations of the crisis-oriented treatment model upon which these services depend, and the scientific limitations of the investigations upon which effectiveness data depend (Wells & Biegel, 1991).

FUTURE RESEARCH

There are some pressing decisions with respect to societal values and priorities that need to be debated before a coherent research agenda for children and family services in general, and family preservation services in particular, can be formulated.

However, a range of research initiatives could be undertaken at the system, community, and program levels to inform the development of such an agenda. Indeed, there is some consensus in the field that research is needed in several areas (Wells & Biegel, 1990, 1991, 1992). Longitudinal investigations pertaining to the use of family preservation services within each system are needed to illuminate the consequences of differing contexts and populations upon the outcomes of family preservation services.[3] Investigations pertaining to the implementation of services within a local context would illuminate the ways in which family preservation services can be introduced into a community and their impact upon use of other services. Investigations pertaining to individual program functioning and effectiveness would illuminate issues pertaining to implementation and replicability. In addition, careful descriptions of families that have failed and those families that have succeeded are especially needed to develop more clinically sophisticated hypotheses than have been tested to date.

POLICY ISSUES

Nelson (1988b) has noted that in order to make the case for the policy relevance of family preservation services, the affordability, replicability, and effectiveness of these services must be demonstrated. As suggested in prior sections, the evidence is insufficient with respect to all three.

Therefore, this section identifies some of the policy issues pertinent to the development and support of family preservation services because of the strong moral foundation upon which such services rest and the initial positive short-term results of service provision for some samples of families. The first issue pertains to the feasibility of the implementation of family preservation services within the context of public agencies (Frankel, 1988). Until quite recently, these services have been implemented largely within the context of private agencies. Family preservation services do not fit easily into existing public agencies: They focus upon families (not individuals) and a wide range of needs; they demand small caseloads; they assume that workers will exert control over key clinical functions—diagnosis, treatment, and follow-up; and they require worker familiarity with the community context of families in need—its resources and limitations. These features may be difficult to transport to large bureaucratic systems. Clearly, policies will have to be developed to provide the administrative support upon which faithful replication of family preservation services depend (Knitzer & Cole, 1989).

In fact, a wide variety of state-level policies pertaining to the implementation of family preservation services have been tried (Knitzer & Cole, 1989). These policies revolve around the role of state leadership in promoting services, the extent to which services are being expanded under careful planning, approaches to reimbursement for the family preservation services, and arrangements for promoting cross-system collaboration with respect to funding and referrals. Yet several areas of cross-system collaboration have not been exploited fully—areas such as linking family preservation services to services provided in schools, services provided through the Family Support Act of 1988 (Knitzer & Cole, 1989), services provided through the Education of the Handicapped Act Amendments of 1986, and services provided "through the 1986 and 1988 set-asides for maternal substance abuse treatment in the Alcohol and Drug Abuse Mental Health Administration Block Grant Program" (Ooms & Beck, 1990, p. 24).

The final policy issue pertains to the potential of family preservation services to act as a catalyst for reform. As Knitzer and Cole (1989) have noted, "in the broadest sense, . . . [family preservation services] represent an effort to shift the ecology of the service system for troubled children and families away from a placement orientation to one where home-based alternatives are equally available. . . . Perhaps most importantly, the family preservation 'movement' has called our attention to the possibility of success in a field where too often, either with or without evidence, the threshold assumption is that nothing works" (pp. 27–28).

However, the majority of policy initiatives pertaining to family preservation services have not been part of a larger plan to reform systems serving children (Knitzer & Cole, 1989). To achieve this potential, what is needed is a comprehensive child and family service system that includes a wide range of preventive, crisis-oriented, and treatment and support services for children and families. Kamerman and Kahn (1989), in their review of patterns of service delivery in public social service agencies, have identified a range of policies that would support such reform. They caution against a reliance upon services that are "targeted" for specific groups and the promotion of one type of service (e.g., family preservation services) through the denigration of another (e.g., the foster care system). Such practices are exclusionary and work against the development of a comprehensive system of services for children.

This overview of family preservation services covers origins and practices and raises some policy, ethical, and research issues. It points to the challenge for individuals involved in family preservation services: to assess what can be learned from this important initiative to keep more American children with their families than is currently the case and to elaborate what has been learned into proposals for reforms that are needed to enhance family and child functioning in light of the commitments we want to make to all American children.

Notes

1. New federal legislation was passed in August 1993 to strengthen troubled families. Hailed as the most significant reform of federally funded child welfare services since the Adoption Assistance and Child Welfare Act of 1980 [P.L. 96-272], the Omnibus Budget Reconciliation Act of 1993 [P.L. 103-66] provides $1 billion to the states, over a five-year period, for early intervention, prevention, and family support services (Binder, 1993). The legislation calls specifically for family preservation services.

2. Recent reviews of intensive family preservation services include one by myself in *Child Welfare* (1994) and one by Rossi (1992) in *Children and Youth Services Review*. The literature I review here includes reports available through roughly early 1992. Some have not been subjected to peer review (e.g., reports from state departments of human services); see Knitzer & Cole (1989) for a list of some recent outcome studies that have been conducted as a part of a state evaluation effort. As a result, this literature has not been subjected to as much scientific scrutiny, effort to integrate findings, and debate as has literature pertaining to more established services.

3. Adequate attention has not been paid to differences in outcome expected as a function of the system in which services are provided. While the focus and purpose of family preservation services within the child welfare system are well described, they have been altered when services have been transported to and described in the language of other systems. However, the overriding purposes of these systems differ, and the impact of these differences upon the target and goals of family preservation services has not been debated. For example, a major limitation of the child mental health system is its inability to provide services to all the children who need them, whereas a major limitation of the juvenile justice system is its inability to reduce the number of children under its purview. The implications of these differing contexts for service provision need to be delineated. Indeed, it may be asking too much of services designed to stabilize family crises to achieve meaningful treatment goals (one major purpose of the child mental health system) in some populations of severely emotionally disturbed children, or to eliminate recidivism (one major purpose of the juvenile justice system) with some chronic juvenile offenders.

References

Adoption Assistance and Child Welfare Act of 1980, 42 U.S.C. § 670.

Alcohol and Drug Abuse and Mental Health Services Block Grant Program of 1981, 42 U.S.C. § 300x et seq.

AuClaire, P., & Schwartz, I. (1986). *An evaluation of the effectiveness of intensive home-based services as an alternative to placement for adolescents and their families.* Minneapolis: University of Minnesota, Center for the Study of Youth Policy, Hubert H. Humphrey Institute of Public Affairs.

AuClaire, P., & Schwartz, I. (1987). *Home-based services as an alternative to placement for adolescents and their families: A follow-up study of placement utilization.* Minneapolis: University of Minnesota, Center for the Study of Youth Policy, Hubert H. Humphrey Institute of Public Affairs.

Bandura, A. (1977). *Social learning theory.* Englewood Cliffs NJ: Prentice-Hall.

Barth, R. (1988). Theories guiding home-based intensive family preservation services. In J. Whittaker, J. Kinney, E. Tracy, & C. Booth (Eds.), *Improving practice technology for work with high risk families: Lessons from the "Homebuilders" Social Work Education Project* (Monograph No.6, pp.91–113). Seattle: University of Washington, Center for Social Welfare Research.

Barth, R., & Berry, M. (1987). Outcomes of child welfare services under permanency planning. *Social Services Review, 61,* 71–90.

Binder, H. (1993, Fall). Federal update. *Front Line Views* (Newsletter of the Intensive Family Preservation Services National Network), 1 (1), p. 3.

Bremner, R. (1971). *From the depths: The discovery of poverty in the United States.* New York: New York University Press.

Bronfenbrenner, U. (1979). *The ecology of human development: Experiments by nature and design.* Cambridge: Harvard University Press.

Bryce, M. (1988). Family-based services: Preventive intervention. In D. H. Olson (Ed.), *Family perspectives in child and youth services* (pp. 177–203). New York: Haworth Press.

Burt, M., & Pittman, K. (1985). *Testing the social safety net.* Washington DC: Urban Institute.

Caplan, G. (1964). *Principles of preventive psychiatry.* New York: Basic Books.

Child Abuse Prevention and Treatment Act of 1974, 42 U.S.C. § 5101.

Children's Defense Fund. (1988). *A call for action to make our nation safe for children: A briefing book on the status of American children in 1988.* Washington DC: Author.

Children's Defense Fund. (1991). *S.4, The Child Welfare and Preventive Services Act.* Washington DC: Author.

Cohen, L., & Nelson, D. (1983). Crisis intervention: An overview of theory and technique. In L. Cohen, W. Claiborn, & G. Specter (Eds.), *Crisis intervention* (2nd ed., Vol. 4). New York: Human Sciences Press.

Community Mental Health Centers Act of 1963, 42 U.S.C. § 2681–2687.

Education for All Handicapped Children Act of 1975, 20 U.S.C. § 1400n, 1401n.

Education of the Handicapped Act Amendments of 1986, 20 U S.C. § 400.

Family Support Act of 1988, 42 U.S.C. § 1305n.

Feldman, L. (1991). Evaluating the impact of intensive family preservation services in New Jersey. In K. Wells & D. Biegel (Eds.), *Family preservation services: Research and evaluation* (pp. 47–71). Newbury Park CA: Sage.

Frankel, H. (1988). Family-centered, home-based services in child protection: A review of the research. *Social Service Review, 62,* 137–157.

Fraser, M., Pecora, P., & Haapala, D. (1988). *Families in crisis: Findings from the family-based intensive treatment project* (Final Report for Grant No. 90-CW-0731, Office of Human Development Services, Administration for Children, Youth and Families). Salt Lake City: University of Utah, Graduate School of Social Work.

Garbarino, J. (1982). *Children and families in the social environment.* New York: Aldine.

Geismar, L. (1957). *The family centered project of St. Paul* (Report to the research section of the Kansas Conference of Social Work). (Available from the Minnesota Historical Society, St. Paul.)

Germain, C., & Gitterman, A. (1980). *The life model of social work practice.* New York: Columbia University Press.

Glasscote, R., Fishman, M., & Sonis, M. (1972). *Children and mental health centers.* Washington DC: Joint Information Service of the American Psychiatric Association and the National Association for Mental Health.

Hawkins, J. D. (1984). *Executive summary of the ADAMHA/OJJDP state-of-the-art research conference on juvenile offenders with serious drug, alcohol and mental health problems.* Seattle: University of Washington, Center for Social Welfare Research.

Hawkins, J. D., & Doueck, H. J. (1987). Juvenile offender diversion and community-based services. In A. Minahan (Ed.), *Encyclopedia of Social Work* (Vol. 2, pp. 10–15). Silver Spring MD: National Association of Social Workers.

Joint Commission on Mental Health of Children. (1969). *Crisis in child mental health: Challenge for the 1970's* (Report of the Joint Commission on Mental Health of Children). New York: Harper & Row.

Juvenile Justice and Delinquency Prevention Act of 1974, 42 U.S.C. § 5601.

Kamerman, S., & Kahn, A. (1989). *Social services for children, youth and families in the U.S.* New York: Columbia University, School of Social Work.

Kinney, J., Haapala, D., Booth, C., & Leavitt, S. (1988). The Homebuilder model. In J. Whittaker, J. Kinney, E. Tracy, & C. Booth (Eds.), *Improving practice technology for work with high risk families: Lessons from the "Homebuilders" Social Work Edu-*

cation Project (Monograph No. 6, pp. 37–68). Seattle: University of Washington, Center for Social Welfare Research.

Kinney, J. M., Madsen, B., Fleming, T., & Haapala, D. A. (1977). Homebuilders: Keeping families together. *Journal of Consulting and Clinical Psychology, 45*(4), 667–673.

Knitzer, J., Allen, M., & McGowan, B. (1978). *Children without homes: An examination of public responsibility to children in out-of-home care.* Washington DC: Children's Defense Fund.

Knitzer, J., & Cole, E. (1989). *Family preservation services: The policy challenge to state child welfare and child mental health systems.* New York: Bank Street College of Education.

Maas, H., & Engler, R. (1959). *Children in need of parents.* New York: Columbia University Press.

Magura, S. (1981). Are services to prevent foster care effective? *Children and Youth Services Review, 3,* 193–212.

Maluccio, A., Fein, E., & Olmstead, K. (1986). *Permanency planning for children: Concepts and methods.* New York: Tavistock.

McGowan, B. (1983). Historical evolution of child welfare services: An examination of the sources of current problems and dilemmas. In B. McGowan & W. Meezan (Eds.), *Child welfare* (pp. 45–90). Itasca IL: F. E. Peacock.

McGowan, B. (1988). Family-based services and public policy: Context and implications. In J. Whittaker, J. Kinney, E. Tracy, & C. Booth (Eds.), *Improving practice technology for work with high risk families: Lessons from the "Homebuilders" Social Work Education Project* (Monograph No. 6, pp. 69–89). Seattle: University of Washington, Center for Social Welfare Research.

Mental Health Systems Act of 1980, 42 U.S.C. § 9401.

Minarik, J. (1988). Fiscal reality and exploding myths. *Challenge: The Magazine of Economic Affairs, 31*(4), 4–13.

Minuchin, S. (1974). *Families and family therapy.* Cambridge: Harvard University Press.

National Resource Center on Family-Based Services. (1988). *Annotated directory of selected family-based service programs* (6th ed.). Iowa City: University of Iowa, School of Social Work, Author.

Nelson, K. (1988a). Program organization description. In Y. Y. Yuan & M. Rivest (Eds.), *Evaluation resources for family preservation services* (pp. 23–42). Alexandria VA: Center for the Support of Children.

Nelson, K. (1988b). Recognizing and realizing the potential of "family preservation." In J. Whittaker, J. Kinney, E. Tracy, & C. Booth (Eds.), *Improving practice technology for work with high risk families: Lessons from the "Homebuilders" Social Work Education Project* (Monograph No. 6, pp. 19–35). Seattle: University of Washington, Center for Social Welfare Research.

Omnibus Budget Reconciliation Act of 1993, P.L. 103–66.

Ooms, T., & Beck, D. (1990). *Keeping troubled families together: Promising programs and statewide reform.* Washington DC: Family Impact Seminar, American Association for Marriage and Family Therapy Research and Education Foundation.

Pecora, P. J., Fraser, M. W., Haapala, D., & Barlome, I. A. (1987). *Defining family preservation services: Three intensive home-based treatment programs* (Research Rep. No. 1). Salt Lake City: University of Utah, Social Research Institute.

Proceedings of the conference on the care of dependent children (Vol. 13), 60th Cong., 2nd sess., 1909, S. Doc.

Rossi, P. (1992). Assessing family preservation programs. *Children and Youth Services Review, 14,* 77–97.

Satir, V. (1967). *Conjoint family therapy* (rev. ed.). Palo Alto CA: Science and Behavior Books.

Shyne, A., & Schroeder, A. (1978). *National study of social services to children and their families* (Publication No. OHDS 78-30150). Washington DC: U.S. Department of Health, Education and Welfare.

Social Security Act of 1935, Title IV-B, 42 U.S.C. § 620 et seq.

Stein, T. (1987). Foster care for children. In A. Minahan (Ed.), *Encyclopedia of Social Work* (Vol. 1, pp. 639–650). Silver Spring MD: National Association of Social Workers.

Stinson, M., & Associates. (1955). *What are we up to in St. Paul?* Paper presented at the meeting of the Twin City Chapter of the American Association of Social Workers, St. Paul.

Stroul, B., & Friedman, R. (1986). *A system of care for severely emotionally disturbed children and youth.* Washington DC: CASSP Technical Assistance Center, Georgetown University Child Development Center.

Tracy, E. (1991). Defining the target population for family preservation services: Some conceptual issues. In K. Wells & D. Biegel (Eds.), *Family preservation services: Research and evaluation* (pp. 138–158). Newbury Park CA: Sage.

Turner, J. (1984). Reuniting children in foster care with their biological parents. *Social Work, 29*(6), 501–505.

U.S. Congress, Office of Technology Assessment. (1986). *Children's mental health:*

Problems and services—A Background Paper (OTA-BP-H-33). Washington DC: U.S. Government Printing Office.

Vinter, R., Downs, G., & Hall, J. (1975). *Juvenile corrections in the states: Residential programs and deinstitutionalization* (Preliminary Report). Ann Arbor: University of Michigan, Institute of Continuing Legal Education.

Wells, K. (1994). A reorientation to knowledge development in family preservation services: A Proposal. *Child Welfare, 73*(5), 475–488.

Wells, K., & Biegel, D. (1990). *Intensive family preservation services: A research agenda for the 1990s. Brief report from the Intensive Family Preservation Services National Research Conference.* Cleveland: Bellefaire/Jewish Children's Bureau.

Wells, K., & Biegel, D. (1991). Conclusion. In K. Wells & D. Biegel (Eds.), *Family preservation services: Research and evaluation* (pp. 241–250). Newbury Park CA: Sage.

Wells, K., & Biegel, D. (1992). Intensive family preservation services research: Current status and future agenda. *Social Work Research and Abstracts, 28*(1), 21–27.

Whittaker, J., & Tracy, E. (1988). Family preservation services and education and social work practice: Stimulus and response. In J. Whittaker, J. Kinney, E. Tracy, & C. Booth (Eds.), *Improving practice technology for work with high risk families: Lessons from the "Homebuilders" Social Work Education Project* (Monograph No. 6, pp. 9–18). Seattle: University of Washington, Center for Social Welfare Research.

Wood, K., & Ludwig, L. (1989). *Families at risk.* New York: Human Sciences Press.

Yuan, Y. Y. (1990). *Evaluation of AB 1562 in-home care demonstration projects: Volume 1* (Final report). Sacramento CA: Walter McDonald & Associates.

2

Homebuilders:
Helping Families Help Themselves

Jill Kinney and Kelly Dittmar

When we opened the Homebuilders[1] program in Tacoma, Washington, in 1974, most of us thought families whose children were placed outside the home were probably hopeless. We presumed that those families probably did not really care about their children and did not deserve to have them. At that time, all child welfare workers had high caseloads. Large amounts of time and expertise for children had typically been available only in residential settings. We did not know what would happen if we allocated similar resources to children while they were in their own homes.

During our work over the past 20 years, our clients have shown us that even seriously troubled families have more capacity for growth than we had previously dreamed. Now, Homebuilders is recognized as a pioneer in a unique social service known as *intensive family preservation* and has helped to guide an international movement to strengthen families. The Homebuilders experience is not only a story of the ability of people to change their lives; it is also a story about the ability of social services to be compassionate, responsive, and cost-effective.

Today, intensive family preservation services (FPS) are available to families in crisis in more than 30 states and a growing number of countries abroad, including Canada, Denmark, The Netherlands, New Zealand, and Australia. At least 10 to 15 states, including New York, New Jersey, Maryland, Michigan, Kentucky, Missouri, New Mexico, and Tennessee, have made substantial commitments to these types of programs and are moving to institutionalize them as a matter of state policy.

Program Context

When a family's problems become so severe that the usual community resources cannot address them, public agency caseworkers frequently seek out-of-home foster care for the children. The Homebuilders intensive family preservation model is designed to give caseworkers and families another option: services that are more intensive, accessible, flexible, and goal-oriented than traditional supports. Instead of workers removing children, additional resources are brought into the home to relieve pressure and to facilitate the development of a safe, more nurturing environment for children within the context of the family.

When Homebuilders began, it was not clear whether intensive help for families would work. By spending large amounts of time with families, FPS workers knew that they would learn much about the families' problems, but they were pessimistic that big changes could occur.

They were wrong. The home-based approach was surprisingly effective. Homebuilders workers quickly learned that they did not actually have to move in with families in order to facilitate significant change. After the first year, many of their other initial assumptions were shattered as well. Families initially assumed to have minimal capacity for nurturing and minimal potential for change could eventually display more strength, sense, and compassion than initially thought possible. People could and did change significantly.

Intensive family preservation services programs, like Homebuilders, are not designed to replace our system of child welfare placements. Placements will always be necessary because there will always be some families who are unable to raise their own children safely and productively. Intensive family preservation services provide communities, service providers, and families with one last option to prevent unnecessary family dissolution. When the advantages and disadvantages of all potential settings have been weighed, when all the factors have been considered, and when the equation yields more positives on the side of placement than on the side of family, placement should occur. When the balance shifts against placement, it should not occur.

Program Characteristics

The Homebuilders model has a number of important components, which are discussed in the following sections. The way in which these characteristics interact makes them much more powerful than if they are utilized in isolation.

Homebuilders is often called a *crisis intervention program*. Crisis theory postulates that when people go through periods of high stress, their regular coping mechanisms break down, leaving them more open to change in either a positive or negative direction.

Clients referred to Homebuilders are usually experiencing one of two basic crises: (1) Local child protective services staff have said that the family is not providing adequate child care and have threatened to remove one or more children, or (2) problems between parents and children have grown so severe that a parent is about to refuse to allow the child to live at home, or the child is about to run away. With either crisis, it is difficult for family members to deny their pain or their problems. Their old habits are dislodged. Family members' increased vulnerability under such conditions can serve as a catalyst for seeking help to resolve their immediate problems. They may be more willing to consider new ways of coping.

Placement Is Imminent

Referrals to the Homebuilders program come from public agency workers who have the authority to remove children from their homes. Both the referring workers and family members must believe that without immediate intensive intervention, out-of-home placement is imminent. They must also have tried or ruled out other less intensive services for preventing placement.

Therapist Availability

Workers are available to see intakes within 24 hours of referral. The program has no waiting list and operates on a space-available basis. Once cases are accepted, workers are on call to families 24 hours a day, seven days a week.

Workers give families their home phone numbers and the number of their supervisor, as well as a team beeper number. During periods of crisis, counselors also let families know additional numbers at which they might be reached. Homebuilders want families to call their counselors when they need to, and FPS workers believe that families will feel more comfortable doing so if someone they know is on the other end of the line. Crisis calls also provide an opportunity for the worker to respond to emergencies, to teach, and to gain new critical information.

Although the amount and time of visits to families vary, workers average between eight and ten hours per week face to face with families. A typical case might require three hours the first day, three hours the second day, telephone contact the third day, two hours the fourth day, three hours every other day for about a week, and two hours three or four times a week for the remaining time. Often there will be one or two additional emergency sessions. It is possible, if necessary, for workers to take shifts with severely disrupted families, or even to stay overnight, but these extreme measures are not usually needed.

Appointments are scheduled at the convenience of the families rather than at the convenience of the workers. Therapist availability means that they are there when families need them. All family members are more likely to participate if it is convenient for them. Further, FPS workers can closely monitor potentially dangerous situations because they can be there when things are the most volatile.

Intervention in the Family Environment

Except on rare occasions when families request otherwise, all Homebuilders services are delivered in family homes, schools, work settings, and neighborhoods. Working in the natural environment makes it possible to reach a much wider range of families and to reach more seriously disturbed families. Many families are too disorganized to get themselves scheduled for and transported to office visits. In addition, many have experienced unsuccessful social services in the past and feel ambivalent about trying again, so any barriers to service delivery may discourage them completely. It is more likely that each family member will eventually participate even though some may choose not to at first. Even if family members do not participate directly, workers often are surprised to learn how much family members pick up just by hanging around in the background.

When family preservation services workers are in the family's natural environment, they see what is really going on in the family home. They observe the family lifestyles and routines. They can assess some of the environmental conditions and constraints, such as the number of rooms, furniture, toys, and so on. They see and experience the natural kinds of disruptions and

32

interferences that routinely occur, such as television, telephone, neighbors dropping in. The family knows that the counselors see and understand what is happening. Being there gives FPS workers more credibility, and the family is more likely to accept their advice.

Ultimately, families need to be able to use new skills at home. If they learn them in the office, skill generalization is often a problem. Many new behaviors never transfer to the environment where they are really needed. The Homebuilders counselor can model and shape new behaviors in the environment where they need to occur. Then FPS staff can watch family members try them, revising them if needed, and provide support until success is achieved.

In-home services are more convenient and functional, and many families comment that it helps with some of their embarrassment at having to ask for help. They feel less subservient and vulnerable and say that it seems more like having a friend or family member come over to help. This conceptualization is more comfortable for most families than the traditional caseworker-client or doctor-patient roles.

FLEXIBILITY
Scheduling of Sessions

Sessions are scheduled at times selected by family members for as long as they need. Counselors are available when it is convenient for the family and stay long enough to hear their whole story. The FPS worker can take advantage of new crises and opportunities for change.

Work and school schedules often prevent families who need services from receiving them. If family members do not have to "give up" favorite activities or rearrange their work and school schedules to see their counselor, they are likely to feel more positive about the counseling and be more willing to participate. Encouraging family members to actively participate in setting up the time for appointments is a potentially useful teaching tool since it rewards them for taking control over part of their learning process.

This flexibility does not mean that counselors have no say in when appointments occur. Particularly after the crisis period has passed, times can be negotiated, and some can be set up in advance so workers can plan their personal lives.

Services and Options

The Homebuilders model provides a wide range of services. Rather than

33

fitting the family to the service, workers aim to tailor the services to individual needs and preferences. Homebuilders attempt to accommodate the values, style, resources, and energy levels of their clients and to approach treatment from many angles, including behavioral, cognitive, emotional, and environmental. Concrete services are also provided as needed.

FPS workers do not require all family members to be present. They will work with whoever is present or whoever is interested in change at that particular time. They might use family sessions to assess interactions between people, to teach communications and negotiations, to set up contracts, or to review progress. They might use individual sessions when family members are blaming one another at a high rate, when feelings are escalated, when working on individual goals, or when only one person is willing to work with them.

INTENSITY: LOW CASELOADS

All intensive family preservation services workers serve few families at a time in order to provide time for crises and for monitoring dangerous situations. At Homebuilders, workers serve two families at a time, the lowest level of FPS caseloads.

With this low caseload, FPS counselors have the time to help families learn new skills as well as resolve their presenting crises. A small caseload allows FPS workers to stay long enough during the first session to hear the whole story, even though the story is five hours long. It allows them to come back the next day to get to work on problems, without waiting until next week when the problems may all be different. The smaller the caseload, the more feasible it is to meet emergencies. The larger the caseload, the more likely that meeting emergencies will disrupt planned visits.

Since safety is a big issue, the ability to respond with as much flexibility as possible is important. Frequent contact with a family for hours at a time increases the opportunity to assess and promote a safe home environment for children and parents. It can reassure child protective workers that Homebuilders is different from traditional services, and can provide the degree of protection and surveillance necessary to help them feel comfortable referring very difficult families.

Continuous, intensive involvement with families facilitates gathering more complete and qualitatively different information. Since the counselors are with their families for long periods of time, the counselors "live their life with them" and see the problems and conflicts firsthand. This intensive involvement with families also helps the counselor transcend the traditional involvement between worker and client and develop a more equal, and deeper, relationship, closer to a supportive friendship. With frequent contact and massed time, more work and better quality work can be accomplished than with conventional methods because little time has to be spent on reviewing the problems each visit. Problems and solutions can be discussed exhaustively. Quick successes can be followed with additional success experiences, and initial failures can be corrected quickly to find more successful interventions.

Low caseloads make it possible to manage delivery of concrete services. In places like New York, it may take all day for a client to see a doctor, or to begin to straighten out red tape regarding public assistance. Low caseloads also facilitate administrative scheduling. Coverage for vacations, compensatory time, crises, or sick leave is much easier than it would be if there were more cases.

A small caseload also helps workers stay on top of issues. Most families served by the program have needs in a number of areas, and the worker's experience with each family is intense. A small caseload allows workers to keep all of the complicated problems, relationships, and plans clearly in mind.

Low caseloads make it possible to give out home phone numbers. Having two families as potential callers is only one third the hassle of having six families who might call, and only one sixth the hassle of having twelve families who might call. Workers feel the low caseload is critical to both client safety and prevention of counselor burnout.

BREVITY: LENGTH OF SERVICE PROVISION

By traditional standards for counseling, all intensive family preservation services programs are brief. The duration of individual FPS programs usually correlates with the number of families seen at one time. If costs are held constant and the length of programs is increased, it is necessary for counselors to serve more families at one time. FPS programs range from four weeks to six months. Because of the correlation between duration and caseload, families are seen for a similar number of total hours.

Homebuilders is the briefest approach: Cases are seen for only four to six weeks. Often, people are skeptical that significant change can occur in a month. Clients often say that they would like more time, and therapists sometimes say that they would like more time. It is possible that with some families more could be accomplished if the intervention were longer.

A four- to six-week time frame has a number of differences that make it possible for change to occur more rapidly. Clients are in crisis. They are seen for intensive periods of time in the settings where the problems are occurring. They see workers when they need to see them, for as long as they need. Because of the counselor's low caseload, it is possible for families to get the equivalent number of hours to a year's outpatient therapy in only four weeks.

A short time frame has other advantages as well. One of the most important is the expectation that change can occur rapidly. Workers discuss the four-week time frame with the family during the first visit and continue to refer to it frequently throughout the intervention period. The short time frame helps keep the worker and the family focused on specific goals and making progress toward reaching them. The message for families is that change can occur right away, and indeed it must in order to fit into the time period. For many families, this expectation is a relief: their problems may not have to drag on for many more weeks or even years.

After four to six weeks, most families are no longer in crisis. They have reached a plateau and are ready to take a break from the hard work of changing their lives. Both family member and workers state that it is easier to give their full commitment for a short period of time.

This short time frame can help prevent worker burnout. Some families are extremely draining. Many are challenging. Workers say that they can cope with anything for four weeks. If they thought they were going to continue for six months, their tolerance might be different.

The short period also diminishes the potential for dependence. When workers have abundant time and resources to help families, these clients could easily come to rely on the workers in ways that would not be functional in the long run. If their time together is short, workers and family members are able to realize that family members need to care for themselves. The longer the duration of the intervention period, the less meaningful that limited time is as a motivator for a worker and family.

Moreover, the success rate in averting out-of-home placement does not appear to be influenced by the length of the intervention. Indeed, some comparisons have indicated no relationship between length of treatment and success in preventing placement.

Informal data indicate that most families who are unable to benefit from a four- to six-week intervention do not benefit from a longer period either. If what FPS programs have to offer is not working for families, even more of it does not seem to help. From the point of view of the referring worker or funding agency, the increased cost of a longer intervention is difficult to justify if four to six weeks accomplishes the goal of placement prevention for 85–90% of the families referred. Although programs for most families can be terminated in four weeks, there will be some families that need and get more time, and other families in which placement can be averted in less than four weeks.

TRAINING

As the number of intensive family preservation services programs continues to expand, training becomes a bigger priority. The more differentiated FPS worker roles become, and the more geographically and culturally different their locations, the more work needs to be done to articulate goals, values, and methods.

Family preservation is still new enough that new Homebuilders staff members are not totally ready for the job. New employees do best if they are given considerable training and support during the whole first year of their employment. Like our hiring process, the training occurs in several phases, with the first-line staff training occurring within the first month or two of employment. New staff never begin seeing families without a supervisor or senior counselor along with them.

Initial Plan

Shortly after the initial training, new staff meet with their supervisors to develop an initial plan for individualized on-the-job training. Staff are given many materials: personnel policies, a resource guide with interventions for common client problems, an overview of the program, a book written jointly by Homebuilders' administrators and various social work faculty members throughout the country, and a reading list. Supervisors go over a checklist with new employees regarding skills that they are expected to learn within their first year of employment.

First Cases

Supervisors or senior counselors always accompany new staff on visits to their first families. Sometimes supervisors go along for the first several families, gradually phasing out as new counselors gain experience and skill. With the first family, the supervisors carry the bulk of the responsibility. They discuss the family with the trainees before the visit, model skills during the visit, and begin coaching the trainees. Supervisors give feedback after each session and provide individual tutorials as needed; or supervisors might arrange for the trainees to meet with training staff to increase their skills.

During the first case, trainees observe their supervisor, try new behaviors, ask questions, and listen to feedback. Supervisors stress that there are no stupid questions and that trainees are expected to indicate if they are having trouble with any aspect of the job.

Second-Line Staff Training Session

Usually in the third or fourth month, trainees go through another three-day session of formal group training. This training focuses more intensively on how to teach families to communicate and to change their own behavior. Assertiveness training, anger management, problem solving and negotiating, and working with depressed and suicidal clients are presented. Discussions take place on what to do if progress is not occurring and how to use Multiple Impact Therapy. Work continues on trainees' own listening and stress management skills. Role-playing is emphasized, and trainees receive much individual coaching as they develop skills.

Ongoing Training

Staff training is an ongoing function. Counselors are intensively trained the entire first year. Thereafter, training is coordinated by a supervisor who meets individually with each counselor at least monthly to discuss additional training needs and personal and professional growth plans.

Staff are always trying to learn more. Homebuilders frequently has outside experts provide staff training, or staff members might attend workshops. Group case consultation and other group training events offer the opportunity for continued growth and learning.

Group case consultation occurs frequently because team members meet at least one or two mornings a week with their supervisor to discuss all their caseload families. Each supervisor has approximately six counselors. Group consultation sessions foster professional growth by increasing options available for families, identifying professional strengths and weaknesses in each team member, improving skills in weak areas, and developing supervision skills for present or future job positions. The sessions also serve to foster team building and to keep team members up to date on one another's caseloads, which can be helpful if counselors are called to accompany or provide backup for another worker.

In case consultation, counselors first give a concise account of the case, including the source of the referral, presenting problems, family social history, their goals, and Goal Attainment Scaling. General updates keep others informed of timeliness, new ideas that did or did not work, and progress on goals. Feedback is solicited from other team members as well as from the supervisor; they listen for feelings as well as content, reinforce the presenting counselor's attempts to deal with his or her situation, and offer suggestions if solicited.

Staff routinely seek individual case consultation from supervisors and other counselors outside regular group meetings. There are certain situations when counselors are required to seek consultation: if they are uncertain whether a case is appropriate to accept, if they are having difficulty defusing family members, or if they are unable to formulate goals after one week. Staff are encouraged to contact supervisors if they dislike the family, if little progress is being made on goals, or if they think out-of-home placement of the children may be the best option for family members. Counselors are also expected to consult with their supervisors if they are working overtime— perhaps more than ten hours a week—or if they find themselves staying awake nights or obsessing about a family. Any time counselors feel pressured to make a decision and think a better decision could be made with help, they should consult a supervisor or manager.

Because emergencies do arise, supervisors and administrators are on call 24 hours a day, seven days a week, just like counselors. Staff *must* immediately contact supervisors if at any time they become concerned for the safety of any family member or themselves. If their supervisor is unavailable, they are to contact other agency administrative staff. Counselors must discuss with their supervisors daily any families whose members present serious threats to themselves or others.

Program Assessment

From the beginning, the Homebuilders program has been heavily evaluated. Program directors have been committed to both understanding the process of the Homebuilders service and the treatment outcomes. The data gathered provide the rudder for management decisions and agency policy.

Over the years we have received a number of public and private grants that have allowed us, and others, to study the Homebuilders program in some detail. These efforts are often humbling experiences. Research endeavors are never as simple, inexpensive, or definitive as we envision.

Each of the studies discussed below has limitations. These studies are difficult to compare with one another because many have small samples. The definitions of avoidance of placement vary, or follow-up times vary. The most critical issue has been, and remains, the assumption that children served by Homebuilders would have been placed outside the home if Homebuilders had been unavailable. Quasi-experimental studies indicate between 76% and 100% of overflow cases do get placed, yet a tight control study with random assignment of cases and a long follow-up period to assess placement rates has yet to be done.

JUVENILE DELINQUENT AND STATUS OFFENDERS STUDY
In 1976 the Office of Child Development in the U.S. Department of Health, Education and Welfare funded a randomly assigned controlled research study to evaluate Homebuilders treatment effectiveness with juvenile delinquent status offenders referred by the Pierce County Juvenile Court in Tacoma, Washington. The authors worked closely with the Washington State Department of Social and Health Services (DSHS) Office of Research. Whenever DSHS got a referral, the design of the study required them to contact their DSHS referral liaison, who would then randomly indicate whether to assign the case to the control group or the treatment group.

The results of this study showed that 30 of the 41 treatment cases (73%) averted out-of-home placement for 12 months after at intake. In the comparison group, 5 of the 18 youths (28%) targeted for out-of-home care avoided placement. Average cost for treatment cases was $2,182 per case, while average cost per comparison case was $4,991, for an average difference of $2,809 per case (Kinney, 1982).

CHILDREN'S MENTAL HEALTH STUDY
In 1979 the Washington State Legislature funded a demonstration project to evaluate the effectiveness of the Homebuilders model with mentally ill and severely emotionally disturbed children and youth. Thirty youths (25

40

treatment and 5 "overflow" comparison group cases) were referred to Home-builders from the Pierce County Office of Involuntary Commitment as an alternative to inpatient psychiatric hospitalization.

It was predicted that these children and their families would need a higher impact service, and the basic Homebuilders model was supplemented in the following ways: The three most experienced Homebuilders counselors were used most frequently for these "mental health" cases and received twice as much supervision time. It was expected that the cases would require more than the normal four weeks of intervention, so the three counselors were responsible for seeing a total of 25 "mental health" cases during the year, as compared to the 54 regular Homebuilders cases that they would normally see in one year. The counselors received additional training in psychotropic medication, suicide prevention, and dealing with violent clients. In addition, psychiatric consultation was available as needed.

Improvements in individual and family functioning were measured by Achenbach's (1979) Child Behavior Checklist (CBCL) and through Global Assessment Scales (GAS). Average scores are reported in aggregate form, so it is not possible to provide additional statistical information, and the original data are currently unavailable for access due to changes in Homebuilders' parent agency.

☐ CBCL scores: Average pretreatment score = 81.7; average posttreatment score = 43.9. The higher the CBCL score, the more problematic the child's behavior. A score of 38 indicates the high end of the "normal range," so these children, with an original average score of 81.7, were demonstrating severe behavior problems. At the end of treatment, their average score of 43.9 indicates that they were approaching the "normal" range.

☐ GAS scores: Average pretreatment score was 29.1, indicating "moderate" impairment in functioning; average posttreatment score was 57.6, closer to "slight" interference with functioning.

☐ Parent ratings of improvement: Parents were asked at termination to rate their children's presenting problems as "better," "worse," or "the same."

Children's living situations were tracked by research staff for 12 months after intake into the study, yielding the following results:

19 (76%) of the 25 youths remained at home.
2 (8%) were placed in psychiatric hospitals.

3 (12%) were placed in group homes.

1 (4%) was placed in juvenile detention.

Project cost-effectiveness was evaluated by a comparison of costs for the Homebuilders program with costs for those clients who were assessed as appropriate for hospitalization by the Office of Involuntary Commitment, referred to Homebuilders, but not accepted because the program was full. The Homebuilders program costs were calculated by dividing the first-year budget ($128,240) by the number of clients (25) to yield an average cost per client of $5,130.

All five comparison cases were immediately placed, four in psychiatric hospitals and one in a correctional institution. Costs were projected using average costs and lengths of stay for those settings and indicated an average cost per client of $17,623, $12,463 more than the costs for Homebuilders.

DEVELOPMENTAL DISABILITIES PROJECT

In 1981 a study was begun to test whether Homebuilders could prevent a developmentally delayed client's move to a more restrictive environment or could facilitate a client's move to a less restrictive placement. Thirteen out of fifteen of the clients referred (87%) were able to prevent a move to a more restrictive setting. Two out of two of those referred (100%) were successful in moving to a less restrictive placement with Homebuilders. Referring workers saw an improvement in 88% of clients who had been referred because of aggressive or destructive behavior and in 82% of clients who had been referred because of recurring episodes of problem behaviors such as stealing, tantrums, or self-injurious behavior.

SPECIAL NEEDS ADOPTION PROJECT

The Homebuilders intensive, home-based family preservation services were provided to 22 special needs children living in 20 adoptive family homes (Haapala, McDade, & Johnston, 1988). All adopted children were at imminent risk of out-of-home placement due to problems such as a child's noncompliance or mental health problems, a parent's poor parenting skills, or a lack of parent-child bonding. On average, Homebuilders therapists spent 63 hours in case-related activities for each of the 20 families. Cases were open for an average of 27 days. At the three-month follow-up point, 77% of the children avoided formal out-of-home placements. These children were living either in their adoptive homes or with relatives. For 18 of the 20 families, Goal Attainment Scale scores were above 50, indicating that the goal was achieved at a level beyond the therapist's expectations. At termination, 12 families showed positive change, 6 families showed no change, and 1 family showed a worsened condition on the Family Risk Scales. According to referring caseworkers (N = 17), no progress was made on 9 of the caseworkers' family treatment goals, some progress was made on 9 of the caseworkers' treatment goals, and considerable progress was made on 14 of the caseworkers' treatment goals. Primary caretakers from 16 of the 20 families completed goal checklists at service intake, and 15 of them completed the checklists at termination.

The status of these children looked much different at the 3- and 12-month follow-up points. Of the 22 children, 10 (46%) had spent some time in at least one formal out-of-home placement, and another 4 (18%) had run away or had lived on the streets for some period of time. Only 8 (36%) of the 22 children completely avoided any time away from the home of their adoptive family or relative. Over the course of the 12-month follow-up period, some of the children went through a series of placements or runaway episodes. It should be noted, however, that at the point of 12-month follow-up, only 32% of these youth were actually reported to be living in formal out-of-home care.

These findings support other research demonstrating less successful placement-avoidance outcomes for children who have previously been formally placed in out-of-home care (Fraser, Pecora, & Haapala, 1991). Some of these children had experienced multiple placements and may, therefore, be at even greater risk for additional placement experiences.

Because little is known regarding the reasonable expectations for maintaining a disrupted special needs adoption placement once the child or family has seriously considered terminating the relationship, it is difficult to determine the potential placement-avoidance impact of a service like Homebuilders. Based on other measures of treatment success gathered at the termination of Homebuilders programs (such as Goal Attainment Scale scores and Family Risk Scale scores), there appears to be, at least initially, a success effect attributed to the Homebuilders service. This report did not collect extended longitudinal data on these measures, so it is not clear how long the discrete positive clinical effects lasted. The Homebuilders approach may provide a valuable option to cases of special needs adoptions disruption, yet further study is needed to more clearly determine its impact on placement prevention as well as behavior change.

FAMILY-BASED INTENSIVE TREATMENT RESEARCH PROJECT

The Family-Based Intensive Treatment (FIT) Research Project was designed to describe the outcomes of intensive home-based family treatment services based on the Homebuilders model. The research question providing the focal point for the investigation was, What factors are associated with family-based child welfare service failures? Data on child, parent, family, service, and system characteristics were collected and used to describe the differences between successful and unsuccessful family-based treatment.

"Service failure" was defined in such a way as to include an unusually broad number of out-of-home conditions. Conventional out-of-home placements such as foster care, group care, and inpatient psychiatric hospitalization were included in the definition along with short-term placements such as shelter care, crisis or receiving care, and detention. In addition, if a child was on the run or moved out of the home to live with a neighbor, friend, or other nonrelative, this was considered to be equivalent to an out-of-home placement. The "placement" of a child in any of these conditions outside the home for two weeks or more during the provision of family preservation services (FPS), or within 12 months following intake into the treatment project, was defined as "treatment failure." Follow-up interviews with parents and management information system reports were used to collect placement data on all children in the families participating in the study.

From these data, two kinds of placement outcomes were computed. First, a family preservation outcome was created by classifying families from which no child was placed as "successful." If even one child from the family was placed, the family's treatment was considered to have failed—that is, family preservation services were unsuccessful. Hence, this measure was called "family preservation." A second placement measure, based on individual children who were designated as being at risk of placement, was also used. It is a direct measure of the number of children at risk who were placed, regardless of whether they were in the same family. In this study, family preservation is used as the major outcome measure, and data analyses focus on identifying those system and family characteristics that distinguish successful family preservation services from unsuccessful services.

A total of 453 families from the states of Utah and Washington participated in the FIT study (Fraser, Pecora, & Haapala, 1991). The services in Washington were provided by Homebuilders in four counties: Pierce (Tacoma), King (Seattle), Spokane, and Snohomish. The services in Utah were modeled after the Homebuilders program and delivered through two public child welfare agency offices. The characteristics of services in each state were measured carefully using over 100 variables, and the key elements of service were identified and described.

A quasi-experimental longitudinal design was used, supplemented by a small case overflow control group (N = 26) in Utah that consisted of families who were referred for home-based services, met the criteria for admission, but could not be served because workers' caseloads were full. Data regarding child and family functioning for the total study sample were collected at four distinct points: at intake, at service termination, 12 months after service intake, and whenever a service failure (child placement or runaway behavior) occurred. Of the 453 families, 263 started treatment sufficiently early in the study to permit a 12-month follow-up. Outcome data for this group are reported separately.

Even with a conservative definition of treatment success (failure defined as any placement with a nonrelative or any runaway episode for two weeks or more), the FPS workers were able to achieve success in preventing placement at the 12-month follow-up point with 71.4% of the children in the Washington sample and 61.9% of the children in Utah, all of whom were at risk of placement in the total sample.

A variety of child and family outcome measures, such as the Child Welfare League of America Family at Risk Scales (Magura, Moses, & Jones, 1987), and instruments that measured changes in family cohesion and adaptability, such as the Family Adaptability and Cohesion Scales (FACES III), and social support (Milardo, 1983) were used. As indicated earlier, the placement locations of children in the treatment and control group families were tracked using management information system reports and interviews with primary caretakers.

Based on FPS worker ratings of pretreatment and posttreatment functioning, families experiencing treatment success made significant positive changes on 21 measures (see Table 2.1). These gains ranged from a decreased use of physical punishment to increased motivation to solve family problems.

FIT study families who were considered service failures showed significant improvements on only nine measures during treatment. These improvements, however, could be beneficial to any children remaining in the home, or to children currently placed out of the home when they return home.

Table 2.1 Successful Families

Families that were classified as successes made significant improvements during treatment on the following 21 measures:

1. Habitability of residence
2. Suitability of living conditions
3. Social support
4. Primary caretaker's mental health
5. Supervision of young children (primary caretaker)
6. Parenting of older children (primary and secondary caretakers)
7. Use of physical punishment (primary and secondary caretakers)
8. Verbal discipline (primary and secondary caretakers)
9. Motivation to solve family problems (primary and secondary caretakers)
10. Attitude toward placement (primary and secondary caretakers)
11. Knowledge of child care and development (primary and secondary caretakers)
12. Primary caretaker's abuse of substances (primary and secondary caretakers)
13. Child's mental health (first, second, and third oldest)
14. Child's physical health (second oldest)
15. Child's physical needs, such as meals, clothing, bathing, and shots (first oldest)
16. Child's school adjustment (first, second, and third oldest)
17. Emotional care and stimulation of children (first and second oldest)
18. Child delinquency (first, second, and third oldest)
19. Child's home-related behavior (first, second, and third oldest)
20. Sexual harassment of child in the home (second oldest)
21. Adult relationships

Source: Families in crisis: The impact of intensive family preservation services by M. W. Fraser, P. J. Pecora, and D. A. Haapala, 1991, Hawthorne NY: Aldine de Gruyter.

Social Support

Three stable and reliable dimensions of social support were found to characterize the social networks of primary and secondary caretakers. During the course of treatment, most caretakers' relationships with their spouses (when there was one) became less aversive. Primary caretakers reported their contacts with extended family members and friends became more empathetic and understanding. Both successful and unsuccessful families receiving treatment were distinguished by a greater order of change in the aversive nature of their social interactions. Caretakers in families avoiding placement appear to have been relatively more effective in reducing negative contacts with spouses, extended family members, coworkers, and friends.

Family Satisfaction

In terms of general satisfaction with family preservation services, primary caretakers rated home-based family treatment as very helpful. Even in families where a child had been placed out of the home, 78% of the primary caretakers felt placement was the best alternative for their family. Conversely, when the child remained in the home, 89% of the primary caretakers thought avoidance of placement was best for their family. Primary caretakers rated both the home-based nature of service and its skills focus as important service elements.

BRONX HOMEBUILDERS PROGRAM

Between 1987 and 1990, Behavioral Sciences Institute operated a Homebuilders program in the Bronx, New York. Based upon the same concept as the institute's Homebuilders programs in Washington State, the Bronx Homebuilders program was an experiment on many levels. Despite the challenges of extreme poverty and drug abuse, the program achieved remarkable success in keeping children out of publicly funded care.

The following information indicates some key preliminary information about the program and also compares some Washington State Homebuilders program data with comparable data from the Bronx Homebuilders program. Data from the Washington State sample represent 376 families with 532 children at imminent risk of placement that were referred to Homebuilders programs in King, Pierce, Spokane, and Snohomish Counties from September 1987 through August 1988. Data from the Bronx represent 58 families with 101 children at imminent risk of placement referred to the Bronx Homebuilders program from May 1987 through August 1988.

While the age groupings of the Washington and Bronx client children appear quite similar, the race of the children, family structure, and family income are quite different. The Bronx families are poorer, have more single parents, and are predominantly Hispanic and Black.

The Bronx program serves its families for about a week longer than the Washington families are served. Staff in the Bronx program also spend more time face to face and in telephone contact with their client families. The length of treatment and number of hours may represent a learning phase associated with the Bronx program since it is a new Homebuilders program.

Preliminary placement outcome data indicate notable differences in the rates of child placement between the New York and Washington State Homebuilders programs. Due to the social conditions, poverty, newness of the Homebuilders program in that community, and other problems in New York, it seems likely that New York would have a lower success rate in preventing out-of-home placements.

Cost-Effectiveness

An initial analysis of the first six months of the Bronx project has many limitations in terms of sample size, length of follow-up, and lack of a control group, as well as serious difficulties in retrieving data from New York systems. It is also impossible at this time for us to know if clients referred to Homebuilders would have been in placement for average lengths of stay, or if clients who are ultimately placed following the Homebuilders treatment remain for average lengths of stay. Nevertheless, we can get a rough idea of the potential of the Homebuilders program for cost-effectiveness.

Costs for Homebuilders services during this period were $211,892, which is $2,306,068 less than the total average costs for placement of all the children would have been. Even if we figure in average costs of placement for the five Homebuilders clients who were placed during this period (one foster infant = $34,649; one nine-year-old child, foster care = $35,763; and three group home placements = $294,909), costs for Homebuilders clients are $1,940,747 less than if they had all been placed.

A more conservative assessment of potential for cost-effectiveness would not assume that all clients would be placed without Homebuilders involvement. In more and more communities, placements do not exist, and even families whose problems are so severe that the children should be placed often struggle along for years, or the children live on the street indefinitely. Yet it is certain that some of the cases referred to Homebuilders would have been placed. But even a few placements would justify the program's costs. For example, the costs for the first six months of the Homebuilders program in New York (including large amounts of start-up costs) were $211,824. In terms of average costs of placements, it would be necessary to avert only 2.2 group home placements, 2.3 psychiatric placements, or 6.1 infant foster care placements to make the Homebuilders program worthwhile.

AUDITORS AND OUTSIDE EVALUATORS

Over the years, the Homebuilders program has been more or less formally evaluated by many groups, including the American Criminal Justice Institute, a National Science Foundation Committee in conjunction with the Boys Town Centers for Youth Development, the National Institute for Mental Health, the Washington State Department of Social and Health Services, Division of Mental Health and Office of Research, the Washington State Legislature, and the Oregon Council on Crime and Delinquency. All reports have been highly positive.

ROUTINE PROGRAM EVALUATION PROCEDURES

The Homebuilders staff have wanted to know not only if they were achieving the anticipated outcomes, but also whether they were achieving them in a way that was satisfactory to all involved. They continuously gather feedback regarding their treatment methods and processes, using this feedback to revise and refine procedures.

Goal Attainment Scaling

Homebuilders has used Goal Attainment Scaling as the foundation of all their recordkeeping to monitor client progress on individual presenting problems. Goal Attainment Scaling was first developed by Kiresuk and Sherman (1968) as an evaluation method for community mental health centers. It allows for the development and monitoring of individualized goals pertinent to each family as opposed to general criteria of improvement.

Goal Attainment Scales at Homebuilders are used to clarify goals, to retain an accurate index of events for recordkeeping purposes, and to assess whether change or progress is occurring in any one area of concern. The potential outcome levels are represented numerically by $+2$, $+1$, 0, -1, and -2. The qualitative breakdown of these ratings is as follows:

Goal: Statement of specific goal

$+2$ = Best Anticipated Success

$+1$ = More than Expected Success

0 = Expected Level of Success (in conjunction with treatment plan)

-1 = Less than Expected Success

-2 = Most Unfavorable Outcome Likely (Kiresuk & Sherman, 1968)

The therapist works with the clients to insert potential outcome levels in the rating scale which are relevant to clients' specific goals. For example:

$+2$ = 80% school attendance this week

$+1$ = 60% school attendance this week

49

0 = 40% school attendance this week

−1 = 20% school attendance this week

−2 = No school attendance this week

As the example specifies, a "0" or expected level of success is 40% school attendance, with the other scale points representing deviations from this expected level. It is desirable to calibrate the scale so there is equal distance between points. Outcome levels should ideally be expressed in clear, measurable terms.

Therapists must also be careful to avoid including numerous aspects or problems in one goal and having too many goals per client. Four ongoing goals per family is probably the maximum number that is manageable. The potential outcome levels on a Goal Attainment Scale are usually rated weekly in conjunction with a summary of the week's goal-relevant activity to clarify and to substantiate the rating choice.

These ratings allow clients, therapists, supervisors, and auditors to monitor progress on client presenting problems. The struggle for clarification of goals by therapists and clients can be an important treatment intervention. Written goals, monitored weekly, force therapists to be more focused on how they spend their time.

Client Feedback

Homebuilders staff have solicited feedback from all client families since the beginning of the program. They always collect this information within one week of program termination. Depending on personnel resources, they also collect feedback three and twelve months after intake. Homebuilders staff want to know not only if out-of-home placement occurred, but also how clients felt they were treated, whether their therapists did as claimed, and, most importantly, whether the clients felt the intervention was helpful.

Policy Encouragement and Development
PUBLIC POLICY SUPPORT

Twenty years have passed since the development of the intensive family preservation services (FPS) model. Despite numerous replications throughout the United States and abroad, widespread adaptation of FPS or, at the very least, some form of services designed to support and preserve the family unit whenever possible, is hampered by the lack of clear public policy guidelines and financial support.

In 1974, when the original Homebuilders demonstration project began, state and federal legislation mandating efforts to preserve families threatened by placement did not exist. The passage of the Adoption Assistance and Child Welfare Act in 1980 marked a dramatic policy shift in favor of "reasonable efforts" to prevent the unnecessary dissolution of families. Despite the act's landmark status, long-term federal funding was not established, and a consistent policy of implementation from state to state never occurred. As a result, children are still being placed in foster care in record numbers. The cost to taxpayers is high; the human cost is even higher.

The latest effort at reform on the federal level ended in a presidential veto. The 1992 Urban Aid and Tax Bill passed by Congress supported widespread efforts to expand FPS and attempted to address some of the shortcomings of the Adoption Assistance and Child Welfare Act. Without strong federal legislation and substantial monetary support, children and families remain dependent upon the creativity and initiative of private funders and local and state governments. Throughout the country, major policy initiatives are being passed which will affect families not only in child welfare but in the juvenile justice and mental health systems as well.

INNOVATIVE APPROACHES

Several examples of successful private, public, and professional nurturing of the FPS movement stand out. Throughout the 1980s the Edna McConnell Clark Foundation spearheaded efforts among private foundations to support new strategies to prevent the unnecessary out-of-home placement of children. The foundation initially supported pilot testing of programs and ideas and sponsored forums at which professionals could share ideas and collaborate on possible solutions. Finally, the foundation began a concerted effort to promote the replication of the FPS model and the large-scale training of workers to provide family preservation services. The Annie E. Casey Foundation is currently leading efforts to define the underlying principles of FPS and to study issues of case targeting and client referral processes.

The successful delivery of intensive family preservation services by public agencies is being demonstrated in states such as New York and Tennessee, where large-scale efforts to train state workers to provide FPS are under way. Behavioral Sciences Institute (the Homebuilders parent agency) is also working with the state of Hawaii on the innovative Families Together Initiative (FTI). There is particular interest in FTI as it is the first statewide interagency

FPS initiative. The program coordinates referrals from the Department of Human Services, Department of Health, Family Court, and the Office of Youth Services. Special action taken by the 1992 Washington State Legislature is historic for both Homebuilders and FPS. The Family Preservation Services Bill (R.C.W 74.14C) is significant in concept because it mandates that every family with a child in danger of immediate out-of-home placement be offered the option of receiving Homebuilders services. The bill also requires that children in long-term out-of-home care be eligible to receive FPS in order to reunite them with their families. The bill significantly nudges public policy and child welfare practice in a direction that is more supportive to families without diminishing our society's responsibilities and concern for children and individual safety.

Other examples of innovative efforts to expand the availability of FPS include the development of social work training programs and national professional networks. Behavioral Sciences Institute and the University of Washington School of Social Work cooperated in the development of a master's-level degree track with a specialization in family preservation. In 1993, the Intensive Family Preservations Services National Network was incorporated in New York. The network is dedicated to nurturing the development, expansion, and quality of FPS programs modeled after the Homebuilders program.

RESEARCH NEEDS

The rapid growth of intensive family preservation services has resulted in greater interest in evaluating the efficacy of these programs and their replications. This is a logical and necessary course for an evolving model that is causing social services to reexamine how to provide services to families.

Landmark legislation passed by the Washington State Legislature in 1992 included a provision for a one-year study of child placement decision making and accurate targeting of families for Homebuilders programs. This is just the beginning. Current research in other states indicates that identifying and referring appropriate cases to FPS programs will be of increasing importance to the long-term survival of these programs, especially in terms of demonstrating that widespread investment in FPS will result in the significant reduction of placement costs. Still, little will be achieved until large-scale studies are funded.

EXPANDING SERVICES TO NEW CLIENTS AND PROBLEMS

The potential for FPS to help families is not limited to just the prevention of out-of-home placement. As with any successful movement, completion of one set of goals raises awareness of new horizons and opportunities for greater contribution and change. In family preservation, emphasis is shifting away from installation of projects to solidifying past gains and addressing needs for research data supporting the approach.

Leaders of the family preservation movement are also interested in spreading core concepts of that effort more broadly. Six key principles of effective services have been documented and operationalized in terms of actual worker behavior with clients: building on strengths; a holistic approach; tailoring of services; decision-making partnerships; short-term, specific goal setting; and an emphasis on worker characteristics and skills. These efforts to apply the values and principles of family preservation to more traditional services hold promise for promoting service integration. The potential for these new directions, for both client and worker empowerment and, ultimately, taxpayer savings, is high.

The changing needs of FPS clients is driving us to be responsive to families unable to receive help through more traditional sources. This is especially true in the case of drug-affected families. In many FPS families, drug use and abuse is a critical factor contributing to instability in the home. In 1990 Homebuilders began a formal effort to study this problem and develop new approaches to helping these families address drug-related problems while still keeping the children in the home. Collaborative efforts between Homebuilders and chemical dependency treatment providers have demonstrated the promise of this combined approach.

Summary

Within a confusing, complicated, and at times disintegrating social service context, intensive family preservation services offer a promising first step to helping families and individuals help themselves. These services offer a cost-effective alternative to placement outside the home at a time when wise investment of social service dollars is a critical consideration. Viewed from a broader context, the philosophy and strategies of FPS can also serve as a model for many types of services to families which can be flexible, responsive, and tailored to client and community needs.

Note

1. Homebuilders is a trademark of Behavioral Sciences Institute (BSI). BSI, a private, nonprofit organization founded by the creators of Homebuilders, is dedicated to strengthening families and communities and enabling individuals to lead safe, independent, and more enjoyable lives. Headquartered in Federal Way, Washington, near Seattle, BSI operates five regional offices in Washington State and one in New York City.

References

Achenbach, T. M. (1979). *Child behavior checklist* (ADM 512). Bethesda MD: National Institute of Mental Health.

Adoption Assistance and Child Welfare Act of 1980, P.L. 96-272 H. R. 3439, 94. Stat. 500. (1980).

Fraser, M. W., Pecora, P. J., & Haapala, D. A. (1991). *Families in crisis: The impact of intensive family preservation services.* Hawthorne NY: Aldine de Gruyter.

Haapala, D. A., McDade, K., & Johnston, B. (1988). *Preventing the dissolution of special needs adoptive families with children in imminent risk of out-of-home placement.*

Kinney, J. (1982, November). *Gaps between problems and solutions in child welfare.* Presentation to National Child Welfare Leadership Center, West Region Legislative Strategy Seminar, Sacramento CA.

Kinney, J., Strand, K., Hagerup, M., & Bruner, C. (in press). *Beyond the buzzwords: Operationalizing key principles in effective frontline practice.* Falls Church VA: National Center for Service Integration and National Resource Center for Family Support.

Kiresuk, T. J., & Sherman, R. E. (1968). Goal attainment scaling: A general method for evaluating community mental health programs. *Community Mental Health Journal, 4,* 443–453.

Lloyd, J. (1982). Prevention: At what cost? *Prevention Report.* Iowa City: University of Iowa, National Resource Center for Family Based Service.

Magura, S., Moses, B. S., & Jones, M. A. (1987). Assessing risk and measuring change in families: The Bundy risk scales. Washington DC: Child Welfare League of America.

Milardo, R. M. (1983). Social networks and pair relationships: A review of substantive and measurement issues. *Sociology and Social Research, 68*(1), 1–18.

3

Network Interventions with High-Risk Youth and Families Throughout the Continuum of Care

Elizabeth M. Tracy, James K. Whittaker, Francis Boylan,
Paul Neitman, and Edward Overstreet

Delivery of services to families in their own homes provides a unique opportunity to identify, assess, and enhance ways in which formal and informal supportive services can complement each other. The home-based worker is in a better position to understand and appreciate social support needs and resources of the family and the family's usual ways of coping with the environment. In addition to gaining greater access to all family members, home-based interventions allow for more effective facilitation of natural helping relationships within the neighborhood or community. It is through these forms of social network interventions that the social environment can be enlisted as a resource and aid in service to the family.

This chapter describes methods and techniques for network assessment and intervention at various points in the continuum of work with families. It is our conviction that social network interventions must be individualized to fit each family's unique needs, based on an assessment of the family's social network resources and perceptions of social support (Tracy & Whittaker, 1990). We also believe that family support is an appropriate service strategy at all points in the continuum, even when placement has occurred or when reunification efforts have failed (Maluccio & Whittaker, 1988).

The potential for supporting families is greatly enhanced, though, when programs define the family in its broadest context, as consisting of a family surrounded by a social network of friends, relatives, neighbors, and other helping resources. Social network interventions attempt to facilitate or mobilize positive changes in the social environment, the primary goal being to help the family maintain the changes achieved during professional intervention. For this reason, home-based services can benefit from inclusion of social network interventions in addition to their many other services.

We begin with a brief overview of social support definitions and rationale for including social network assessment in youth and family services. The findings of two agency-based research and development projects designed to identify, enhance, and augment the social network resources of at-risk families also are presented. Finally, we offer a discussion of social network interventions throughout the continuum of care, followed by a summary of practice implications.

Significance of Social Networks and Social Support

Our interest in social networks and social support was stimulated by the growing recognition in youth and family services that resources of neighborhood and extended family networks are frequently correlated with outcomes of interest. Intervention efforts can be made more enduring and permanent through the supportive assistance of kin, friends, neighbors, and other informal helpers who can help youth and families consolidate the gains made in professional helping. A classic 1960s follow-up study of youth leaving residential treatment captures the critical nature of a youth's environment in postdischarge adaption: "Only when the situation to which the child returned was taken into account were performances at Bellefaire related to post-discharge adequacies. In a stressful community situation, strengths nurtured within the institution tended to break down, whereas in a supportive situation, these strengths tended to be reinforced" (Allerhand, Weber, & Haug, 1966, p. 140).

These findings were similar to those obtained by Lewis (1982) and Nelson, Singer, and Johnsen (1978) in subsequent studies of youth leaving residential treatment. Jones, Weinrott, & Howard (1981), in a comprehensive follow-up of perhaps the most widely studied group home model of the 1970s, put it this way: "The message is simple, a program could be an apparent success if the criterion is modification of target behaviors during the program experience. The same program may be seen as far less successful if the criterion is the postprogram adjustment and reintegration of the youth [into the community]" (1981, p. 134).

Nearly thirty years later, carefully executed empirical studies from the same institution originally studied by Allerhand and his colleagues yielded a refined analysis of the particular types and loci of support that are crucial for particular outcomes (Wells, Wyatt, & Hobfoll, 1991). For example, the study by Wells and her colleagues provides additional empirical evidence of the criticality of family support as a correlate of postdischarge adaptation and the importance of studying the combined effects of family support, stress, and stability related to adaption (Wells et al., 1991). A parallel discussion has more recently arisen in the area of intensive family preservation services stressing the importance of postintervention supports in the family's natural environment (Tracy & Whittaker, 1991) and the importance of certain types of support (e.g., concrete helping) during the treatment intervention (Fraser, Pecora, & Haapala, 1991).

There is, however, a wide gap between outcome studies that highlight the importance of a particular type of social support and interventions designed to strengthen and enhance existing networks of kin, friends, and neighbors. While a few pilot network interventions with neglectful families—for example, those by Gaudin, Wodarski, Arkinson, & Avery (1990–91)—show initial promise, we are certain that network interventions offer no panacea. In fact, they are best seen as part of a more comprehensive service intervention. Moreover, we are well aware that existing client networks often reinforce life-injurious behavior (such as drug use) and often are themselves a source of stress through the placement of excessive demands. Indeed, if *only* to better understand these negative influences, we believe that family workers—whether in family preservation, foster care, or residential services—need a more systematic and detailed understanding of their clients' personal networks and social exchanges.

To further that end, we initiated a research and development project, the Social Networks Project at Boysville of Michigan in mid-1989, to further test the clinical utility of a social network assessment tool (Tracy & Whittaker, 1990) as a means of identifying the support needs of families in the agency's newly created family preservation program in inner-city Detroit and Saginaw (Whittaker & Tracy, 1990; Whittaker, Tracy, Overstreet, Mooradian, & Kapp, 1994). This project replicated and built upon an earlier effort with Homebuilders in the state of Washington to understand the support needs and network resources of families at risk of out-of-home placement (Whittaker, Tracy, & Marckworth, 1989).

As Michigan's largest voluntary youth services agency, Boysville provided an interesting laboratory for testing the development of new practice technology designed to identify and intervene with the extended networks of the families that the agency served. While our work to date has focused on placement prevention services, we believe that much of what we have identified as helpful in assessment and intervention will have wide applicability across the range of in-home and placement services offered by the agency. Ultimately, we hope that strategies and techniques developed in successful family preservation programs and designed to improve social supports for clients will also prove useful in aftercare efforts of family-based programs as well.

In developing a rationale for our focus on networks and support, we identified a number of reasons why this information is critical to informed practice, including the following:

1. Better understand culturally specific patterns of help giving
2. Identify potential sources of support to aid in the maintenance of treatment gains
3. Aid in understanding family system boundaries
4. Gain an appreciation of the client's perception of support
5. Pinpoint sources of conflict within the personal social network
6. Pinpoint sources of particular types of help within the network
7. Encourage the client to actively restructure the immediate social environment
8. Encourage efforts at self-help
9. Identify patterns of reciprocal helping
10. Identify relevant others who may participate in future network interventions (Tracy, Whittaker, & Mooradian, 1990)

Second, in developing a common language on networks and social support, we began with the idea that social support refers to the actions that others perform when they render assistance. There are several different types of social support:

☐ Emotional support: having someone listen to your feelings, comfort you, or offer encouragement

☐ Informational support: having someone teach you something, give you information or advice, or help you make a major decision

☐ Concrete support: having someone help out in tangible ways, loaning you something, helping with a chore, or taking you on an errand

Social support can take place within naturally occurring helping networks of family, friends, neighbors, and peers, or in groups and organizations that have been specifically created or contrived for this purpose. Formal support includes services delivered by paid human service professionals. Informal support can be delivered by kinship networks, volunteers, or local community groups.

The term *social network* refers to the structure and number of people and groups with whom you have contact or consider yourself to be in contact. A person's social network can be described in a number of ways:

☐ Size: the total number of people in the network

☐ Composition: the variety of people or groups in the network interacting with one another

☐ Frequency of contact: how often people in the network interact with each other

☐ Durability or length of relationship: how long people in the network have known one another, how stable the relationships have been

☐ Intensity: the strength of relationships within the network

☐ Density: the extent to which network members know and interact with one another independently

☐ Multiplexity: the extent to which network relationships serve more than one function or provide more than one type of support

☐ Reciprocity: the amount of give and take, the extent to which support provided is balanced by support received

☐ Dispersions: how easy it is for network members to make contact with one another

☐ Homogeneity: the extent to which network members are similar to one another

The terms *social network* and *social support* do not necessarily refer to the same concept. People may be surrounded by large social networks, but may not feel supported or perceive support from others. Also, they may not be receiving the types and amount of support that they need. A social support network as defined by Whittaker and Garbarino (1983) refers to a set of interconnected relationships among a group of people that provides enduring patterns of nurturance (in any or all forms) and provides contingent reinforcement for efforts to cope with life on a day-to-day basis (p. 5).

Not all social ties are supportive. Patterns of negative social networks may be evident. For example, social network members may be overly critical or demanding of one another, or they may reinforce or encourage harmful or antisocial behavior, such as drug abuse or gang violence. Some social networks fail to support efforts to change behaviors, such as a parent changing from punishment approaches to more positive forms of child management. Without support from the network, it is more likely that changes will not be maintained over time.

Several related concepts are important to note. Enacted support refers to the actual utilization of support resources. Perceived support refers to the extent to which an individual feels his or her support needs are or would be fulfilled. Network orientation refers to beliefs, attitudes, or expectations concerning the usefulness of network members in helping to cope with a problem. Some people may have adequate social networks but may not make use of or access their network in times of need due to a negative network orientation. Another barrier to use of one's social network may be inadequate social skills in requesting help, developing network relationships, and maintaining supportive social ties over time.

A third reason for our focus on networks and support is that we have identified several possible directions for social support interventions that we believe have relevance in foster care and residential services as well as in the context of intensive family preservation services. For example, social support goals may include one or any combination of the following:

1. Increase sources of emotional support (e.g., people who support and reinforce positive change efforts, people who listen to you without making judgments)
2. Increase sources of concrete assistance (e.g., people who will help you out or give you a break)
3. Increase sources of information or advice (e.g., people who teach, model, or give constructive advice)
4. Increase skills in dealing with people in the network (e.g., how to deal

with people who do not reinforce change efforts or do not provide social support, or balancing relationships which are not reciprocal)

Steps that might be taken to achieve social support goals include the following:

□ Changing the structure of the network:
1. Increase or decrease size of social network
2. Change composition of social network (e.g., decrease reliance on formal services)
3. Increase or decrease frequency of contact with others
   □ Increasing skill level:
1. Develop or increase skills in making friends
2. Decrease negative beliefs about self (if this is a barrier to developing or maintaining supportive relationships); increase positive self-statements and increase ability to identify personal strengths
3. Develop strategies for handling criticism from others
4. Increase assertive skills (if this is a barrier to developing or maintaining supportive relationships)
5. Increase communication skills (if this is a barrier to developing or maintaining supportive relationships)
6. Teach reciprocity skills (if this is a barrier to developing or maintaining supportive relationships)
7. Develop a plan to reach out to others during a crisis period (Tracy et al., 1990; Whittaker, Tracy, & Marckworth, 1989)

Network Interventions throughout the Continuum

Social network intervention methods fulfill different functions at various points in the continuum of care. For example, the support needs of a family in a brief, intensive intervention designed to prevent placement may be different from those of a family awaiting the reintegration of a youth following long-term residential treatment. The type of support and the preferred source of support may differ depending on the timing of its delivery. Support needs may vary depending on whether an event is being anticipated, experienced, or concluded (Jacobsen, 1986).

The experience of placement for youth and families may require different

Table 3.1 Social Network Interventions throughout Continuum

	Placement prevention	Preplacement services	During placement	Aftercare services
Assessment issues and tasks	What supports are available to help defuse precipitating factors?	What supports are available to facilitate the transition?	What supports are available to facilitate changes?	What supports are available to maintain changes?
Social support goals	Increase quality and quantity Link with pro-social networks	Provide informational support about placement	Provide informational, emotional, and concrete support	Increase quality and quantity Mobilize pro-social network
Examples of interventions	Parent-parent Peer counseling Network Volunteer linking	Connect with parent support	Connect with formal and informal support systems Mobilize change efforts	Booster sessions Peer counseling Mutual aid Support groups
Challenges and obstacles	Mobilizing sufficient informal resources Linking with formal supports	Mobilizing sufficient formal resources and services	Maintaining contact between parent and child	Maintaining change over home Fostering new connections

supportive services before, during, and after placement. Among the key variables to consider at each point in the continuum are (1) assessment issues; (2) social support goals; (3) interventions; and (4) challenges and obstacles. These variables are illustrated in Table 3.1.

PLACEMENT PREVENTION SERVICES

Placement-prevention services attempt to avert the need for placement by intervening intensively to defuse the precipitating crisis event and to restore safety within the family. The key social support assessment issue is determining what supports are needed to help defuse the crisis situation that precipitated the need for placement. For some families, concrete assistance in the form of household chores, transportation, and procurement of furniture or child care equipment will be priorities. Other families may need respite from the demands of child care, or emotional and informational support in their roles as parents. Still others may need to rely on supportive resources as a backup to maintain child safety and supervision.

Social network interventions are highly congruent with placement-prevention program goals, as the following examples indicate:

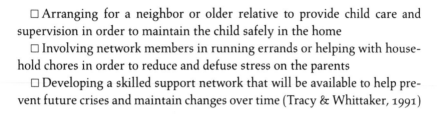

☐ Arranging for a neighbor or older relative to provide child care and supervision in order to maintain the child safely in the home

☐ Involving network members in running errands or helping with household chores in order to reduce and defuse stress on the parents

☐ Developing a skilled support network that will be available to help prevent future crises and maintain changes over time (Tracy & Whittaker, 1991)

Since most placement-prevention services are provided on a short-term, time-limited basis, social support goals will, out of necessity, be limited in scope. Some families may be socially isolated or have few network members to rely upon for help. The goal may be to increase the quantity of social support resources via volunteer linking, parent-to-parent matching, or parent support groups. An individual family member may benefit from more supportive social connections, such as in linking a youth with a Big Brother or Big Sister.

Other families may need assistance to enhance the quality of existing network relationships through network facilitation techniques. This might involve, for example, helping parents learn better ways to handle criticism from relatives in order to improve relationships in the extended family. Network members may be involved in training and educational sessions so they are better prepared to perform supportive roles vis-à-vis the family (Barsh, Moore, & Hamerlynck, 1983).

Social network interventions are highly congruent with the empowerment philosophy of placement-prevention programs. In addition, the home-based worker's knowledge of the family situation and the variety of roles ordinarily held by the worker provide a firm groundwork for these forms of intervention.

There are, however, a number of service challenges and obstacles to avoid. For example, families with extensive substance abuse problems present special concerns. It may be difficult to mobilize sufficient network resources from within the existing network. The family may be surrounded by a network that supports and reinforces substance abuse. Or the network may be overwhelmed by caregiving demands and be unwilling or unable to provide further help. Rebuilding of new nonabusing networks, including involvement in Alcoholics Anonymous or other 12-step programs, may be necessary.

Another challenge is the process of linking families to community resources in a timely manner. In some areas, follow-up supportive services may be lacking. In others, the waiting period before services begin or before intake is complete may extend well beyond the time period of placement-prevention services. Often, families need considerable support to follow through on referrals.

PREPLACEMENT SERVICES

Parent involvement and family support are key factors in facilitating the child's return home from placement, and in maintaining and generalizing the changes achieved during the placement (Lewis, 1984; Taylor & Alpert, 1973). Parent involvement is best begun even before the child's placement takes place. Various strategies have been proposed to engage families in all phases of the placement process (Jenson & Whittaker, 1987). Intake activities, such as preadmission orientations, arranged visits, and written treatment plans, help ensure that parents understand the placement experience and become part of the decision-making process. Supportive services to the family at this stage attempt to define the roles and responsibilities of all parties, to assess the family situation at the time of placement, to help parents and children cope with emotional reactions to separation, and to set expectations for future parent involvement and visitation.

In terms of social support assessment at preplacement, it is important to consider the degree to which the family will be supported during the transition period. For example, do other relatives and key family friends understand the reasons for the placement? Will the network be willing and able to help parents cope with feelings of depression, guilt, and failure, or will they exacerbate these feelings? Are there network members who might provide concrete supports, such as child care for siblings or transportation, to enable the parents to participate fully in the child's placement?

While any number of social network interventions might be employed during preplacement services, perhaps the most important is informational support to the parents and family about the placement experience. Roles and responsibilities will likely vary depending on the type of placement—foster family, group home, or residential treatment. In any event, parents need an introduction to new roles.

Home-based services at this point in the continuum could help with the transition and also yield valuable assessment information about the child, family, and environmental factors contributing to the need for placement, since ultimately these factors must be reduced or resolved during the placement period. One promising network approach is for parents of children currently in placement to reach out to newly enrolled families. The parents can provide firsthand information about the program and help prepare the new parents to become involved in the helping process (Mitchell, 1982).

One of the main challenges to service delivery at this point is mobilizing sufficient formal services and resources to address multiple family problems. Accurate assessment is a prerequisite to adequate service provision. In addition, the family must be positively engaged in the helping process and receptive to the services offered. This may mean that the worker initially must supply the motivation and hope that the family will need to engage and invest energy in change efforts.

DURING PLACEMENT

Parental involvement during placement requires a shift in focus from child-centered to family-centered services, meaning that the entire family becomes the unit of attention. Traditionally, parents of children in out-of-home care were not involved in the placement process, being viewed as part of the problem rather than as part of the solution (Whittaker, 1979). A number of practical considerations also limited parental involvement: lack of financial resources, the location of placement facilities in rural or isolated areas, sociocultural differences between treatment personnel and parents, parental guilt, and the presence of multiple family problems (Whittaker, 1981).

Placement is now more commonly viewed as a support to parents, and parents are involved in all phases of the placement process (Whittaker, 1979). Services to parents of children in placement seek to maintain contact between family members, improve parent-child relationships, enhance parenting skills, and generalize and maintain the child's behavioral gains (Blumenthal & Weinberg, 1984). While biological families are the most common resource for permanency planning, they may also be the most vulnerable. In many cases, the original parent-child problems and family problems precipitating the need for placement have not been resolved at the time of reunification (Turner, 1986). Upon the child's return, many biological families have continuing needs for the most basic of services: housing, medical/ dental, counseling, special educational, recreational, legal (Fein, Maluccio, Hamilton, & Ward, 1983).

As a result, a number of follow-up studies have documented that the least stable and productive type of permanent plan is return to the biological family (Barth & Berry, 1987; Lahti, 1982; Rzepnicki, 1987; Seltzer & Bloksberg, 1987). It is estimated that as many as 43% of children reunited with their biological parents reenter foster care within one to two years (Maluccio, 1988). At least one study has shown that the continuation of problems which led to placement was directly linked to the reason for the child's reentry into foster care (Folaron & Hess, 1991).

It is essential that families receive services during the child's placement in order for successful reunification to occur. In most placement settings, this takes the form of involvement in treatment activities, parent training and education, parent support groups, or conjoint family therapy (Jenson & Whittaker, 1987). The key issue in terms of social support assessment is whether supports are available to facilitate change. In other words, will the family's network be willing and capable of reinforcing behavior changes, or will the network sabotage interventions in unanticipated ways?

It is during the child's placement that families will require the most informational, emotional, and concrete support. Support may be provided, for example, by placement staff, group home parents, child care staff, and social workers. But unless informal helping resources are mobilized as well, behavioral changes may be more difficult to sustain over time.

A challenge during this phase of family support is maintaining contact between parent and child. Many factors will mitigate against regular parental visiting, and yet parental visiting remains the strongest predictor of whether a child remains in care or returns to the biological family (Lawder, Poulin, & Andrews, 1986; Turner, 1986). The family's social network may be able to play a key role in supporting visitation, either through emotional support and encouragement or through concrete assistance in traveling to and from visits. Preliminary analysis of family contact data during placement at Boysville highlights the critical function of regular telephone contact between youth and their extended families and suggests several tantalizing possibilities for network interventions (Whittaker, Overstreet, Kapp, Fine, & Mooradian, 1991).

Social network assessments may also reveal other significant relatives or network members who should be considered part of the visiting plan. These significant others may have special influence with the child. They also may represent culturally significant patterns of help seeking and giving, as in the special role of grandparents in African-American families. In situations in which reunification with the parents is not possible, the child may well be able to maintain connections with some other key family members, and regular contact with these individuals during placement would help facilitate continued contact upon emancipation (Maluccio, Krieger, & Pine, 1990).

The focus on the components of social support and the use to which social network data are put for a youth in care may result in a reconceptualization of the family-helping role in placement services. Here, we are inclined to agree with Bernheim that "Families generally want some combination of information, education, opportunities for emotional ventilation and support, professional availability during times of crisis and contact with other families who have similar difficulties. They wish to understand what constitutes reasonable expectations for them . . . [and] to have meaningful participation in treatment and discharge planning" (1989, p. 562). Her definition of the "Family Consultant" role best captures the nonhierarchical, strength-based, educational approach to family work that we believe ought to inform family work for children and youth in out-of-home care.

AFTERCARE SERVICES

Social support also plays a key role in aftercare services. Family, peer, and school supports at the time of discharge are related to long-term adjustment upon return to the community (Jenson, Hawkins, & Catalano, 1986). In addition, the parent's attitude toward the return, the amount of planning for the return, and the perception that the return is permanent have been found to be factors in successful reunification, as is the role of the foster parents or group caretakers and their relationship with the biological family (Green & Bremseth, 1986).

Several efforts are under way to provide intensive family reunification services prior to discharge, based on the practice principles of home-based family preservation programs (Fein & Staff, 1991). Other means of achieving community reintegration include the use of family support groups just prior to and just after discharge, posttreatment youth groups, aftercare teams, and liaison specialists (Jenson & Whittaker, 1987). Key social support issues in-

67

clude increasing the quantity and quality of support available both to the youth and family.

Most placement and treatment settings provide a rich mix of supportive services, which are often difficult to replicate in the community setting. For example, the youth who has benefited from positive peer culture will need help locating a similar reference group upon return to the community. The teenage mother who is discharged from foster care will need to be connected to supports for her new single-parenting role; she may also need help renegotiating a new form of relationship with her former foster parents (Maluccio et al., 1990). Practical support may be most important—for example, help in obtaining a vocational program, employment, or housing. In addition, some youth and families—for example, in cases of substance abuse or gang activity—will need to have a pro-social network mobilized on their behalf. Peer counseling with others in a similar situation may be effective, either on an individual basis or via mutual aid groups.

The challenge is to maintain change over time and to be able to foster new social connections that will be mutually satisfying to all concerned. This may require more cooperative working agreements and linkages between residential programs and community-based services in order to help youth and families maintain positive changes. Case advocacy and community development efforts may be needed in order to ensure that appropriate services are available. As Wells and Whittington (1990) pointed out, social and community deficits in terms of housing, food, education, medical care, and employment may be responsible for putting a greater number of youth at risk for placement and may make it more difficult for children and youth to return home once removed. It is also important to remember that both the youth and family may have distinctly different social support needs, especially for those youth who have emancipation or adoption as the end goal. Whether the goal is reintegration or emancipation, recent research on post-discharge adaptation of troubled youth suggests the critical role that family support plays in determining adaptation (Wells et al., 1991).

Conclusion

The preceding sections have outlined the importance of family support and involvement at each point in the continuum of care. In our view, social network interventions are an essential component of family support services because these interventions are designed to build a skilled support system for the family that will help maintain changes over time once professional involvement has been completed. Moreover, we believe that the focus on the "basics" of social support—emotional, informational, and concrete aid— ought to be considered as part of the essential assessment for youth and families at all points on the service continuum. Our goal is to help youth and families acquire new competencies and skills in dealing with their environment. At the same time, it is essential that we help to restructure and enrich these environments so that they are more supportive and nurturing (Whittaker, Schinke, & Gilchrist, 1986).

As Maluccio (1981) has suggested, assessment of the person needs to be complemented by a careful evaluation of that person's environment and its contribution to needs, problems, or solutions. Maluccio poses a number of environment assessment questions:

☐ Does the environment support, nourish, and challenge the person?
☐ What is interfering with efforts to use available supports and resources?
☐ What needs to be added, removed, or otherwise changed in order to achieve a better person-environment fit?

Incorporating social network assessments and interventions on a routine basis will not be achieved without some accommodations on the part of family workers. There are a number of institutional, professional, and conceptual barriers to adoption of social network interventions (Whittaker, 1986). No doubt these interventions would require a new knowledge base for practice, expanded practice roles such as the role of family consultant suggested by Bernheim (1989), and reformulations of worker-client relationships. In terms of outcome research, the long-term effects of many social network interventions remain largely untested and unknown. It seems clear, though, that while social network interventions would not replace the need for skilled professional involvement with families, they do have the potential to enhance and extend the impact of these interventions for children and their families.

As a short-term goal, we think it important that family preservation and other community-based prevention programs work together with special foster care, residential treatment, and other placement services to identify ways in which promising network and social support strategies can be transferred from one setting to another. We believe that those involved in aftercare efforts can learn much from those involved in prevention and vice versa. Building a truly family-supportive service continuum means breaking down some of the artificial barriers that have evolved between various types of care and service. We believe a focus on extended youth and family networks and on identifying basic support needs provides a particularly good vehicle for launching that discussion.

References

Allerhand, M. E., Weber, R., & Haug, M. (1966). *Adaptation and adaptability: The Bellefaire follow-up study.* New York: Child Welfare League of America.

Barsh, E. T., Moore, J. A., & Hamerlynck, L. A. (1983). The Foster Extended Family: A support network for handicapped foster children. *Child Welfare, 62,* 349–359.

Barth, R., & Berry, M. (1987). Outcomes of child welfare services under permanency planning. *Social Service Review, 61,* 71–90.

Bernheim, K. F. (1989). Psychologists and families on the severely mentally ill: The role of family consultation. *American Psychologist, 44,* 561–564.

Blumenthal, K., & Weinberg, A. (Eds.). (1984). *Establishing parent involvement in foster care agencies.* New York: Child Welfare League of America.

Fein, E., Maluccio, A. N., Hamilton, V., & Ward, D. (1983). After foster care: Outcomes of permanency planning for children. *Child Welfare, 62,* 485–558.

Fein, E., & Staff, I. (1991). Implementing reunification services. *Families in Society, 72,* 335–343.

Folaron, G., & Hess, P. (1991). Placement decisions: Teaching effectiveness in child welfare practice and policy. Paper presented at Annual Program Meeting, Council on Social Work Education, March 1991, New Orleans LA.

Fraser, M. W., Pecora, P. J., & Haapala, D. A. (1991). *Families in crisis: The impact of intensive family preservation services.* Hawthorne NY: Aldine deGruyter.

Gaudin, J. M., Wodarski, J. S., Arkinson, M. K., & Avery, L. S. (1990–91). Remedying child neglect: Effectiveness of social network interventions. *Journal of Applied Social Sciences, 15*(1), 97–123.

Green, R., & Bremseth, M. (1986). *California foster parent training survey final report.* Atlanta GA: Child Welfare Institute.

Jacobsen, D. E. (1986). Types and timing of social support. *Journal of Health and Social Behavior, 27,* 250–264.

Jenson, J., Hawkins, J., & Catalano, R. (1986). Social support in aftercare services for troubled youth. *Children and Youth Services Review, 8,* 323–347.

Jenson, J. M., & Whittaker, J. K. (1987). Parental involvement in children's residential treatment: From preplacement to aftercare. *Children and Youth Services Review, 9,* 81–100.

Jones, R. R., Weinrott, M. R., & Howard, J. R. (1981). *Impact of the Teaching Family*

Model on troublesome youth: Findings from the National Evaluation. Rockville MD: National Institute of Mental Health (reproduced by National Technical Information Service, U.S. Department of Commerce, Springfield VA, PB82-224353).

Lahti, J. (1982). A follow-up study of foster children in permanent placements. *Social Service Review, 56,* 556–571.

Lawder, E., Poulin, J., & Andrews, R. (1986). A study of 185 foster children 5 years after placement. *Child Welfare, 65*(3), 241–251.

Lewis, W. W. (1982). Ecological factors in successful residential treatment. *Behavioral Disorders, 7,* 149–156.

Lewis, W. W. (1984). Ecological change: A necessary condition for residential treatment. *Child Care Quarterly, 13,* 21–29.

Maluccio, A. N. (Ed.). (1981). *Promoting competence: A new old approach to social work practice.* New York: Free Press.

Maluccio, A. N. (1988). *Promoting reunification through agency collaboration* (Proposal summary). Hartford: University of Connecticut, Center for the Study of Child Welfare.

Maluccio, A. N., Krieger, R., & Pine, B. A. (1990). *Preparing adolescents for life after foster care: The central role of foster parents.* Washington DC: Child Welfare League of America.

Maluccio, A. N., & Whittaker, J. K. (1988). Helping the biological families of children in out-of-home placement. In E. W. Nunnally, C. S. Chilman, & F. M. Cox (Eds.), *Troubled relationships: Families in trouble series* (Vol. 3, pp. 205–217). Newbury Park CA: Sage.

Mitchell, C. A. (1982). Planning with parents: The use of groups in residential treatment. *Social Work with Groups, 5*(4), 32–45.

Nelson, R. H., Singer, M. J., & Johnsen, L. O. (1978). The application of a residential treatment evaluation model. *Child Care Quarterly, 7,* 164–175.

Rzepnicki, T. (1987). Recidivism of foster children returned to their own homes: A review and new direction for research. *Social Service Review, 61,* 56–68.

Seltzer, M., & Bloksberg, L. (1987). Permanency planning and its effects on foster children: A review of the literature. *Social Work, 32*(1), 65–68.

Taylor, D. A., & Alpert, S. W. (1973). *Continuity and support following residential treatment.* New York: Child Welfare League of America.

Tracy, E. M., & Whittaker, J. K. (1990). The Social Network Map: Assessing social support in clinical social work practice. *Families in Society, 71*(8), 461–470.

Tracy, E. M., & Whittaker, J. K. (1991). Social network assessment and goal setting in intensive family preservation services practice. In E. M. Tracy, J. Kinney, D. Haapala, & P. Pecora (Eds.), *Intensive family preservation services: An instruc-*

tional sourcebook (pp. 193–202). Cleveland OH: Case Western Reserve University, Mandel School of Applied Social Sciences.

Tracy, E. M., Whittaker, J. K., & Mooradian, J. (1990). *Training resources on social networks and social support.* (Available from authors, Mandel School of Applied Social Sciences, Case Western Reserve University, Cleveland OH.)

Turner, J. (1986). Successful reunification of foster children with their biological parents: Characteristics of parents and children. *Child Care Quarterly, 15*(1), 51–55.

Wells, K., & Whittington, D. (1990). Prior services used by youth referred to mental health facilities: A closer look. *Children and Youth Services Review, 12,* 243–256.

Wells, K., Wyatt, E., & Hobfoll, S. (1991). Factors associated with adaptation of youths discharged from residential treatment. *Children and Youth Services Review, 13*(3), 199–217.

Whittaker, J. K. (1979). *Caring for troubled children.* San Francisco: Jossey-Bass.

Whittaker, J. K. (1981). Family involvement in residential treatment: A support system for parents. In A. N. Maluccio & P. A. Sinanoglu (Eds.), *The challenge of partnership: Working with parents of children in foster care* (pp. 67–88). New York: Child Welfare League of America.

Whittaker, J. K. (1986). Formal and informal helping in child welfare services: Implications for management and practice. *Child Welfare, 65,* 17–25.

Whittaker, J. K., & Garbarino, J. (1983). *Social support networks: Informal helping in the human services.* New York: Aldine.

Whittaker, J. K., Overstreet, E., Kapp, S., Fine, D., & Mooradian, J. (1991). *Differential patterns of family involvement in residential youth care and involvement: An empirical analysis.* Unpublished manuscript, Boysville of Michigan, Clinton MI.

Whittaker, J. K., Schinke, S., & Gilchrist, L. (1986). The ecological paradigm in child, youth and family services: Implications for policy and practice. *Social Service Review, 60,* 483–503.

Whittaker, J. K., & Tracy, E. M. (1990). Social network intervention in intensive family-based preventive services. *Prevention in Human Services, 9*(1), 175–192.

Whittaker, J. K., Tracy, E. M., & Marckworth, M. (1989). *Family Support Project* (Final Report). Seattle: University of Washington.

Whittaker, J. K., Tracy, E. M., Overstreet, E., Mooradian, J., & Kapp, S. (1994). Intervention design for practice: Enhancing social supports for high risk youth and families. In J. Rothman & E. J. Thomas (Eds.), *Intervention Research: Design and development for human service* (pp. 195–212). New York: Haworth Press.

4

Parent Support and Education Programs: Their Role in the Continuum of Child and Family Services

Robert Halpern

"No, my friend," said Bacon softly, ". . . If you people were that worried about the children you would build the day-care center yourself and hire the best professional people to work in it, people with experience. You wouldn't even talk about hiring the people off the streets. What do the people of the streets know about running a day-care center? No, my friend, you're investing in something else. You're investing in steam control." – Tom Wolfe, *Bonfire of the Vanities*

Deliberate intervention to strengthen the ability of parents—particularly low income parents—to protect, nurture, and guide their children has a long history in the United States (Boyer, 1978; Grubb & Lazerson, 1982). Whatever the socially defined problems of children in a particular era, inadequate parenting has been implicated as a causal factor. Historically, the principal thrust of efforts to address problems attributed in whole or part to inadequate parenting has been to supplement or compensate for parental care. But there have always been efforts to strengthen such care as well. Examples include the "moral guidance" provided by the nineteenth-century friendly visitors, the settlement workers' advice and assistance in child-rearing matters, and the family casework of the first child and family service agencies (Lubove, 1968). In this chapter I examine one of the principal strategies to emerge in the current era to strengthen parenting: parent support and education programs for families with infants and young children. These programs provide guidance, assistance, and encouragement to parents, and sometimes direct developmental services to children, with the objectives of promoting attentive parenting, parents' personal development, and healthy child development.

Today's parent support and education programs represent both a continuation of and a departure from the efforts of earlier eras. Like those prior efforts, current programs tend to be targeted at low-income families and to be oriented toward helping families adjust to difficult life conditions rather than toward changing those conditions. But the current generation of programs is the first to focus so clearly on child rearing during infancy and early childhood and the first to be subject to systematic empirical scrutiny. Finally, today's parenting programs are struggling more fully to develop helping strategies that balance authoritative guidance in the child-rearing norms of the era with support for families' own self-directed child-rearing and coping efforts.

Formative Influences on Parent Support and Education

Today's parent support and education programs are, in part, a legacy of the War on Poverty's community action programs. At a generic level, today's programs have incorporated many of the philosophical and strategic tenets of community action, such as the use of indigenous paraprofessionals to provide direct services; advocacy and service brokerage on behalf of families; and attempts to embed programs physically and socially in community life. More specifically, it was in this period that the notion of early childhood intervention for economically disadvantaged children and their families first emerged. Initially, this notion was translated into the largely child-focused Head Start program. (Although Head Start involved parents in a variety of roles, it did not provide services designed to strengthen parenting per se.) But by the late 1960s, Head Start's managers and their academic consultants began to feel that in order to prepare poor children for the demands of formal schooling, it would be necessary to strengthen the family environment, beginning in infancy (Skerry, 1983). This concern sparked an era of increasing, and increasingly heterogeneous, interest in parent support and education, fueled by a number of key social trends.

Beginning in the mid-1970s, after having declined for 15 years, poverty among families with young children began increasing. It would continue to increase until 1986, leveling off at about 10% for white children and families and close to 50% for nonwhites. Moreover, poverty among families with young children was increasingly coming to be associated with single parenthood, onset of childbearing during adolescence, and social and geographic isolation from the mainstream of society (Wilson, 1987). Together these trends exacerbated not only school failure but such related problems as child abuse and neglect and juvenile delinquency, simultaneously suggesting new purposes for and complicating the tasks of preventively oriented, family-level interventions.

During this same period there was growing public (and, indeed, provider) frustration with the inability of the major human service systems to effectively address persistent social problems, resulting at once in a search for new helping paradigms (e.g., application of social support theory to formal helping) and relative decline in the resources granted to human service agencies to meet the needs of growing numbers of high-risk, multistressed young families (Reischauer, 1986; Whittaker, 1986). Ironically, this growing sense of frustration coincided with enormous progress in the understanding of both normal development and developmental risk in infancy and early childhood, creating for the first time a solid knowledge base for preventively oriented professional help focused on promoting development and reducing risk.

Questions Facing the Genre

Today's parent support and education programs, then, are seeking a useful social role in a context of worsening social conditions for young families; a troubled human service system in transition to an as yet undefined future; a rapidly emerging knowledge base for clinical intervention in infancy; and a policy climate characterized at once by renewed interest in addressing poverty-related problems and few new dollars for social problem solving. This context, together with the inherent tensions embodied in parenting interventions, has yielded a genre characterized by a number of unresolved strategic dilemmas and identity issues.

For example, are parent support and education programs more appropriately conceived as formal helping services, or as an additional source of social support for hard-pressed families? Should they concentrate on helping new parents adjust to parenting and coping as best as possible with poverty-related stresses, or should they actually strive to alter parents' childrearing styles and capacities, and perhaps promote other kinds of personal change? Who, therefore, should do the helping in parent support and education programs, and what kinds of skills should these helpers have? Should parent support and education programs cast a broad net, or strive to serve families whose personal history and/or social situation suggest heightened risk of inattentive parenting? Questions of strategy aside, why should these programs, often the least adequately funded, have to be on the front line of efforts to address the worsening conditions of families with young children? Further, what can reasonably be expected of any kind of family-level interventions, given American society's seeming indifference to the well-being of families with young children?

A Closer Look at Parent Support and Education Programs

There have been a number of recent efforts at defining parent support education (Halpern, 1990; Kagan & Shelley, 1987; Weiss & Halpern, 1988; Weissbourd, 1987; Weissbourd & Kagan, 1989). But in spite of such efforts, there is only moderate agreement on the purposes and helping strategies that characterize the genre. Lack of consensus on definition is due in part to ideological and theoretical differences among those working in this field. It is due also to variability in actual practice flowing not only from differences in conceptualization but also differences in the characteristics of families served by different programs, in program auspices, disciplinary background and social characteristics of service providers, amount of funding, and the mandates of funders. Yet there is also a recognizable core to the field, consisting of a certain approach to helping described by numerous observers and participants.

TWO PROGRAMS, TWO APPROACHES

To illustrate both the heterogeneity and the shared elements of parent support and education, I discuss briefly two examples, both carefully conceived and implemented demonstrations widely considered within the purview of the genre. The first is the Yale Child Welfare Research Project (Provence & Naylor, 1983). In this program a highly skilled interdisciplinary team consisting of a clinical social worker, nurse, pediatrician, day-care worker, and psychologist provided an individually tailored mix of supportive services from birth to 30 months to 18 low-income families in New Haven. The program included twice monthly home visits by the social workers, primary health care, from 2 to 28 months of high-quality day care (average: 13 months), and developmental exams. Activities other than home visits took place at a remodeled house located in the neighborhood in which participating families lived. The second project is the Maternal and Infant Health Outreach Worker (MIHOW) program, part of the Ford Foundation's Child Survival/Fair Start Initiative (Clinton, 1989; Halpern & Larner, 1987). In the MIHOW program, implemented in Appalachia and the mid-South, specially trained and supervised community women delivered monthly home visits from midpregnancy to age two to low-income families in five geographically and socially isolated rural communities. The average family that completed the program received 5 prenatal and 17 postnatal home visits.

The two intervention programs were obviously different in the amount and kinds of intervention that each family received, the involvement of professionals (and, conversely, of the community), and the resources each could bring to bear. Even the common element of home visits in the two programs differed substantially. The Yale Child Welfare home visitors were experienced psychiatric social workers, with years of problem-centered, psychodynamically oriented clinical experience. Because there were other team members focusing on the needs of the children, they could be "the parent's person" (Provence & Naylor, 1983, p. 19). Their highly individualized work with families had a strong mental health orientation based on the idea that "better parenting may be possible mainly as an indirect result of helping the [parent reduce her] own psychological neediness and stress" (p. 20).

The MIHOW "natural helpers" were residents of the isolated low-income communities that they served; many had limited formal education; a number began as MIHOW clients. Their work with families, while also responsive and individualized, was guided by a common health and parenting curriculum that focused primarily on the parents' role in meeting children's developmental needs, and secondarily on parents' own support needs. The use of a curriculum was based on the rationale that community women with no prior formal helping experience would work more effectively with some external resources (i.e., methods, information, activities) on which to draw. In contrast to a mental health model, MIHOW was better characterized as an "information and resources" model (Booth, Barnard, Mitchell, & Spieker, 1987). The use of community women in the MIHOW project was in part driven by necessity; unlike the New Haven setting, there were few formal human services in the communities involved. But it was also the result of the program initiator's commitment to self-help and mutual support among community women as paths to community development.

In spite of the numerous differences between the two programs, there were similarities as well, and these point to what seems to bind this "hetero-geneous genre." Both met people "where they lived," not only physically but psychologically and socially as well. Both provided emotional support, encouragement, and assistance in the framework of families' own efforts to master parenting and other developmental tasks and to cope with various reality problems associated with poverty. In both programs, the home visi-tors tried to act as sympathetic listeners responding to the needs that each family expressed. In both, the home visits represented not just a physical reaching out to families but an expression of caring and commitment to the family extended over a long period of time.

COMMON CHARACTERISTICS: A WORKING DEFINITION

Parent support and education programs, then, are those in which specially trained community members (or, less commonly, professionals) provide sus-tained support to families during pregnancy, infancy, or early childhood. Because families vary in support needs, and because family workers vary in social background, child development knowledge, theoretical orientation, and helping skills, support provided takes many forms.

As the two program illustrations suggest, support might be focused more on parents' own psychological or developmental needs, on parenting knowl-edge and skills, or on feelings about parenting. Support might include provi-sion of information about basic infant care, about the ways in which infants express their needs, or about what feelings an expectant parent can anticipate when the new baby comes. It might include discussing with a parent some of the things that she has observed about her baby; commenting on the positive and effective things she does with the baby; directly "engaging the infant in social, play, motor or language activity" as a way of modeling activities that the parent might want to try herself (Bromwich, 1978, p. 181); or drawing a parent's attention to how much her baby seems to enjoy (or be distressed by) certain stimuli. It might include active assistance with practical problems such as child care or transportation; advocacy for a family's efforts to secure entitlements and services; or a reminder of a coming medical appointment. It might mean providing a sympathetic ear as well as concrete suggestions for a teen mother struggling with her own mother's refusal to allow the baby's father to be involved with the baby. It might mean helping a young mother find strategies for managing her toddler's oppositional behavior, or even helping her become aware of how her own emotional and behavioral responses are contributing to that behavior. It might mean encouragement and assistance for a young mother who expresses interest in continuing or renewing her education.

These discrete dimensions of support are provided in the context of a gradually nurtured relationship between family and program staff. Given many low-income families' negative history with formal helping institutions, program staff often must work patiently to earn trust by being reliable and responsive to immediate concerns and pressing problems. Ideally, as trust solidifies, parents begin to volunteer issues meaningful to them in the personal sphere, in the parent-child relationship, or in general family functioning. Once "certain core issues are identified, the repeated articulation, confrontation and resolution of these issues, whether on a verbal or more concrete problem-solving basis," creates the conditions for gains to be consolidated (Heinicke, Beckwith, & Tompson, 1988, p. 137).

The immediate objectives of the multifaceted support provided in parent support and education programs are to promote attentive and nurturant parenting, parent's psychological well-being, and personal development. The ultimate objective is to promote healthy child development, or in child welfare–oriented terms, to prevent developmental harm. In some cases, parent support and education programs are also conceptualized as a community development strategy designed to identify and activate latent helping resources in a community, to foster enduring helping relationships among community members, to provide community members a voice for communicating to dominant institutions their own assessment of what their lives are like, and, less commonly, to stimulate collective action to address community problems.

Some parent support and education programs work with families primarily through a single modality, most commonly home visits or parent groups located in a convenient neighborhood setting. A growing number provide numerous services through a variety of modalities based at and emanating from a "family support center." In addition to home visits and parent support groups, such services might include parent-child activities, health and developmental screening, personal counseling on a range of family life issues, GED and adult education classes, meals, respite care, developmental day care, transportation, and primary health care. Some family support centers have a drop-in dimension which permits families to draw on support

79

when and how they need it and allows for a gradual nurturing of ability and commitment to participate in formal activities.

Distinct Helping Philosophy

Parent support and education programs are defined not only by a set of helping purposes and strategies but by a set of helping principles as well (Weiss & Halpern, 1988). Participation in these programs is generally voluntary. At the same time, program staff feel responsible for reaching out to families unwilling or unable to seek support themselves and for nurturing their capacity to accept and use support. Physically, most programs are easily accessible, and most have relatively simple, nonthreatening intake procedures. Parent support and education programs strive to be sensitive to each family's sociocultural heritage, viewing such heritage as a critical source of identity and self-esteem. Participants have a voice in shaping the emphases and content of their interactions with the program and, in some cases, in shaping basic program design. In general, services provided are shaped by community conditions and concerns and by the gaps in other helping services.

Target Population

The majority of parent support and education programs serve low-income families. Programs typically make their services available to any family in a specific population of low-income families, defined by residence in a particular neighborhood or human service agency catchment area. On its surface this makes sense, since poverty is so strongly implicated with the child welfare and child development problems that parenting programs strive to prevent. The rationale for relatively broad targeting is that the stressful familial and extrafamilial environments in which low-income families live pose inherent threats to both parents' and infants' well-being and development.

Alternatively, some programs focus on low-income families identified as being at risk of inattentive or inappropriate parenting due to extreme parental youth (i.e., teen-parenting programs), maternal depression, prior history of parenting problems, a difficult-to-care-for child, or other risk factors. The rationale here is based more on the heterogeneity of low-income families in functioning and support needs. These more focused programs may serve families identified and referred by one or more institutional sources—for example, a public hospital or health department clinic, a child and family service agency, or even protective services staff. Or they may both accept referrals and seek their own participants. Programs for pregnant and parenting teens often employ this latter strategy.

Sponsorship

Most often parent support and education programs are initiated by neighborhood agencies as service programs responding to perceived neighborhood needs. Funding is typically modest and usually secured opportunistically on a year-to-year basis. Weissbourd (1987) describes the growth of programs in the 1970s: "Program initiators used the available resources around them and patched together a web of mutual aid, information and linkages to other resources to begin meeting the needs they saw" (p. 50). There is also a "demonstration" stream in parent support and education, single- and multi-site efforts with significant research components. This program stream provides the empirical base for the field.

In the past few years, a number of states have initiated what are in different stages of becoming statewide networks of programs. Initiatives in Connecticut, Florida, Illinois, and Maryland are linked to their social service systems; in Kentucky, Minnesota, and Missouri to their education systems. These "pioneering" initiatives vary considerably in resource richness, target population, policy objectives, degree of local autonomy, and quality control mechanisms and thus bear careful watching for lessons useful to other states (Weiss, 1989).

The Logic of Parent Support and Education Programs

The main theoretical rationale for parent support and education programs is found in the notion of parents as the primary influence on the developing infant and young child. Obviously, parenting is not the only influence on young children's development. Children need adequate housing, medical care, nutrition, safe environments in which to play, and, not least, good-quality child care and education programs. But in early childhood, parents constitute children's primary environment. Parental guidance, encouragement, and praise form the scaffolding for young children's efforts to master developmental tasks. Parent and infant create a style of interacting in which the infant gradually transforms into his or her own style of adjusting to events in life (Massie, Bronstein, Afterman, & Campbell, 1988, p. 214). Parents also play a critical role in mediating between children and the larger environment, protecting children from threats to their well-being, seeking

81

out such community resources as early childhood education programs, and interpreting and giving meaning to the worlds inside and outside the family context (Musick, 1987).

An additional rationale for parent support and education can be found in the importance of this phase of life to parents themselves. The way in which young adults adjust to parenting and cope with other developmental tasks sets a foundation not only for their children's future but for their own as well. Becoming a parent is a critical event in the long-term processes of separation from one's own parents and identity consolidation. Indeed, it is a point where these two processes meet as new parents (unconsciously) select and internalize those characteristics of their own parents with which they will identify and reenact features of their own parenting.

For all young adults, but especially for those with difficult personal histories, becoming a parent is thus a time not only of promise but of heightened vulnerability as issues from the past, present, and future converge and have to be integrated. Low-risk environments provide resources that help reduce the stresses and buffer the vulnerabilities activated by parenthood. But high-risk environments tend to magnify both the stresses and vulnerabilities (Solnit, 1983). It is in such environments that ever greater numbers of young adults are struggling to master parenting and related developmental tasks.

One of the most important social trends of the current era is the increasing concentration of poverty in the United States in families with young children (Halpern, 1987). Families can and do cope adaptively with the stresses associated with poverty. But the grudging and sometimes dehumanizing way in which our society provides basic supports to poor families undermines efforts to cope adaptively and, especially, to attend to young children's pressing needs. The inherent stresses associated with poverty in the United States have been compounded in recent years by a deterioration in the social fabric holding low-income communities together, a fabric that traditionally provided at least a measure of support and nurturance for low-income families (Wilson, 1987). Further, an increasing proportion of young adults embarking on parenting under conditions of poverty were themselves reared in poverty, personally experiencing its physical and psychological injuries. These young parents are disproportionately likely to have experienced poor or erratic nurturance as children and to bring the residue of such experience to their own parenting (Egeland, Jacobovitz, & Papatola, 1987; Solnit, 1983).

Granting that parents constitute young children's "primary environment,"

and that worsening poverty among young families is producing or exacer-
bating stresses that make parenting difficult, especially for parents with
few "self" resources on which to draw, why focus on parent support and
education per se? For the majority of low-income families, why not address directly the contextual factors that impinge on parenting and child
development, such as dangerous neighborhoods, overcrowded and dilapi-
dated housing, unstable and poor-quality day care, constant scrambling to
make ends meet? For the highest-risk families, in whom stresses may in fact
be centered and played out in the parent-child relationship, why not assure
access to sustained and skilled therapeutic interventions focusing on both
concrete needs and psychodynamic obstacles to nurturant parenting?

Addressing directly the situational stresses that make parenting difficult
in American society would require a significant reorientation of social arrangements and public priorities. Such a reorientation does not appear to
be forthcoming. While public awareness of the fragile situation of families
with young children is growing, the social and political will to address that
situation is barely discernible (Hart, 1989). That leaves what de Lone (1979)
has called "secondary strategies": predominantly personal helping services
designed to promote individual well-being, adaptation, and development.

The value of such services is in part a matter of perspective. Some prefer
to focus on their limitations: for example, de Lone (1979), who argues that
services "can counter some of the injuries of inequality . . . [but] are insufficient by themselves to alter the powerlessness, the limited life options, and
the hardships of everyday experience that are the bottom line of inequality"
(p. 68). In effect, services do not alter the social conditions that produce or
exacerbate and ultimately reproduce individual and family problems. Others
prefer to emphasize the (largely unrealized) potential of personal helping
strategies. For example, Schorr (1988) argues that we now have the knowledge and experience to design a carefully orchestrated set of helping services
that not only can improve the odds of favorable long-term outcomes for
high-risk children but that can also alter the causal processes that lead to
intergenerational transmission of child and family problems.

Even within an optimistic framework, personal helping services that could
facilitate coping and adaptation have not reached the great majority of low-
income families, at least not before individual child and family problems
become critical. Categorical mandates, large caseloads, and socialization of
professionals into narrowly conceived helping roles have conspired to pre-

vent the major human service systems from providing prevention-oriented, multifaceted, responsive, and sustained personal assistance to young families (Halpern, 1986; Schorr, 1988). Providers working within the framework of formal helping agencies have demonstrated limited capacity to reach out to families who are unwilling or unable to seek help themselves and to nurture the families' capacity to identify problems and use help. Most providers have been unwilling or unable to go halfway toward bridging cultural, linguistic, and social gaps by starting with families' own child-rearing and coping traditions (Musick & Stott, 1990).

There are only a relative handful of agencies around the country with staff trained to attend to the therapeutic needs of families in which there are signs of serious problems in parent-infant interaction. What are variously called clinical infant programs or infant mental health programs, both built on a qualitative leap in the last two decades in our understanding of infant development, have only just begun to make inroads into the major helping systems. Meanwhile, the need for preventively oriented but clinically informed services built on an understanding of infancy appears to be growing as more and more young adults embarking on parenting bring with them the residue of poor or erratic nurturance (Musick & Halpern, 1989).

The major human service systems have begun to recognize that their services too often reflect "the ambulance service at the bottom of the cliff," and have begun to struggle to find new paradigms and strategies (Farrow, 1988; Weiss, 1989). Parent support and education has been embraced as a vehicle for the working through of one such new strategy in which providers strive to reproduce the beneficial effects of informal support systems in deliberately constructed support programs mobilized around the critical developmental task of adjustment to the parenting role (Gottlieb, 1988; Tracy & Whittaker, in press; Whittaker, 1986).

Ironically, it is not just the beneficial effects of social support that have drawn the interest of human service providers; there is also a growing recognition that informal support does not always provide the validation, encouragement, and assistance that contribute to attentive and nurturant parenting (Bronfenbrenner, 1987). A number of observers have argued that low-income families' strong informal support networks compensate for lack of support from formal helping institutions in mastering developmental tasks and coping with contextual sources of stress (Stack, 1974). But low-income families' network support has always come with costs, which sometimes seemed to equal or outweigh their benefits (Belle, 1982). Moreover, not all the "costs" of using support are external; a young parent may lack the personal psychological resources to seek and accept support where it is available (Rook & Dooley, 1985). Especially in the central cities, there is evidence that informal support systems are "thinning out" and becoming less protective and nurturing (Musick, 1987).

The presumed advantages of deliberately constructed social support, as provided in parent support and education programs, are that it is provided by persons who themselves are not psychologically needy and therefore will not make "draining" reciprocal psychological demands; it provides a direct and knowledgeable link to a range of community resources; and it serves to mediate between the child-rearing norms of a family's reference group and those of the larger society. For young parents whose own families cannot provide the validation, encouragement, guidance, and practical assistance needed to nurture growth and development, deliberately constructed support presumably can fill these family functions, at least at some level.

Parent support and education programs cannot be expected to alter basic parenting capacities and styles acquired through a lifetime of experience in a particular familial and social world and often continually reinforced in the present. Nor can they alter parents' and infants' basic life situations. But success with particular developmental tasks such as parenting is not completely dependent on one's nurturance history, adequacy of family income and supports designed to meet basic needs, neighborhood characteristics, and other less easily alterable factors. The quality of contemporaneous support also influences success with such tasks, and that is where parent support and education programs take their cue.

On the one hand, if deliberately constructed support can set the parent-child relationship, parents' own personal development, and child development on a slightly more positive course, this positive "nudge" should be self-reinforcing, picking up momentum over time. On the other hand, because parent support and education can influence only a few of the many determinants of parenting, and because there are many threats to healthy development in low-income children over which parents may have little control, the effects of parenting programs should theoretically be modest. That, indeed, appears to be the case.

Selection of Studies for Review

In searching for studies that would shed some light on the effectiveness of parent support and education for families at higher than average risk of inattentive parenting, four primary criteria were used: Target children had to be at risk of compromised well-being and development primarily due to environmental rather than biological risk factors (although the latter could be present); direct services had to be primarily parent-focused or, at a minimum, equally focused on parent and child; the study had to have a reasonably strong design; and parent outcomes had to be examined. Each of these criteria eliminated numerous studies, leaving a sample of 20 studies undertaken over a 22-year period. The sample, while not exhaustive, is characteristic of the field.

Before discussing these studies, I would like to comment briefly on the first two criteria because they affect the character of the evidence. Many reviews have mixed studies involving services for parents of disabled infants together with studies involving low-income families (Casto & Mastropieri, 1986; Heverly, Newman, & Forquer, 1982). I am excluding the former from consideration here largely because sources and nature of risk to compromised child development are substantially different in the two populations. Programs for parents of disabled infants generally do not focus on poverty-related obstacles to attentive parenting, but rather employ trained specialists to impart specific skills to parents to meet their children's special developmental needs. Studies of such programs have displayed a more consistent pattern of short-term effects on selected parental behaviors than have studies involving low-income families, in part because investigators measured behaviors that parents were being trained to employ with their children. The exclusion of studies involving disabled infants nonetheless weakens the case for parent support and education if one prefers not to differentiate populations and intervention strategies.

I have also chosen to exclude programs providing primarily direct services to children, supplemented by parent services, to avoid the confounding that occurs when it appears that the services for children are primarily (though not necessarily exclusively) responsible for outcomes found. Among the studies affected, two well-designed experimental studies are particularly notable. The first, the Perry Preschool Study, provided a daily preschool education program for three- and four-year-old children supplemented by weekly home visits (Berrueta-Clement, Schweinhart, Barnett, Epstein, & Weikert, 1984). In the second, the Early Training Project, three- to four-year-old children were provided three summers of daily center-based preschool, complemented during the two intervening nine-month periods by weekly home visits in which the home visitor worked directly with the child as well as with the mother (Gray, Ramsey, & Klaus, 1982).[1]

The Parent Support and Education Evaluation Studies

Table 4.1 illustrates the diversity of helping strategies in parent support and education. Fourteen of the studies provided home visiting exclusively, four provided a mixture of home- and center-based services, and two provided exclusively center-based services. Nine employed professionals as family workers, eight employed paraprofessionals (typically community women), and three employed a mixture of both. Intervention duration ranged from 4 to almost 60 months (average: 12 to 24 months); frequency of contact ranged from four days a week to once a month (average: about twice monthly).

The studies in Table 4.1 are arranged in loosely chronological fashion, and it is possible to observe evolution in the field on many fronts: theoretical orientations, program services and emphases, and target populations. The first generation of studies (Gordon, 1969; Lambie, Bond, & Weikert, 1974; Madden, O'Hara, & Levenstein, 1984) was designed by educational psychologists concerned with improving the teaching and socialization skills of low-income mothers and thereby the cognitive and language development of their children. The educational psychologists were joined in the early 1970s by academics and clinicians concerned with psychosocial obstacles to attentive and nurturant parenting (Bromwich, 1978; Provence & Naylor, 1983; Siegel, Bauman, Schaefer, Saunders, & Ingram, 1980). Their programs tended to focus on "strengthening the psychological milieu and development of emotional or affective relationships between the infant and her/his family" (Silver, 1979, p. 11). During that same period, the whole field became gradually more infused with ecological child development theory. Such theory posited that the "parenting system" is significantly affected by broader support systems, and ecological child development theory has contributed, in some programs, to a broadening of program purposes and activities, such as the provision of health and social services, meals, transportation, and even adult basic education (the Syracuse Family Development Research Program/Lally & Honig, 1977; the Parent Child Development Centers/Andrews et al., 1982; the Child and Family Resource Program/Travers, Nauta, & Irwin, 1982). In the late 1970s and early 1980s, parent support and education also began drawing the attention of the maternal and child health community,

Table 4.1 Summary of Parent Support and Education Evaluation Studies

Name/Reference	Sample/Design	Attrition	Intervention	Treatment Effects
Florida Parent Education; Gordon, 1969; Gordon & Guinagh, 1974	276 low-income, rural southern black families, randomly assigned to treatment (T) or control (C) conditions in 3 cohorts, each cohort varying in child age at entry (3 months, 12 months, 24 months)	30%, not reported by treatment condition	Weekly home visits by specially trained community women, each with a caseload of 10 families; 3 different ages of entry and 2 different program lengths for each yielded 6 treatment lengths from 1 to 3 years; the home visiting worked from Piagetian orientation, bringing activities and games into home for mother to do with her child; strong emphasis on play; when children reached 2 years of age they met in small groups in backyards of different T group families	T children had higher IQs than C children immediately posttreatment; at ages 4–6 children in 2–3-year treatment groups were higher on various achievement measures; no reported parent effects; no residual long-term effects on parents or children
Ypsilanti-Carnegie Infant Education; Lambie, Bond, & Weikart, 1974; Epstein & Weikart, 1979	88 low-income families with infants 3–11 months, 58 white, 30 black, randomly assigned to professional home visit group, paraprofessional visit group, or control; paraprofessional group later dropped because it did not get organized	20%, disproportionately white	Professional home visitors provided an average of 4 weekly visits of 60–90 minutes over 16 months; goal of the visits was to help mothers understand that they were primary teachers of their infants; mothers were encouraged to try out different teaching strategies, think up means of supporting infants' development, make sense of infants' behavior; visitors were encouraged to be sensitive to parental preferences in joint work with mothers	T mothers had more positive, facilitative patterns of verbal interaction than C mothers immediately posttreatment; they expanded more, asked more questions, used less negative language; no short-term effects on maternal perceptions of or expectations for children, or on child IQ

				In follow-up when children ages 6, 7, and 7½ years, researchers found no residual treatment effects on mother-child interaction patterns or children's academic progress
Mother-Child Home Program; Madden, O'Hara, & Levenstein, 1981	166 low-income families, 88% black, majority on welfare, randomly assigned to T (N = 86) or C (N = 80) groups in 4 waves	23% Ts; 27% Cs	Twice weekly, 30-minute home visits by college-graduate volunteers; in the first year families received 40–43 visits, in the second year 16–39, depending on cohort; home visitors acted as "toy demonstrators" who used toys and books to model verbal interaction with the child in the first weekly visit; the second visit was to review and encourage mother to practice	For 1972, 1975, and 1976 cohorts, T mothers had more positive interactions with children in cognitive domain (provided labels, used color name, verbalized numbers and shapes) but not in affective domain (verbalized praise, provided nonverbal expressions of warmth)
				Follow-up in the first grade showed no effects on teacher rating of children's problem behavior, adjustment; some residual maternal behavior effects for 1976 cohort only
Syracuse Family Development Research Project; Lally, Mangione, & Honig, 1989	108 low-income families, 85% single parents, mean maternal age 18 years, majority of families black, constituted T group; matched pairs formed C group (N = 108) constructed when T children were 36 months old	17% Ts; 30% Cs	5-year intervention, beginning after birth; daily developmental program for children from 6 months to 5 years (half-day program up to 15 months, full day thereafter); weekly home visits from enrollment to 5 years; modeled interaction with the children, demonstrated parent-	At 5 years of age, no differences between T and C children on cognitive ability; in first grade, T children had more positive social interaction with other children, but were more negative toward teachers
				In follow-up at age 14, researchers

Table 4.1 Continued

Name/Reference	Sample/Design	Attrition	Intervention	Treatment Effects
			child games, supported parents' efforts at personal development; linked to needed social services; center-based parent meetings	found 65 of 82 T children completing the program, 54 of 74 Cs; T girls had better school attendance and grades; T boys had fewer and less serious types of juvenile offenses
Birmingham Parent-Child Development Center; Andrews et al., 1982	251 low-income, black families, average maternal age 22 years, education 11 years, randomly assigned to treatment or control conditions	57% Ts, 27% Cs; not random; Ts lost women returning to work, also lowest IQ mothers	Duration: infants aged 3–36 months; in first year mothers spend 3 half-days weekly in parenting/child development classes and participate with infants in nursery, where more experienced peers serve as models; in second year mothers are "understudies"; in third year they become peer models themselves; program provided broad view of child development, attention to family strengths, also transportation, health and social services as needed	In nonsocial stress situation: T mothers comforted children more at 24 months, refrained more from verbal control at 24 and 36 months; in teaching situation: T mothers better at 24 and 36 months on quality of instruction, praise; exit interview: T mothers had greater reported life-satisfaction, use of community resources; T children 8 points higher on Bayley at 24 months, 8 points higher on Stanford-Binet at 36 months
Houston Parent Child Development Center; Andrews et al., 1982	216 low-income, Mexican-American families, average maternal age 28 years, education 7.5 years, randomly assigned to treatment or control conditions	50% Ts, 51% Cs; main reason both groups: high mobility	Duration: infants aged 12–36 months; in first year 30 weekly home visits by trained lay visitors; in second year mothers attended 3-hour sessions at center, 4 days a week; children simultaneously	On teaching situation: T mothers talked and elaborated more to children, used less criticism at 36 months; on Caldwell HOME: Ts higher at 36 months, especially on provision of play materials, emo-

Program; Study	Sample	Attrition	Treatment	Results
			received developmental program; weekend family workshops, evening meetings for family; broad view of child development, with attention to family strengths, also transportation, health, and social services as needed; specific activities to engage fathers	tional responsiveness; T children 8 points higher on Bayley at 24 months, higher on S-B at 36 months
New Orleans Parent-Child Development Center; Andrews et al., 1982	126 low-income, black families, average maternal age 24 years, education 11 years, randomly assigned to treatment or control conditions		Duration: infants aged 2–36 months; two classes, 3 hours each per week, for full 3 years, one on child development, other on community resources; also strong health education component, broad view of child development; attention to family strengths, also transportation, health, and social services as needed	On waiting room situation: T mothers more sensitive, accepting, cooperative at 24 to 36 months, T children 6 points higher on S-B at 36 months; cohort 2 alone, 10 points higher
Child and Family Resource Programs; Travers, Nauta, & Irwin, 1982	82 low-income families from each of 5 different local programs, randomly assigned to T or C conditions; total N = 199 T families; 210 C families; sample 39% white, 47% black, 4% Hispanic, 10% other; 70% single parents; 50% completed high school	45% Ts, 35% Cs	Lay home-visiting programs for families with infants from birth to 3 years of age; 11 local programs around the country; each program was designed to link into formal social services, through Head Start or other agencies; frequency of home visits varied from monthly to bi-monthly; focus of visits varied across programs, but reportedly	No program effects on child health or development; marginally significant effects on parent-as-teacher measure; no effects on parents' ability to recognize family needs and find resources to meet them; T mothers had greater feelings of efficacy, of ability to control events than Cs; T mothers increased in employment or training 37% from

Table 4.1 Continued

Name/Reference	Sample/Design	Attrition	Intervention	Treatment Effects
			was mostly on service brokerage, general family problems, parents' personal support needs; very uneven attention to parent-child interaction, children's needs	baseline vs. 28% for C mothers
Yale Child Welfare Research; Provence & Naylor, 1983; Seitz, Rosenbaum, & Apfel, 1985	Treatment group consisted of 18 low-income families, 12 black, 2 Puerto Rican, 2 white, 2 "mixed"; 50% single parents; matched control group, from same pool of mothers in clinic records from which Ts were drawn, constructed when T children were 30 months	not a factor	Duration: birth to 30 months; regular pediatric care at project "Children's House"; developmental exams at 2, 3, 6, 9, 12, 18, 24, 30 months by physicians and psychologists; an average of 13 months of day care for each child, with 3 to 1 staff-child ratio; biweekly home visits throughout by clinical social workers who focused on parents' own needs for support, encouragement, nurturance; program focus on family functioning as well as parent-child relationship; strong mental health focus throughout	Immediately post-treatment, T children had better language development than controls

In a 10-year follow-up, T boys had less need for remedial services than C boys; T children had better school attendance than Cs; T mothers reported more pleasurable, involved relationships with children and were more involved in children's school life; 13/15 T families vs. 8/15 families self-supporting (an apparent result of mediating factors: T mothers were more likely to delay subsequent childbearing and to seek additional education) |
| Parent-Infant Interaction Project; Brom- | Treatment group drawn from a population of families with preterm infants considered "high risk" at 9 | not a factor | 15 months of biweekly home visits, child aged 9–24 months; home visits by nurses built around | No effects on children's cognitive development; T mothers more attentive to their infants than Cs; |

92

	%	Intervention	Results
wich, 1978; Bromwich & Parmalee, 1981 — months; matched controls drawn from same population; 30 T families, 33 C families; 67% sample low SES; 50% white, 33% Hispanic, remainder black		structured clinical assessments of nature of and primary issues in parent-infant relationship; focus on affective dimensions; attempt to identify and build on parents' and infants' strengths, at same time encourage greater parental self-awareness of what was happening in interactions	T mothers had more reciprocal, positive interactions than C; more of T child time spent on intellectual activities; intervention was more effective for families with discrete obstacles to an enjoyable parent-infant relationship, less helpful for those with multiple, overwhelming problems and in which infant was low priority; with T groups, 11 cases rated successful, 14 mixed success-failure, 5 largely unsuccessful
Hospital and Home Support During Infancy; Siegel, Bauman, Schaefer, Saunders, & Ingram, 1980 — 321 low-income women, mostly black, receiving prenatal care in public clinic of community hospital, semi-rural setting; 202 of these women with a normal delivery randomly assigned to 1 of 3 treatment conditions or control; T1: early and extended hospital contact only, T2: home visits only, T3: both treatment; 119 families with infants needing 24 hours observation in hospital assigned to extended contact and home visits, or control		Early and extended contact: 45 minutes of mother-infant contact during first 3 hours after delivery and 5 additional hours during hospital stay; 9 home visits by specially trained community woman during first 3 months of infancy; home visits designed to promote mothers' involvement with their infants, and to support mothers in coping with a range of situational stresses	Modest effects of early and extended contact alone, but not in combination with home visits, on attachment; no intervention effect on acceptance of infant, or measures of interaction, stimulation from any treatment combination; no intervention on effects on reported child abuse and neglect or appropriate health care utilization
Efficacy of Prenatal and — 115 mother-infant pairs; urban low-income working-class fami-	30%	Home visits by BA-level professionals in child psychology; focus	In general, there appeared to be no treatment effects for the group

Table 4.1 Continued

Name/Reference	Sample/Design	Attrition	Intervention	Treatment Effects
Postpartum Home Visits; Larson, 1980	lies, randomly assigned to 1 of 2 treatment conditions or control; T1 (N = 16) prenatal and infancy home visits, T2 (N = 27) infancy home visits beginning 6 weeks; C (N = 37)		on enhancing basic infant care skills, more reciprocal mother-infant interaction, more effective, enjoyable interaction patterns; also more appropriate utilization of medical care; one treatment group received 1 prenatal visit, 1 postpartum visit, 4 visits in first 6 weeks, 5 visits from 6 weeks to 11 months; the other received 5 visits from 6 weeks to 11 months	beginning home visits at 6 weeks; the prenatal onset treatment parents had fewer feeding problems, better mother-child interaction patterns, more appropriate preventive and episodic health care utilization, and higher Caldwell HOME scores than either the control or the other treatment group
Parent Training with Teen-age Mothers; Field, Widmayer, Stringer, & Ignatoff, 1980	Part of a research study with 6 groups; 2 groups were low-income teenagers who had given birth to preterm babies and who were randomly assigned to T (N = 20) or C (N = 28) conditions		Biweekly half-hour home visits by a 2-person team—a trained professional interventionist and a teenage, black college student; total of 12 visits over first 8 months; focus of the visits was on educating mothers on developmental milestones, teaching exercises to stimulate development and promote interaction	At 4 months, T babies were heavier and longer than CS, and T mothers expressed more realistic expectations, rated infant temperament as less difficult than did C mothers; at 8 months, T mothers were higher than CS on Caldwell HOME subscales, emotional and verbal responsivity, maternal involvement
Parent-Infant Project; van Doornick, Dawson, Butterfield,	Pregnant women aged 16 or older recruited in health department maternity clinic; sample 50% teens, 75% white, 25% Hispanic, most	32% TS, 40% CS	Weekly home visits by lay home visitors, from mid-pregnancy to 15 months; emphasis on provision of emotional support and concrete	C infants slightly fuller gestation, higher birth weights; T mothers with inadequate baseline diet less likely to improve diet (21% vs.

	Sample	Participation	Program	Results
& Alexander, 1980	low-income; random assignment to T (N = 92), (N = 53) conditions		assistance with immediate concerns, hypothesized to lead to enhanced self-esteem, personal relations, use of resources; not a direct emphasis on parenting behaviors, rather indirect path of influence	45%); no overall program-favoring effects on parenting (except for modest trend at 4 months on maternal warmth); higher-risk mothers seemed to benefit most from services
Perinatal Coaching; Jacobson, undated	Low-income WIC recipients, 39% married, 93% white, 52% welfare dependent; randomly assigned to T (N = 31), (N = 80) conditions	no report (36% of those invited to participate declined)	One year of home visits, beginning at birth, by trained middle-class volunteers; number of visits received ranged widely, but seems to have averaged 15–30; not clear if visits more supportive or didactic, but did focus on parenting issues, encouraging more maternal interaction and involvement with infants	No program-favoring effects on Caldwell HOME, a mother-infant interaction measure, an attachment measure; many mothers in both groups reportedly seemed depressed and at 13 months had difficulties expressing positive affection toward baby
United Charities of Chicago; Slaughter, 1983	Low-income, urban inner-city women; 100% black, most welfare dependent, single-parent families; clusters of buildings in each of 3 public housing projects randomly assigned to toy demonstration home visiting (TD), mothers' discussion groups (MD), or control; all families in a cluster with infants 8–24 months offered one particular choice; at baseline, 41 in TD, 53 in MD, 38 controls	37% (15/41 TDs, 27/53 MDs, 7/38 controls)	Toy demonstration home visiting modeled after mother-child home program described above (Madden, O'Hara, & Levenstein, 1984); 32 visits during school year for 2 years; mothers' discussion groups (10 mothers in each) met weekly, focus on mothers' own agendas and interests: sharing of personal experiences, discussion of child-rearing issues, etc.; some formal presentation of child development	General pattern of program-favoring effects modest, but favoring MD group most; MD mothers superior to controls at 1 or 2 testing points on ego maturity, future orientation, use of community resources, endorsement of risk taking, expectation of children to become self-directing; MD mothers most likely to elaborate on children's play; MD children most likely to use expressive language; some modest

Table 4.1 Continued

Name/Reference	Sample/Design	Attrition	Intervention	Treatment Effects
			activities; both treatments provided/run by professional black social workers	program-favoring effects for each T group at one point in time, but not at others (a mixed picture)
Prenatal/Early Infancy Project; Olds, Henderson, Tatelbaum, & Chamberlain, 1986a, 1986b, 1988	Women with no previous live births and one or more of 3 risk factors—under age 19, single parent, low SES; randomly assigned to (1) infant health and developmental screening (N = 90), (2) screening and transportation (N = 94), (3) above plus prenatal home visits (N = 116), (4) above plus prenatal and infancy home visits (N = 116); in sample, 47% under age 19, 62% unmarried, 61% low SES, 23% with all risk factors; analytic sample all white, excluding 46 blacks in program	15–21%, depending on group	Biweekly nurse home visits mid-pregnancy till birth of baby, weekly the first month, decreasing in frequency till 24 months; home visits focused on parent education (80% of effort), but included service brokerage and effort to involve mothers' informal support systems; postnatal visits emphasized interpreting infant behavior, infant emotional needs, and need for progressively more complex experience; full treatment was 40 visits	No overall prenatal effects, but nurse-visited teens under 16 had babies 324 grams heavier than controls; few overall program-favoring postnatal effects, except for fewer emergency room visits for those visited to 12 and 24 months; but low SES, unmarried teens in control group (N = 32) and prenatal visit group (N = 18) had much higher incidence of abuse and neglect than those visited to 24 months (N = 22), 19%/18% vs. 4%; finding supported by same trend on two Caldwell subscales for restrictiveness, appropriate control; in a 2-year follow-up the same highest risk subsample had fewer subsequent pregnancies
Menninger Infant Project; Ware, Osof-	140 pregnant adolescents from city-county health department program randomly assigned to T or C condi-		Both Ts and Cs were clients of a health department program providing prenatal care, social services,	No treatment effects on infant cognitive or language development; effects on maternal-infant inter-

96

sky, Culp, & Eberhart-Wright, 1987	tions; 60% white, 40% nonwhite; low-income sample		and nutritional guidance for first 18 months; τs received in addition a lay home-visiting program, weekly 1st month, biweekly next 6 months, then monthly until 18 months; τs also had access to phone counseling for 24-hour emergency help and professional back-up for teens needing crisis or mental health consultation; home visitors used simple activity sheets describing developmental tasks that the mothers could do with infants and demonstrated activities as well; important goal was to encourage fun and play with infants	action during play and feeding, not on attachment or Caldwell HOME; within group analysis of home-visited teens found higher maternal-infant play and Caldwell HOME scores among teens considered actively involved in and accepting of the program (N = 25) than those harder to engage (N = 31)
Intervention with Disadvantaged Parents of Sick Pre-terms; Beckwith, 1988, undated	92 low-income and working-class parents, with low-birth-weight infants with respiratory and other problems randomly assigned to τ (N = 37), c (N = 55) groups; 50% on welfare, 39% single mothers	5% τs; 36% cs (the pattern of attrition left a more disadvantaged τ group, regarding parents' own nurturance history, use of prenatal care)	2 clinically skilled home visitors, a pediatric nurse and an early childhood educator; visits began in the nursery and continued for a year, at first weekly, and in some cases evolving to biweekly; purpose of intervention was to increase mothers' involvement and level of responsive interactions with their babies; the home visitors' primary task was to nurture the mothers, to enable them to nurture	Significant program-favoring effects on maternal involvement and reciprocal interaction with their infants, also developmental expectations, including the τ group mothers with abusive, alcoholic, and otherwise troubled families of origin; also program-favoring effects on mothers' self-appraisal and appraisal of their impact on their children; there were no apparent effects on the security of the mother-infant

Table 4.1 Continued

Name/Reference	Sample/Design	Attrition	Intervention	Treatment Effects
			their infants; they also focused on the mothers' perceptions of their infants' behavior; the model was derived from the Bromwich model described above, which works through the foundation of the visitor-mother relationship	attachment or on infant "mastery motivation" or developmental test performance at 13 months; Beck- with reports that the interventions appeared to "unhook maternal behavior from adverse predisposing factors"
Maternal and Infants Health Outreacher Worker Project; Clinton, 1989	Very low income, rural families from 5 communities in Appala- chia and mid-South, many both socially and geographically isolated; mean age 20 years, 67% white/ 33% black, 43% married; matched comparison group constructed from neighboring population pockets to sites served; same on demograph- ics; MIHOW participants slightly more disadvantaged; N = 204 Ts, 124 Cs	44% by 1 year, 65% by 2 years (measurement sample 105 Ts, 102 Cs at 2 years)	Those who completed program re- ceived 5 prenatal and 17 "monthly" postnatal visits till 2 years; home visitors were mostly community women; goals of visiting to encour- age appropriate health self-care and utilization of formal care, to help clients gain access to services, to increase parents' involvement with children, knowledge of children's developmental needs; because most home visitors had no "formal" child developmental knowledge, the curriculum was designed in part to provide basic concepts as well as games, ideas, play activities to share with parents, and advice on infant care	For families who stayed with the program there were significant program-favoring effects on both subscale and total Caldwell HOME scores at 1 and 2 years across all the sites; also, more T mothers breastfed their infants—33% vs. 22%

and a number of studies were undertaken that combined health and parenting concerns (Clinton, 1989; Larson, 1980; Olds, Henderson, Tatelbaum, & Chamberlain, 1986a, 1986b, 1988; van Doorninck, Dawson, Butterfield, & Alexander, 1980). As adolescent childbearing emerged as a social problem, parent support and education studies were undertaken that focused on adolescent parents (Field, Widmayer, Stringer, & Ignatoff, 1980; Olds et al., 1986a, 1986b, 1988; Ware, Osofsky, Culp, & Eberhart-Wright, 1987).

Analysis of Findings

Within the framework of a diverse set of studies, it is still possible to discern central tendencies. The effects of parent support and education do not appear to reach into less easily alterable effective dimensions of the parent-child relationship, or into parents' mental health. For example, only one of five studies that measured security of attachment found program-favoring effects on that variable. None of the four studies in Table 4.1 that reported moderate to high rates of depression in families served found program effects on these variables. An additional study that served women with high baseline rates of depression, but that was excluded from Table 4.1 because of design limitations, also found no effects (see Lyons-Ruth, Botein, & Grunebaum, 1984). Nonetheless, short-term program-favoring effects on one or more dimensions of maternal behavior were found in 13 of 19 studies. (The Syracuse Project either did not measure or did not report short-term maternal outcomes.)

The studies in Table 4.1 reported effects on such important behaviors as involvement and reciprocal interaction with the infant, praise for accomplishments, restrictiveness and appropriate control, verbal and material stimulation, and less commonly in nonverbal warmth and affection, responsiveness to children's bids for attention, and comforting. Effects were also reported in a moderate number of studies on parents' awareness of their role as "teachers" and the appropriateness of expectations of their children. One of only two studies that collected information on child abuse and neglect reported finding program-favoring effects (i.e., Olds et al., 1986a, 1986b), and these were found for a discrete subsample of the larger treatment group.

Only four studies examined indicators of general parent-coping adaptation and efforts at personal development; but three of these four found significant program-favoring effects. It was my impression in reading program reports that if more programs had systematically measured some of

99

these outcomes, this percentage would remain relatively high. Only one program that targeted adolescent parents (Olds et al., 1988) had a program focus and, in a subsequent two-year follow-up, reported program-favoring effects on delayed or subsequent pregnancy. Finally, 6 of 12 studies that measured infants' or young children's developmental test performance found posttreatment program-favoring effects in this domain.

The picture with respect to long-term effects is less promising, albeit much more tentative due to small numbers. Two of seven studies that followed children into middle or later childhood found any residual program effects: the Syracuse Family Development Research Program (Lally & Honig, 1977) and the Yale Child Welfare Research Program (Provence & Naylor, 1983). The Houston Parent Child Development Centers (PCDC) found some enduring behavioral effects for boys between ages 8 and 11 (Johnson & Walker, 1987). But a more recent and comprehensive follow-up of all three PCDC samples found no residual effects on a number of child and family variables. The Yale Child Welfare Research Program was also one of three that examined, and the only one that found, long-term program-favoring effects on parenting or broader family functioning, including more involved and pleasurable maternal relationships with children, greater involvement in school life, and higher rates of family self-sufficiency. The relatively greater effects on parents and more modest effects on children in the Yale study as opposed to the Syracuse study are probably due to the relatively greater programmatic focus of the Yale study on parenting and parents' own well-being. The causal path to altered long-term outcomes for children in the study may have involved parents to a greater degree with parent and child effects reinforcing each other over time.

Summary and Qualifications

The evidence from a quarter century of evaluated program experience with parent support and education suggests positive short-term effects from the majority of evaluated programs on selected, relatively more accessible dimensions of parenting, parents' personal well-being and development, and children's cognitive development, and long-term effects in only a modest proportion of those studies that have followed children and families into their later years. This pattern fits the nature of the interventions. But it is also a reflection of the possibility that different families benefit from participation in different ways, reducing the appropriateness of the dominant approach of examining group differences in central tendency scores. It may also be a function of limitations in what investigators have thought, or perhaps thought possible, to measure. For example, few studies have measured reduction of substantiated abuse or neglect; few have had the will or resources to follow children and families into later childhood; few have measured effects on families' use of community resources; and few have grappled with the genuine difficulty of measuring more subtle dimensions of the parent-child relationship.

More attention should be given to enduring program effects on parents themselves. But enough evidence exists to suggest that parent support services alone do not tend to have long-term effects on child development. This may be in part because parent support and education programs do not get at the most consequential dimensions of parenting, or because these programs have little effect on the ecology of children's lives. Not surprisingly, some mix of parent support and direct developmental services to young children appears to hold the most promise of promoting improved long-term child development outcomes while not neglecting parents' own developmental and support needs.

A particularly notable limitation of many of the studies in Table 4.1 is relatively high attrition. Although the range of attrition rates is wide, there is a noticeable central tendency toward an attrition rate of about 35–40%. This is above the inherent self-selection that occurred at the beginning of studies as samples were being formed, a problem whose magnitude is difficult to ascertain. The reasons for such high attrition vary across studies. For example, the lengthy and intense PCDC interventions, while contributing to improved parenting, may not have been fully consonant with women's efforts to advance their education or to seek or return to work (Andrews et al., 1982). In other studies (e.g., the Maternal and Infant Health Outreach Worker Program, the Parent-Infant Project), high population mobility, inability to engage some families, overwhelming family problems, and like factors contributed to family or staff decisions to discontinue participation. But for the most part, when program-favoring effects are reported in Table 4.1, they are only for those families who remained in the program for most or all of the scheduled duration. The questions of whom parent support and education programs are and are not reaching and likewise for whom they are and are not helpful are going to be of growing importance as these programs move into the human service mainstream in coming years.

Additional Program Design Issues

Beyond the importance of linkage to other service components, parent support and education must be considered in terms of effectiveness within its legitimate purview and acceptability to families as a social support strategy. In that light, Table 4.1 provides much clearer guidance on some program design questions than on others. Perhaps the most consistent pattern revealed in Table 4.1 was a tendency (with the exception of the MIHOW project (Clinton, 1989)) for programs employing professionals to be more effective than programs employing lay family workers. All five of the studies with the weakest pattern of positive outcomes (Jacobson, undated; Siegel et al., 1980; Travers, Nauta, & Irwin, 1982; van Doorninck et al., 1980; Ware et al., 1987) used lay workers; four of these five used "indigenous" community women. Conversely, significant professional involvement in service delivery tended to be associated in these studies with the strongest patterns of positive short- and long-term effects (e.g., Andrews et al., 1982; Olds et al., 1986a, 1986b, 1988; Provence & Naylor, 1983).

Lay workers have some obvious strengths, such as acceptability to families; intimate knowledge of target population beliefs, life experience, and living conditions; and role flexibility in when, how, and where they will work (Halpern, 1990). But there is a growing appreciation that the strengths of indigenous lay workers are not equivalent to formal, particularly clinical, helping skills gained through years of training and supervision in a specific discipline. Specialized helping skills may not be essential if the objective is to provide enriched social support to adequately coping, albeit hard-pressed, young families. But they would seem critical with the growing proportion of parents for whom obstacles to nurturant parenting posed by stressful living conditions are compounded by mental health problems, lack of self-resources, or struggles for their own personal development; specialized helping skills seem critical not least because of threats to the helper's own sense of well-being posed by work with this group of families.

For example, the fact that indigenous lay workers are drawn from the communities served by a program translates into the likelihood that they may still be wrestling in their personal lives with many of the same problems with which they are trying to help families. It may be difficult for them to separate their own, often undigested, experience of these problems from that of the families whom they are trying to help. Or they may have less ability to maintain empathy and at the same time distance themselves in the face of a young parent's rejecting or self-destructive behavior. The Menninger Infant Project team described this latter problem in the stresses that their lay home visitors experienced with the higher-risk teens: "Repeatedly the home visitors were confronted with rejection; no one at home at a mutually agreed upon time, sudden moves, refusal to answer the door, unreturned phone calls. At times it was hard to persevere when one was hardly welcome, where depression and passivity were observed and where the home visitor strongly wished to rescue the child from poverty, harsh discipline and/or uncaring attitudes" (Ware et al., 1987, pp. 10, 15).

A seemingly confusing pattern emerges with respect to relative effectiveness of parent support and education for lower-risk and higher-risk families within a particular program (a pattern not explained by family worker characteristics). Two studies (Beckwith, 1988; Olds et al., 1986a, 1986b, 1988) reported that program services were most effective in promoting attentive and nurturant parenting for the subgroup of their sample that appeared to be at highest risk of inattentive parenting. Other studies (Bromwich, 1978; Ware et al., 1987) reported that their intervention was relatively more effective in influencing parenting in lower-risk mothers in their sample. Likewise, with respect to general maternal coping, van Doorninck et al. (1980) reported that their program was more effective with mothers coping less well at baseline. Travers et al. (1982) reported that the Child and Family Resource Program was more effective with mothers coping better at baseline.

The helping strategies of the various programs do not seem to account for such apparent contradictions. For example, Beckwith (1988) and Bromwich (1978) both provided essentially the same program. Beckwith noted that the intervention appeared to "unhook maternal behavior from adverse predisposing factors" (p. 245). A similar pattern is reported by the Lyons-Ruth et al. study (1984) mentioned earlier. While their intervention did not alleviate often crippling depression or anxiety in mothers, it helped them separate their caregiving somewhat from these conditions. On the other hand, Bromwich and Parmalee (1979) reported that their intervention was less effective in families with multiple, overwhelming problems, in part because in these families the infant was a low priority, and it was hard to motivate the mother to focus on and attend to her infant's needs. Ware et al. (1987) also found that they were more effective in developing productive helping relationships, and consequently in focusing on the parent-child relationship, with better-functioning teen mothers who were less stressed.

In some ways, the overriding issue here is the important influence that mothers' own needs for nurturance played in many of the programs. The difference was in programs' inclination and capacity to respond to such needs. Perhaps the most effective program in this respect was the Yale Child Welfare Research Project, both in its staffing pattern and its helping principles. Children's services in the Yale project were addressed by a pediatrician, nurse, developmental psychologist, and early childhood educator. A social worker was "the parent's person," not only providing help with concrete problems but also supplying the care and nurturance that some parents themselves still needed (Provence & Naylor, 1983). But unlike the Yale project, few parent support and education programs have had the luxury of different staff to attend to mother and infant needs. Family workers thus have been faced with the difficult tasks of finding a balance in their attention and avoiding the temptation of becoming too much the parent's or the child's advocate.

The problem of balance will become increasingly important in parent support and education programs as these programs struggle to serve ever more distressed, troubled families. In my ongoing consultation with supervisory and front-line staff in well-established programs throughout the country, I have repeatedly been told the same thing: the average family served today has more and more severe problems of all sorts than five or ten years ago. This appears to be in part because a greater proportion of young, low-income adults have the multiple disadvantages of poverty, highly stressed support networks, and poor personal nurturance histories and because parent support and education programs are receiving more high-risk referrals.

The growing group of multidisadvantaged families will need far more sustained and skilled helping services than all but a few parent support and education programs provide. Such programs will have to attend simultaneously and coherently to pressing family survival needs, parents' own significant nurturance needs, vulnerable parent-child relationships, and, in some cases, the special needs of young children with biological vulnerabilities. These programs will have to provide a flexible mix of concrete, clinical, and supportive help in a nonbureaucratic, family-like context. In other words, the model that increasingly will be needed for young families is one which reflects the strengths but avoids the limitations of both specialized helping services and innovative community-based approaches like parent support and education.

Parent Support and Education and Broader Human Service Reform

The development and expansion of such a multifaceted model will require a resource commitment far beyond what has been available for prevention-oriented family service programs up to the present and a much greater willingness on the part of skilled professionals to work in low-income communities. Both of these, in turn, will require a rethinking of the mandates, practices, and resource distribution patterns of the large public human service bureaucracies, particularly state child welfare systems. The prospects for such a basic rethinking are guarded.

On the positive side, there appears to be a stronger base of agreement about reforming child and family services than in past reform periods. Fewer stakeholders see a reason to continue business as usual. A number of states and municipalities are struggling to find ways to free up resources for flexible, prevention-oriented, "family-centered" services. For example, some have sought federal waivers to use portions of their child welfare, AFDC, Medicaid, or other categorical funds in new initiatives whose principles and approaches closely resemble those in parent support and education programs. New federal legislation, such as the Family Support Act of 1988, and major program reauthorizations, such as those for Head Start, have provided added impetus for reform, mandating the programs that they fund to work together across categorical boundaries.

Thus far, most state and local service reform efforts have been embedded in efforts targeted at specific policy objectives or populations. Examples include home-based family preservation services, teen pregnancy and parenting programs, and infant mortality reeducation initiatives. These programs have filled in a missing piece in the larger system, but they have had less influence in generalizing their principles and approaches beyond their specific population and categorical boundaries. Currently on the drawing boards are a small number of more ambitious efforts that consciously or unconsciously build on the principles embodied in parent support programs. For example, Michigan and Washington have developed plans for basic reorganization of their specialized child and family service subsystems into one integrated system, the heart of which would be a network of community-based family service centers, and for a less stigmatizing approach to defining eligibility for services. David Dinkins, as mayor of New York City, called for the replacement of the city's fragmented, categorical social service system with a network of "comprehensive, convenient, neighborhood multi-service centers, locally based and responsive to local residents and their needs" ("Dinkins describes plan," 1990, p. B12).

As the example of New York City also illustrates, however, it is most difficult to reform services in just those contexts most in need of new service approaches and paradigms. As Kamerman and Kahn (1989) have illustrated, it is difficult to innovate in a situation characterized by crisis and breakdown. In such situations, overwhelmed and undersupported front-line providers in the categorical systems are in little position to rethink their roles with families—for example, to reach out before serious problems appear, to provide individualized services, or to provide sustained support. Discrete innovations tend to be distorted by the problems of the larger context. Providers may have to serve more troubled families than is appropriate or provide services that they are not equipped to provide.

Even those new initiatives with a strong resource base and clear mandate to provide a responsive, flexible mix of services have struggled with both predictable and unpredictable implications of service reform. For example, the headquarters staff members of the Illinois Parents Too Soon initiative are struggling to provide the same high level of training, monitoring, and support to 30 local programs that they provided when there were one third the number of programs. The organization has also struggled with the challenges that reflect the flip side of those associated with specialized services. For example, it has struggled to find an appropriate meaning for such ideas as supportive services and "generalist" helping roles with family problems requiring specialized, clinically skilled help (Halpern & Percansky, 1989). In a related vein, the Parents Too Soon staff has seen caseloads gradually increase as many local programs struggle to respond each year to greater numbers of referrals and walk-ins. For example, home visitors with caseloads of 15 to 20 families a few years ago now have caseloads of 30 to 40 families.

Conclusion

It is not easy to draw conclusions about the potential and the place of parent support and education programs in the larger continuum of child and family services. On the one hand, within their modest purview, parent support and education programs reflect a genuine effort to forge more helpful, family-level services. They reach families earlier, support families in a more open-ended and sustaining way, and reach out to troubled families more effectively than have mainstream human services. On the other hand, today's parent support and education programs reflect a recapitulation of American society's historic propensity to seek family-level solutions to deeply rooted social problems and to place the burden of change on those experiencing the greatest strains.

As parent support and education programs move into the human service mainstream, they will have to confront a number of issues. Foremost among these issues will be developing a clear but differentiated identity: for example, deciding the appropriate recipients for supportive services provided by community women; deciding how and why to influence deeply embedded parenting practices; and deciding whether to establish discrete programs focused on the adjustment to parenting, or multiservice entities that assemble an array of parent- and child-focused services to respond to numerous evolving parent and child needs throughout early childhood. In this author's view, while parent support and education programs are well suited to serve as an additional social resource for families that are coping adequately, as currently constituted, such programs should not be expected to be the primary helping resource for families experiencing deeply rooted child-rearing and related difficulties. Considerably more clinical backup will be needed for that task.

Note

1. These two research teams would probably agree with my decision to exclude them. None of the causal models articulated by Perry researchers include parent change, and they have argued that "Parent involvement may not be absolutely essential" to change in children (Berrueta-Clement et al., 1984, p. 108). Gray and colleagues (1982) go even further, concluding that they "have not found in these analyses any evidence that strongly supports the belief that parental mediation is a crucial variable in determining the performance of children who have participated in early intervention programs similar to ours" (p. 183).

References

Andrews, S., Blumenthal, J., Johnston, D., Kahn, A., Ferguson, C., Lasater, T., Malone, P., & Wallace, D. (1982). The skills of mothering: A study of the Parent Child Development Centers. *Monographs of the Society for Research in Child Development, 47*(6), 1–81.

Beckwith, L. (1988). Intervention with disadvantaged parents of sick pre-term infants. *Psychiatry, 51*, 242–247.

Belle, D. (1982). *Lives in stress.* Beverly Hills CA: Sage.

Berrueta-Clement, J. R., Schweinhart, L. J., Barnett, W. S., Epstein, A. S., & Weikert, D. J. (1984). Preschool's effects on social responsibility. In D. Weikert (Ed.), *Changed lives: The effects of the Perry Preschool Program on youths through age nineteen* (pp. 61–73). Ypsilanti MI: High/Scope Press.

Booth, C., Barnard, K., Mitchell, S., & Spieker, S. (1987). Successful intervention with multi-problem mothers: Effects on the mother-infant relationship. *Infant Mental Health Journal, 8,* 288–305.

Boyer, P. (1978). *Urban masses and moral order in America.* Cambridge: Harvard University Press.

Bromwich, R. (1978). *Working with parents and infants.* Austin: Pro-Ed.

Bromwich, R., & Parmalee, A. (1979). An intervention program for pre-term infants. In T. Field, A. Sostak, S. Goldberg, & H. Schuman (Eds.), *Infants born at risk.* New York: Spectrum Publishers.

Bronfenbrenner, U. (1987). Family support: The quiet revolution. In S. Kagan, D. Powell, & B. Weissbourd (Eds.), *America's family support programs.* New Haven: Yale University Press.

Casto, G., & Mastropieri, M. (1986). The efficacy of early intervention programs. *Exceptional Children, 52*(5), 417–424.

Clinton, B. (1989). *Maternal and Infant Health Outreach Worker Project* (Final Technical Report). Nashville TN: Vanderbilt University, Center for Health Services.

de Lone, R. (1979). *Small futures.* New York: Harcourt Brace Jovanovich.

Dinkins describes plan to improve social services. (1990, April). *New York Times,* p. B-12.

Egeland, B., Jacobovitz, D., & Papatola, K. (1987). Intergenerational continuity of abuse. In R. Gelles & J. Lancaster (Eds.), *Child abuse and neglect: Biosocial dimensions.* New York: Aldine.

Family Support Act of 1988, 42 U.S.C. § 1305 nt.

Farrow, F. (1988). *A framework for child welfare reform.* Washington DC: Center for the Study of Social Policy.

Field, T., Widmayer, S., Stringer, S., & Ignatoff, E. (1980). Teenage, lower class, black mothers and their pre-term infants: An intervention and developmental follow-up. *Child Development, 51,* 426–436.

Gordon, I. (1969). *Early childhood stimulation through parent education* (Final report to the Children's Bureau, Department of Health, Education and Welfare). Gainesville: University of Florida.

Gordon, I., & Guinagh, B. (1974). *A home learning center approach to early stimu-*

lation (Final report to the National Institute of Mental Health). Gainesville: University of Florida.

Gottlieb, B. (1988). Support interventions: A typology and agenda for research. In S. Duck (Ed.), *Handbook of personal relationships.* New York: Wiley.

Gray, S., Ramsey, B., & Klaus, R. (1982). *From three to twenty: The Early Training Project.* Baltimore: University Park Press.

Grubb, N., & Lazerson, M. (1982). *Broken promises.* New York: Basic Books.

Halpern, R. (1986). Community-based support for high risk young families. *Social Policy, 17*(1), 17–18, 47–50.

Halpern, R. (1987). Key social and demographic trends affecting young families: Implications for early childhood care and education. *Young Children, 42*(6), 34–40.

Halpern, R. (1990). Community-based early intervention. In S. Meisels & J. Shonkoff (Eds.), *Handbook of early intervention.* New York: Cambridge University Press.

Halpern, R., & Larner, M. (1987). Lay family support during pregnancy and infancy: The Child Survival/Fair Start Initiative. *Infant Mental Health Journal, 8*(2), 130–143.

Halpern, R., & Percansky, C. (1989). *Parents Too Soon home visiting services: Report and recommendations.* Chicago: Ounce of Prevention Fund.

Hart, P. (1989). Investing in prevention: Tomorrow's leaders and the problem of poverty. In G. Miller (Ed.), *Giving children a chance.* Washington DC: Center for National Policy Press.

Heinicke, C., Beckwith, L., & Tompson, A. (1988). Early intervention in the family system: A framework and review. *Infant Mental Health Journal, 9*(2), 111–141.

Heverly, M., Newman, F., & Forquer, S. (1982). *Meta-analysis and cost analysis of preventive intervention programs* (Report to the National Center for Clinical Infant Programs). Philadelphia: EPPI/MCP, Systems Research Unit.

Jacobson, S. (undated). *Perinatal coaching study* (Report of Oakland Family Services). Detroit: Wayne State University, Department of Psychology.

Johnson, D., & Walker, T. (1987). Primary prevention of behavior problems in Mexican-American children. *American Journal of Community Psychology, 15,* 375–386.

Kagan, S., & Shelley, A. (1987). The promise and problems of family support programs. In S. Kagan, D. Powell, & B. Weissbourd (Eds.), *America's family support programs.* New Haven: Yale University Press.

Kamerman, S., and Kahn, A. (1989). *Social services for children, youth, and families in the United States.* Westport CT: Annie E. Casey Foundation.

Lally, R., & Honig, A. (1977). *The Family Development Research Program: A program for prenatal, infant and early childhood enrichment* (Final Report). Syracuse: Syracuse University.

Lally, R., Mangione, P., & Honig, A. (1989). The Syracuse University Family Development Research Program: Long range impact of an early intervention with low-income children and their families. In D. Powell (Ed.), *Parent education as early childhood intervention*. Norwood NJ: Ablex.

Lambie, D., Bond, J. T., & Weikert, D. (1974). *Home teaching with mothers and infants*. Ypsilanti MI: High/Scope Press.

Larson, C. (1980). Efficacy of prenatal and postpartum home visits on child health and development. *Pediatrics, 66*, 191–197.

Lubove, R. (1968). *The professional altruist*. Cambridge: Harvard University Press.

Lyons-Ruth, K., Botein, S., & Grunebaum, H. (1984). Reaching the hard to reach: Serving multi-risk families with infants in the community. In B. Coehler & J. Musick (Eds.), *Intervention with psychiatrically disabled parents and their infants*. San Fransisco: Jossey-Bass.

Madden, J., O'Hara, J., &. Levenstein, P. (1984). Home again: Effects of the mother-child program on mother and child. *Child Development, 55*, 636–647.

Massie, H., Bronstein, A., Afterman, J., & Campbell, B. (1988). Inner themes and outer behaviors in early childhood development: A longitudinal study. *Psychoanalytic Study of the Child, 43*, 213–242.

Musick, J. (1987). *Psychological and developmental dimensions of adolescent pregnancy and parenthood: An interventionist's perspective*. Paper prepared for the Rockefeller Foundation.

Musick, J. & Halpern, R. (1989). Giving children a chance: What role community-based early parenting interventions? In G. Miller (Ed.), *Giving children a chance: The case for more effective national policy*. Washington DC: Center for National Policy Press.

Musick J., & Stott, F. (1990). Paraprofessionals, parenting and child development: Understanding the problems and seeking solutions. In S. Meisels & J. Shonkoff (Eds.), *Handbook of early childhood intervention*. New York: Cambridge University Press.

Olds, D., Henderson, C., Tatelbaum, R., & Chamberlain, R. (1986a). Improving the delivery of prenatal care and outcomes of pregnancy: A randomized trial of nurse home visitation. *Pediatrics, 78*, 16–28.

Olds, D., Henderson, C., Tatelbaum, R., & Chamberlain, R. (1986b). Preventing child abuse and neglect: A randomized trial of nurse home visitation. *Pediatrics, 78,* 65–78.

Olds, D., Henderson, C., Tatelbaum, R., & Chamberlain, R. (1988). Improving the life course development of socially disadvantaged mothers: A randomized trial of nurse home visitation. *American Journal of Public Health, 78,* 1436–1445.

Provence, S., & Naylor, A. (1983). *Working with disadvantaged parents and their children.* New Haven: Yale University Press.

Reischauer, R. (1986, Fall). The prospects for welfare reform. *Public Welfare,* pp. 4–11.

Rook, K., & Dooley, D. (1985). Applying social support research: Theoretical problems and future directions. *Journal of Social Issues, 41*(1), 5–28.

Schorr, L. (1988). *Within our reach.* New York: Doubleday.

Seitz, V., Rosenbaum, L., & Apfel, N. (1985). Effects of family support intervention: A ten year follow-up. *Child Development, 56,* 376–391.

Siegel, E., Bauman, K., Schaefer, R., Saunders, M., & Ingram, D. (1980). Hospital and home support during infancy: Impact on maternal attachment, child abuse and neglect, and health care utilization. *Pediatrics, 66,* 183–190.

Silver, B. (1979). Overview of clinical infant research programs. In *Clinical infant research programs.* Washington DC: National Institute of Mental Health.

Skerry, P. (1983). The charmed life of Head Start. *Public Interest, 73,* 18–39.

Slaughter, D. (1983). Early intervention and its effects on maternal and child development. *Monographs of the Society for Research in Child Development, 48,* 4.

Solnit, A., (1983). Foreword to S. Provence and A. Naylor, *Working with disadvantaged parents and their children.* New Haven: Yale University Press.

Stack, C. (1974). *All our kin.* New York: Harper & Row.

Tracy, E., & Whittaker, J. (1987). Evaluating the evidence base for social support interventions in child and family practice: Issues for empirical research and program design. *Children and Youth Services Review.*

Travers, J., Nauta, M., & Irwin, N. (1982). *The effects of a social program* (Final Report; Child and Family Resource Program's Infant-Toddler Component). Cambridge MA: Abt Associates.

van Doorninck, W., Dawson, P., Butterfield, P., & Alexander, H. (1980). *Parent-infant support through lay health visitors* (Final Report; Bureau of Community Health Services, Department of Health, Education and Welfare). Denver: University of Colorado, Health Sciences Center.

Ware, L., Osofsky, J., Culp, A., & Eberhart-Wright, A. (1987). *A preventive men-*

tal program for adolescent mothers and infants. Paper from the Menninger Infant Project presented at the meeting of the American Academy of Child and Adolescent Psychiatry, Washington DC.

Weiss, H. (1989). State family support and education programs: Lessons from the pioneers. *American Journal of Orthopsychiatry, 59,* 32–48.

Weiss, H., & Halpern, R. (1988). *Community-based family support and education programs: Something old or something new?* Paper commissioned by the National Resource Center for Children in Poverty, Columbia University, New York.

Weissbourd, B., (1987). A brief history of family support programs. In S. Kagan, D. Powell, & B. Weissbourd (Eds.), *America's family support programs.* New Haven: Yale University Press.

Weissbourd, B., & Kagan, S. (1989). Family support programs: Catalysts for change. *American Journal of Orthopsychiatry, 59,* 20–31.

Whittaker, J. (1986, Jan./Feb.). Formal and informal helping in child welfare services: Implications for management and practice. *Child Welfare,* pp. 17–25.

Wilson, W. (1987) *The truly disadvantaged.* Chicago: University of Chicago Press.

5

Multisystemic Treatment of
Serious Juvenile Offenders and Their Families

Scott W. Henggeler and Charles M. Borduin

Multisystemic therapy (Henggeler & Borduin, 1990) is a family-based therapeutic approach that has been viewed as a highly promising treatment for
complex psychosocial problems in children and adolescents (see Culbertson,
1990; Miller & Prinz, 1990). This chapter discusses the application of multisystemic therapy to the treatment of serious juvenile offenders and their
multiproblem families. In our discussion, we address the empirical rationale
for the application of this particular therapy as well as the clinical features of
multisystemic therapy that make it especially well suited for treating antisocial behavior in adolescents. More specifically, we address the following
issues: (1) we show that serious juvenile offenders experience numerous
psychosocial difficulties and present significant problems to their communities and that there is a dire need to develop effective interventions for such
offenders and their families; (2) we show that there are multiple correlates
and causes of delinquency and that the key correlates pertain to characteristics of the social systems (i.e., family, peers, school) in which these offenders
are involved; (3) we argue that the identified correlates of delinquency are
consistent with a social-ecological model of behavior, which represents the
theoretical foundation of multisystemic therapy; (4) we summarize findings from controlled evaluations of multisystemic therapy and argue that the
efficacy of multisystemic therapy is largely due to its consideration of the
multiple factors associated with delinquency; and (5) we provide a brief description of the clinical features of multisystemic therapy and delineate nine
principles for designing multisystemic interventions.

Seriousness of the Problem

Chronic and violent criminal activity by adolescents presents significant problems at several levels of analysis, and these problems argue for the development of effective treatment approaches. On a personal level, adolescents who commit serious criminal offenses experience numerous psychosocial difficulties as well as reduced educational and occupational opportunities. Moreover, serious criminal activity by adolescents has extremely detrimental emotional, physical, and economic effects on victims, victims' families, and the larger community (Gottfredson, 1989). Therefore, effective treatment may not only benefit the youth and his or her family, but may also save numerous persons from victimization.

On an epidemiological level, adolescents, especially males, commit higher rates of most criminal acts than any other age group. For example, males under the age of 19 years accounted for approximately 20% of all arrests for violent crimes in 1989 (Federal Bureau of Investigation, 1990). Because the offense/arrest ratio for male adolescents is extremely high for crimes such as aggravated assault, robbery, and rape (Elliott, Huizinga, & Morse, 1985), arrest statistics grossly underestimate the prevalence of adolescent criminal activity. In addition, a relatively small percentage of families account for a large percentage of crime in a community (West & Farrington, 1973; Wolfgang, Figlio, & Sellin, 1972). Thus, if one purpose of treating juvenile offenders is to decrease crime, then serious juvenile offenders and their multiproblem families are a logical target for intervention efforts.

On a social services level, conduct-disordered adolescents consume much of the resources of all the youth service systems (child mental health, child welfare, juvenile justice, and special education). These adolescents are especially overrepresented in the "deep end" of the various youth service systems. Moreover, adults with serious mental disorders commonly develop from the population of youth who engage in antisocial behavior (Levine, Watt, Prentky, & Fryer, 1980). Therefore, the development of effective treatments for delinquency may help to free resources to address other important problems of children and their families.

Unfortunately, as numerous reviewers have concluded (e.g., Mulvey, Arthur, & Reppucci, 1989; Quay, 1987; Romig, 1978), the development of effective treatments for delinquent behavior has been extremely difficult. In part, this difficulty is due to the high stability of aggressive behavior in individuals (Loeber, 1982) and across generations (Huesmann, Lefkowitz,

Eron, & Walder, 1984). However, as Henggeler (1989) has suggested, an even more important reason for the historically poor results of delinquency treatment studies may be that the interventions used in these studies have almost always addressed only a small portion of the possible determinants of delinquent behavior.

Correlates and Causes of Delinquency

A vast number of studies have evaluated correlates of delinquency (for reviews, see Henggeler, 1989; Quay, 1987). In general, these correlates pertain to the individual adolescent and the key systems (family, peer, school) in which he or she is embedded. Identified correlates of delinquency have included cognitive characteristics such as low verbal IQ, deficits in sociomoral reasoning and in problem-solving skills, and low self-esteem. Among the family correlates of delinquency are low family warmth and cohesion, ineffective parental discipline, parental deviance, marital discord, and dysfunctional parent-adolescent communication. In addition, peer characteristics such as association with deviant peers and conformity to antisocial peer pressure have been identified as strong correlates of delinquency. Finally, school factors such as poor academic performance and dropping out have also been linked with delinquency.

In light of the numerous correlates of delinquency, several research groups have developed empirically based multidimensional causal models of antisocial behavior in adolescents (for a review, see Henggeler, 1991). One important advantage of such models is that they allow a determination of variables that contribute to delinquency when the effects of other correlates are controlled. For example, in an integrated model (i.e., integrating strain theory, control theory, and social learning theory), Elliott, Huizinga, and Ageton (1985) conducted a longitudinal evaluation of a representative national sample of adolescents. Delinquency at time-2 was predicted directly by prior delinquency and involvement with delinquent peers. In addition, delinquency at time-2 was predicted indirectly by family difficulties and school difficulties, which predicted involvement with delinquent peers. Similarly, in a cross-sectional study, Patterson and Dishion (1985) concluded that delinquent behavior was predicted directly from low parental monitoring, low academic skills, and high association with deviant peers. These and other causal modeling studies (e.g., Agnew, 1985; LaGrange & White, 1985; Simcha-Fagan & Schwartz, 1986) provide consistent support for the view

115

that variance in delinquent behavior is contributed directly or indirectly by variables at the youth, family, peer, and school levels.

It is logical to conclude, based on the results of the causal modeling studies, that delinquency is multidetermined. Hence, it follows that effective interventions should be relatively complex, considering adolescent characteristics as well as aspects of the key systems in which adolescents are embedded. Similarly, there is a growing consensus among reviewers that potentially effective treatments for antisocial behavior should recognize the multiple determinants of such behavior (e.g., Hazelrigg, Cooper, & Borduin, 1987; McMahon & Forehand, 1988; Tolan, Cromwell, & Brasswell, 1986).

Systemic/Social Ecological Theories of Behavior

Findings from the causal modeling studies of delinquency are consistent with systemic/social ecological theories of psychosocial development and behavior. In Bronfenbrenner's (1979) theory of social ecology, individuals are viewed as being nested within a complex of interconnected systems that encompass individual, family, and extrafamilial (peer, school, neighborhood) factors. Behavior is seen as the product of the reciprocal interplay between the child and these systems and of the relations of the systems with each other. Likewise, systems theory (Minuchin, 1985) emphasizes the reciprocity of interpersonal relations and posits that child behavior problems typically reflect problematic family relations. Indeed, we (Mann, Borduin, Henggeler, & Blaske, 1990) have recently supported two key theoretical assumptions of family systems theory (i.e., child behavior problems are associated with cross-generational family coalitions, and positive changes in family coalition patterns are linked with the amelioration of individual symptomatology).

The multisystemic clinical approach is based largely on family systems (e.g., Haley, 1976; Minuchin, 1974) conceptualizations of behavior and behavior change. Although multisystemic therapy has much in common with traditional family therapies, it also includes substantive differences, the most important of which is that, consistent with the theory of social ecology, the multisystemic approach posits that behavior problems can be maintained by problematic transactions within any given system or between some combination of pertinent systems. Multisystemic treatment, then, is not limited to interventions within the family, but encourages treatment of problems in other systems as needed. In further contrast with most family therapy

116

approaches, multisystemic interventions consider important child development variables (e.g., the child's cognitive developmental abilities) and often
use interventions that are not necessarily systemic (e.g., cognitive behavior
therapy, behavioral parent training). In many ways (e.g., continuous evaluation of outcome, importance of contextual events, concern for treatment
generalization), the multisystemic approach is similar to the behavioral-
systems perspective described by Mash (1989). Most significantly, however,
the conceptual framework of the multisystemic approach fits closely with the
findings from the multidimensional causal models of antisocial behavior.

Controlled Outcome Evaluations of Multisystemic Therapy

We have a firm and continuing commitment to evaluating the efficacy of
multisystemic therapy. This commitment is driven largely by the question-
able ethics of providing children and families with mental health services
of untested effectiveness. In fact, only a handful of the approximately 250
different child and adolescent therapies that are currently used by mental
health professionals have been shown to be more effective than no treatment
(Kazdin, 1988). Although medical associations and the public demand accountability when physicians use untested drugs or other unproven medical
treatments, the use of untested and potentially harmful psychotherapies is
widely accepted in the mental health field. Clearly, for both ethical and pragmatic reasons, it is important that psychotherapies be evaluated rigorously.

Evaluations of multisystemic therapy with juvenile offenders have been
completed at three sites: Memphis, Tennessee; Columbia, Missouri; and
Simpsonville, South Carolina. In each of these sites, our clinical samples
were composed primarily of multiproblem families, many of whom were
of lower social class, minorities, and single parents. Although such families have been typically viewed as highly resistant to therapy, the studies
described below suggest that multisystemic therapy has been very successful in ameliorating a wide range of problems experienced by these families.
As discussed later in this chapter, we believe that the delivery of *home-
based* treatment was one of the key components of our success with these
multi-need families.

GENERAL DELINQUENCY

Our first treatment evaluation focused on inner-city delinquents who presented a wide variety of behavior problems (Henggeler et al., 1986). The

effects of multisystemic therapy were contrasted with the effects of the usual services provided in the community (i.e., mental health, educational, vocational, recreational), and the outcome data were derived from pretreatment and posttreatment assessment sessions involving standardized evaluations. Results showed that multisystemic therapy changed variables that tapped key correlates of delinquency. Youth in the multisystemic condition had decreased behavior problems and decreased association with deviant peers. Likewise, families who received multisystemic therapy showed increased warmth and affection. On the other hand, families in the usual services comparison group showed deterioration in warmth and affection. The results of this study were encouraging and prompted further evaluations.

ADOLESCENT SEXUAL OFFENDERS

Although costly residential treatment programs for adolescent sexual offenders have proliferated, there is little empirical support for their efficacy (Davis & Leitenberg, 1987). We conducted the first controlled treatment study with adolescent sexual offenders (Borduin, Henggeler, Blaske, & Stein, 1990). Sixteen sexual offenders were randomly assigned either to multisystemic therapy or to individual counseling conditions. Although the small sample size did not provide sufficient statistical power to analyze changes in psychosocial functioning, three-year recidivism data were collected. The frequency of rearrests for sexual crimes and for nonsexual crimes was significantly lower in the multisystemic condition than in the individual counseling condition (e.g., $M = .12$ vs. 1.62, respectively, for sexual offenses). Again, multisystemic therapy was relatively effective with a difficult-to-treat clinical sample.

CHRONIC JUVENILE OFFENDERS

The Missouri Delinquency Project (MDP) represents our most comprehensive and extensive evaluation of multisystemic therapy. Two hundred chronic juvenile offenders ($M = 4.2$ arrests) were randomly assigned to either multisystemic therapy or individual therapy conditions. An article presenting data from a subset of the MDP sample has been published (Mann et al., 1990), and the manuscript discussing the results from our entire sample is currently in press (Borduin et al., in press). As in our first outcome study (Henggeler et al., 1986), adolescents who received multisystemic therapy had fewer behavior problems, parents self-reported decreased psychiatric symptomatology, and considerable evidence of positive changes in family relations emerged (e.g., increased family adaptability and positive communication, decreased conflict and hostility). In contrast, such changes did not emerge for adolescents in the individual therapy condition. Moreover, at a follow-up completed an average of four years following treatment, official arrest records revealed that 22% of the adolescents who completed multisystemic therapy had been rearrested, in contrast to 72% of the adolescents who completed individual therapy. Even the adolescents who prematurely dropped out of multisystemic therapy showed a significantly lower recidivism rate than their counterparts who prematurely dropped out of individual therapy (47% vs. 72%).

VIOLENT/CHRONIC JUVENILE OFFENDERS

The Family and Neighborhood Services (FANS) project (Henggeler, Melton, & Smith, 1992), located in South Carolina, focused on violent adolescent offenders and was the first study to use community-based, master's degree–level professionals as therapists in the multisystemic condition. Eighty-four violent/chronic juvenile offenders at imminent risk of incarceration were randomly assigned to receive either multisystemic therapy or the usual services of the juvenile justice system. Results, based on arrest and incarceration data collected an average of 59 weeks following referral to the project, showed that youth who received multisystemic therapy had significantly fewer criminal charges (1.20 vs. 2.48) and arrests (.87 vs. 1.52), a significantly lower recidivism rate (43% vs. 67%), and significantly less time in out-of-home placements (5.8 weeks vs. 16.2 weeks). Thus, multisystemic therapy was more effective *and* less expensive (based on a cost analysis) than usual services. Moreover, results of a 2.4-year follow-up (Henggeler, Melton, Smith, Schoenwald, & Hanley, 1993) showed that multisystemic therapy doubled the survival rate (i.e., percentage of youth not rearrested) of participants when compared with youth in the usual services condition.

SUBSTANCE USE AND ABUSE IN DELINQUENTS

Although treatment approaches for adolescent substance abuse have proliferated, there are few evaluations of treatment efficacy. We (Henggeler, Borduin, et al., 1991) have recently examined the effects of multisystemic therapy on reductions in substance use and abuse in the MDP and FANS samples. In the MDP, analyses of arrest data collected an average of four years following treatment indicated that youth who participated in multisystemic therapy had a significantly lower rate of drug-related arrests than did youths who participated in the individual therapy condition (i.e., 4% vs. 16%). Similarly, in the FANS project, youth in the multisystemic condition reported a significant reduction in soft-drug use relative to youth in the usual services condition.

CONCLUSION

The results from these outcome studies clearly support the efficacy of multisystemic therapy in treating relatively serious psychosocial difficulties in juvenile offenders and their multiproblem families. We should also note that this therapy has been shown to be more effective than behavioral parent training in treating child abuse and neglect (Brunk, Henggeler, & Whelan, 1987). Furthermore, the success of multisystemic therapy has led to funding for several controlled clinical trials that are currently being conducted. These trials include (a) a multisite study of the effectiveness of multisystemic therapy with violent/chronic juvenile offenders residing in rural sites in Orangeburg and Spartanburg, South Carolina; (b) an evaluation of the effectiveness of multisystemic therapy with substance-abusing delinquents in Charleston, South Carolina; (c) a rigorous examination of multisystemic therapy blended with a mobile crisis program as an alternative to hospitalization of youth presenting psychiatric emergencies in Charleston; and (d) an evaluation of multisystemic therapy with Hispanic-American violent/chronic offenders in Galveston, Texas.

Clinical Features of Multisystemic Therapy

The success of multisystemic therapy is linked with at least two distinct characteristics of the approach. First, consistent with findings from the causal modeling literature, multisystemic treatment takes a comprehensive (i.e., encompassing the interrelations among youth, family, peer, and school variables) approach to conceptualizing and treating antisocial behavior. The second characteristic is the commitment to ensuring that changes are made in the youth's naturally occurring environment (i.e., family, peer group, school). This characteristic and other important clinical features of multisystemic therapy are briefly discussed in the next section.[1]

CASE CONCEPTUALIZATION AND MANAGEMENT

Multisystemic therapy is distinguished from other intervention approaches by its comprehensive conceptualization of clinical problems and the multi-faceted nature of its interventions. And, as noted previously, a strong case can be made that a comprehensive, broad-based approach is particularly well suited for treating antisocial behavior. Multisystemic therapy, however, does not involve a "unique" set of intervention techniques. Rather, intervention strategies are integrated from other pragmatic, problem-focused treatment models. These models include strategic family therapy (Haley, 1976), structural family therapy (Minuchin, 1974), behavior therapy (e.g., Blechman, 1985), and cognitive behavior therapy (e.g., Kendall & Braswell, 1985). Thus, it is essential that the therapist have a strong working knowledge of these treatment models, and developing such knowledge is considered an essential component of training in the multisystemic approach.

Therapists who use the multisystemic treatment approach are mental health professionals with master's degrees or doctorates. Due to the complex nature of multisystemic therapy and the high level of requisite skills for therapists, this is not an approach that is appropriate for use by nonprofessionals. The average duration of treatment is expected to be approximately four months (ranging from two to six months), with the final month involving less intensive contact to monitor the maintenance of therapeutic gains. Treatment plans for each family are typically developed, specified, and monitored during group supervisory meetings each week. The vast majority of therapeutic interventions are conducted by the therapist or by the parents under the guidance of the therapist. The therapist is also responsible for closely monitoring the efficacy of all specialized interventions (e.g., special education placement, referral to Alcoholics Anonymous, referral to legal services). In some cases, specialized interventions continue following treatment termination. Generally, however, the therapist and supervisor are accountable for all aspects of intervention.

HOME-BASED SERVICES

In light of the numerous problems in living faced by antisocial youth and their multi-need families, together with their occasional suspiciousness and hostility toward middle-class service providers, it is not difficult to appreciate why this population of juveniles is generally considered "difficult to treat."

Nevertheless, we have adopted several procedures that are of considerable value for dealing with impediments to treatment in this population. These procedures represent a central aspect of the multisystemic approach and are largely responsible for the excellent cooperation that we have obtained from multi-need families treated in our projects.

A cornerstone of multisystemic therapy, when used with economically disadvantaged multi-need families, is the provision of home-based treatment. The therapist usually begins treatment by meeting with the youth and all other family members living in the home. Despite the fact that the family has agreed to participate in treatment, it is often the case that they have done so under the threat of some social or legal sanction. Thus, family members may be extremely anxious or hostile about meeting with a therapist. These feelings may be intensified if the family is also expected to meet with the therapist in an unfamiliar setting, such as a mental health clinic. Thus, the initial family session, and subsequent sessions as well, are usually conducted at the family's residence. Most multi-need families, when given a choice by the therapist, prefer to meet on their own "turf" rather than in an unfamiliar setting. We believe that the therapist's willingness to travel to the family's home conveys a high level of respect for the family members' participation in treatment and helps them to form an image of the therapist as a reasonable and committed professional.

Meeting the family in their home also has pragmatic advantages. A high percentage of missed or canceled clinic appointments occur because a family does not have reliable transportation, or because the meeting time conflicts with a parent's work schedule. Demanding that a lower-income parent adjust his or her work schedule to attend a meeting at a social service agency does little to enhance cooperation or to convey an appreciation for the parent's life situation. Consequently, we have learned that the therapist's time is often used most efficiently when sessions are conducted in the family's home and often at night or on the weekend. A further advantage of this scheduling practice is that it is much easier for unmotivated families to ignore an appointment at a clinic than to ignore the therapist who knocks at their door at the scheduled time.

In those few instances when the family is not home at the appointment time, the therapist will often wait for up to 30 minutes for the family to return. If that is not possible, the therapist will return later that day to briefly meet the family and to reschedule the appointment. Although such an effort is initially time-consuming for the therapist, we have found that persistence in making contact with the family members helps to ease their apprehensions about meeting the therapist and starting treatment. We have also found that this initial persistence ultimately saves time because it allows therapy to begin (and end) sooner and reduces the number of missed sessions during treatment.

The persistence of the therapist also serves an important communicative function for the small percentage of families who have little desire for contact with social service professionals and who have learned strategies for passively avoiding the attention of these professionals. When social service professionals contact these families, the families seem to be agreeable to suggestions but rarely follow through after the professional leaves. The family has learned to present a cooperative front as a strategy for minimizing contact with professionals. The professional, who typically is underpaid and has a high caseload, is often satisfied with the family's apparent cooperation or does not have the time or resources to persist in engaging the family. The multisystemic therapist, however, indicates both verbally and behaviorally (in a friendly and nonpejorative manner) that he or she is willing to devote as much time as is needed to deal with identified problems. When highly resistant families realize that the therapist is persistent, many decide to cooperate with therapy. Obviously, the effective use of multisystemic therapy is predicated on the therapist's having a reasonable caseload.

During interviews with the family, it is necessary that the meeting room (usually the living room or kitchen) be structured to minimize distractions. Thus, the therapist might need to ask the family to turn off the television or stereo and to tell visitors and callers to return or call later. The therapist usually begins the first session with a brief social stage in which an effort is made to help everyone relax. The therapist makes a point of obtaining some social response from each family member to convey that everyone in the family is important and to define the therapy situation as one in which all family members can contribute. The therapist then shifts to a problem stage in which everyone in the family is asked to give his or her view of the presenting problem(s). This strategy provides important information about areas of agreement and conflict in the family and also helps to define therapy as a cooperative endeavor.

The last part of the first interview involves a goal-setting stage during which the family members are asked to specify what changes they would like to seek in therapy. Here the therapist's task is to help the family to develop a clear operational definition of the problem behaviors or complaints that they would like to have solved. By arriving at such a definition, the therapist and family members have essentially entered into a contract about the goals of therapy, and the therapist (and family) will have a yardstick for measuring change and evaluating the success of the treatment. Additional goals for treatment may be added by the therapist after an assessment has been completed in other relevant systemic contexts (e.g., the peer group, school).

Subsequent treatment sessions focus on facilitating the necessary attitudinal and relationship changes to attain the conjoint goals of the family members and the therapist. The therapist addresses treatment goals one at a time or in some logical combination. As substantive progress is made toward meeting one goal, treatment sessions incorporate additional goals. Emphasis is placed on the efficient use of treatment time; thus, sessions rarely last for more than 90 minutes and may last for as few as 15 minutes. At the conclusion of each session, family members are given explicit tasks that are designed to facilitate the attainment of the identified goals. The first item on the agenda of the next session is the family members' performance of the tasks. Depending on the stage of treatment and on any extant crises, sessions may be held every day or as infrequently as once a week. The specific family members who attend will vary with the nature of the particular problem that is being addressed (e.g., youth are usually not included in sessions that address lax parental discipline in order to avoid undermining the parent's authority).

GENERAL PRINCIPLES FOR MULTISYSTEMIC INTERVENTIONS
During the past few decades, the use of therapeutic "techniques" such as systematic desensitization and problem-solving skills training has become popular among many mental health professionals. Techniques can be implemented in a relatively standardized manner because they can be readily described in intervention manuals and applied to certain highly circumscribed problems. However, when dealing with complex social systems that can have a multitude of significant clinical problems, each with its own set of contributing factors, a highly specified treatment approach cannot provide the flexibility that is needed to optimize positive therapeutic outcome. Thus, multisystemic treatment is guided by a set of intervention principles and by strategies of change.

In consideration of the strengths and weaknesses of particular therapists and families, a moderate degree of flexibility is permitted. We do not believe that complete agreement regarding treatment decisions is a necessary condition for effective multisystemic therapy. In fact, multiple paths can lead to efficient and successful behavior change. What is more important is that therapists conceptualize behavior problems within a framework that considers the multidimensional nature of such problems, and that interventions be conducted directly in the systems that have been targeted for change. The following principles and guidelines represent the fundamental nature of multisystemic therapy and are applicable to almost every case.

1. *The primary purpose of assessment is to understand the "fit" between the identified problems and their broader systemic context.* To accomplish this task, the therapist obtains information from multiple sources (e.g., youth, parents, teachers) about the strengths and weaknesses of individual family members, family relations, and relations with extrafamilial systems (e.g., peers, school, neighborhood). Such an assessment strategy relies heavily on the ability of the therapist to synthesize information, which is sometimes conflicting, and to "read" people.

2. *Interventions should be present-focused and action-oriented, targeting specific and well-defined problems.* The use of well-specified treatment goals, reached by consensus, provides necessary direction and purpose for therapy. Such goals also help to motivate the family's efforts toward change.

3. *Interventions should target sequences of behavior within or between multiple systems.* Multisystemic therapy focuses primarily on changing interpersonal relations. Thus, treatment almost always attempts to strengthen positive social bonds and to modify problematic interpersonal relations.

4. *Interventions should be developmentally appropriate.* For example, interventions with younger adolescents usually place greater emphasis on the development of effective parental control strategies, whereas interventions with older adolescents may focus on issues of emancipation and independence.

5. *Interventions should be designed to require daily or weekly effort by family members.* This conveys the message that treatment involves commitment and work on the part of the family members. Also, problems will be resolved more rapidly if family members actively work on them.

6. *Intervention efficacy is evaluated continuously from multiple perspectives.* Frequent feedback keeps the therapist (and family) abreast of treatment

efficacy and avoids the devotion of extensive time and energy to unproductive solutions. Evaluation from multiple perspectives (multiple family members, teachers) also ensures that the therapist will not be misled by false claims of therapeutic gains.

7. *Interventions should be designed to promote treatment generalization and long-term maintenance of therapeutic change.* This principle has several implications. First, interventions should emphasize the development of skills that are to be used in the natural environment. Second, the therapist should assist others in making changes for themselves and should not perform tasks for the family. Third, prior to termination, the therapist should ensure that the youth and family have the motivation and ability to maintain a positive trajectory regarding social relations and school or vocational goals.

8. *Therapeutic contacts should emphasize the positive, and interventions should use systemic strengths as levers for change.* Reframing and positive connotation are used to decrease resistance to treatment. In addition, strengths of the systems are identified and used to attain the identified goals. For example, parental concern for the adolescent might be used in motivating the parent to adopt more effective control strategies; or an adolescent's athletic or artistic talent might be used to promote his or her involvement with prosocial peers.

9. *Interventions should be designed to promote responsible behavior and decrease irresponsible behavior among family members.* Consequences for responsible behavior and for irresponsible behavior are clearly delineated, and the parents learn to implement these consequences consistently and fairly. In addition, an implicit aspect of this principle is that psychiatric terminology is avoided. Common language labels such as *immature, stubborn,* and *irresponsible* replace psychiatric and DSM-III-R interpretations of such behaviors.

Summary and Conclusions

Although there are still gaps in our knowledge concerning the determinants of antisocial behavior, multidimensional causal models of delinquency have pointed to the complex and reciprocal interplay between pertinent characteristics of adolescents and of the key systems in which adolescents are embedded. In light of the fact that most delinquency treatment approaches address only a small subset of the possible determinants of delinquent behavior, it is not surprising that most of these approaches have been unsuccessful. To be effective, treatment should be capable of addressing multiple determinants of delinquent behavior and should intervene in the natural systems in which adolescents transact.

The findings from our outcome studies suggest that multisystemic therapy is effective in decreasing the behavior problems of serious juvenile offenders and in improving the relations within their multiproblem families. We believe that an important component of our success with these adolescents and their families is the provision of home-based treatment services. Such services can enhance cooperation of family members, increase the likelihood of treatment generalization, and promote long-term maintenance of therapeutic changes. Likewise, other aspects of multisystemic therapy (e.g., well-specified treatment goals, emphasis on systemic strengths) may also contribute to the excellent cooperation and long-term gains that have been obtained with many families.

Note

1. Extensive descriptions of multisystemic intervention strategies, including case studies, have been published elsewhere (Henggeler & Borduin, 1990).

References

Agnew, R. (1985). Social control theory and delinquency: A longitudinal test. *Criminology, 23*, 47–61.

Blechman, E. A. (1985). *Solving child behavior problems at home and school*. Champaign IL: Research Press.

Borduin, C. M., Henggeler, S. W., Blaske, D. M., & Stein, R. (1990). Multisystemic treatment of adolescent sexual offenders. *International Journal of Offender Therapy and Comparative Criminology, 34*, 105–113.

Borduin, C. M., Mann, B. J., Cone, L. T., Henggeler, S. W., Fucci, B. R., Blaske, D. M., & Williams, R. A. (in press). Multisystemic treatment of serious juvenile offenders: Long-term prevention of criminality and violence. *Journal of Consulting and Clinical Psychology*.

Bronfenbrenner, U. (1979). *The ecology of human development: Experiments by nature and design*. Cambridge: Harvard University Press.

Brunk, M., Henggeler, S. W., & Whelan, J. P. (1987). Comparison of multisystemic therapy and parent training in the brief treatment of child abuse and neglect. *Journal of Consulting and Clinical Psychology, 55*, 171–178.

Culbertson, J. L. (1990, August). *Clinical child psychology in the broadening of our scope.* Presidential address to the Section on Clinical Child Psychology at the meeting of the American Psychological Association, Boston.

Davis, G., & Leitenberg, H. (1987). Adolescent sex offenders. *Psychological Bulletin, 101,* 417–427.

Elliott, D. S., Huizinga, D., & Ageton, S. S. (1985). *Explaining delinquency and drug use.* Beverly Hills CA: Sage.

Elliott, D. S., Huizinga, D., & Morse, B. J. (1985). *The dynamics of deviant behavior: A national survey progress report.* Boulder CO: Behavioral Research Institute.

Federal Bureau of Investigation, U.S. Department of Justice (1990). *Uniform crime reports.* Washington DC: Author.

Gottfredson, G. D. (1989). The experiences of violent and serious victimization. In N. A. Weiner & M. E. Wolfgang (Eds.), *Pathways to criminal violence* (pp. 202–234). Newbury Park CA: Sage.

Haley, J. (1976). *Problem solving therapy.* San Francisco: Jossey-Bass.

Hazelrigg, M. D., Cooper, H. M., & Borduin, C. M. (1987). Evaluating the effectiveness of family therapies: An integrative review and analysis. *Psychological Bulletin, 101,* 428–442.

Henggeler, S. W. (1989). *Delinquency in adolescence.* Newbury Park CA: Sage.

Henggeler, S. W. (1991). Multidimensional causal models of delinquent behavior. In R. Cohen & A. Siegel (Eds.), *Context and development.* Hillsdale NJ: Erlbaum.

Henggeler, S. W., & Borduin, C. M. (1990). *Family therapy and beyond: A multisystemic approach to treating the behavior problems of children and adolescents.* Pacific Grove CA: Brooks/Cole.

Henggeler, S. W., Borduin, C. M., Melton, G. B., Mann, B. J., Smith, L., Hall, J. A., Cone, L., & Fucci, B. R. (1991). Effects of multisystemic therapy on drug use and abuse in serious juvenile offenders: A progress report from two outcome studies. *Family Dynamics of Addiction Quarterly, 1,* 40–51.

Henggeler, S. W., Melton, G. B., & Smith, L. A. (1992). Family preservation using multisystemic therapy: An effective alternative to incarcerating serious juvenile offenders. *Journal of Consulting and Clinical Psychology, 60,* 953–961.

Henggeler, S. W., Melton, G. B., Smith, L. A., Schoenwald, S. K., & Hanley, J. H. (1993). Family preservation using multisystemic treatment: Long-term follow-up to a clinical trial with serious juvenile offenders. *Journal of Child and Family Studies, 2,* 283–293.

Henggeler, S. W., Rodick, J. D., Borduin, C. M., Hanson, C. L., Watson, S. M., & Urey, J. R. (1986). Multisystemic treatment of juvenile offenders: Effects on adolescent behavior and family interaction. *Developmental Psychology, 22,* 132–141.

Huesmann, L. R., Lefkowitz, M. M., Eron, L. D., & Walder, L. O. (1984). Stability of aggression over time and generations. *Developmental Psychology, 20,* 1120-1134.

Kazdin, A. E. (1988). *Child psychotherapy: Developing and identifying effective treatments.* New York: Pergamon.

Kendall, P. C., & Braswell, L. (1985). *Cognitive-behavioral therapy for impulsive children.* New York: Guilford.

LaGrange, R. L., & White, H. R. (1985). Age differences in delinquency: A test of theory. *Criminology, 23,* 19–45.

Levine, R. R. J., Watt, N. P., Prentky, R. A., & Fryer, J. H. (1980). Childhood social competence in functionally disordered psychiatric patients and in normals. *Journal of Abnormal Child Psychology, 8,* 132–138.

Loeber, R. (1982). The stability of antisocial and delinquent child behavior: A review. *Child Development, 53,* 1431–1446.

Mann, B. J., Borduin, C. M., Henggeler, S. W., & Blaske, D. M. (1990). An investigation of systemic conceptualizations of parent-child coalitions and symptom change. *Journal of Consulting and Clinical Psychology, 58,* 336–344.

Mash, E. J. (1989). Treatment of child and family disturbance: A behavioral-systems perspective. In E. J. Mash & R. A. Barkley (Eds.), *Treatment of childhood disorders* (pp. 3–36). New York: Guilford.

McMahon, R. J., & Forehand, R. (1988). Conduct disorders. In E. J. Mash & L. G. Terdal (Eds.), *Behavioral assessment of childhood disorders.* New York: Guilford.

Miller, G. E., & Prinz, R. J. (1990). Enhancement of social learning family interventions for childhood conduct disorder. *Psychological Bulletin, 108,* 291–307.

Minuchin, P. P. (1985). Families and individual development: Provocations from the field of family therapy. *Child Development, 56,* 289–302.

Minuchin, S. (1974). *Families and family therapy.* Cambridge: Harvard University Press.

Mulvey, E. P., Arthur, M. A., & Reppucci, N. D. (1989). *Review of programs for the prevention and treatment of delinquency* (Office of Technology Assessment). Washington DC: U.S. Government Printing Office.

Patterson, G. R., & Dishion, T. J. (1985). Contributions of families and peers to delinquency. *Criminology, 23,* 63–79.

Quay, H. C. (Ed.). (1987). *Handbook of juvenile delinquency.* New York: Wiley.

Romig, D. (1978). *Justice for our children.* Lexington MA: Lexington Books.

Simcha-Fagan, O., & Schwartz, J. E. (1986). Neighborhood and delinquency: An assessment of contextual effects. *Criminology, 24,* 667–703.

Tolan, P. H., Cromwell, R. E., & Brasswell, M. (1986). Family therapy with delinquents: A critical review of the literature. *Family Process, 25,* 619–650.

West, D. J., & Farrington, D. P. (1973). *Who becomes delinquent?* London: Heinemann.

Wolfgang, M. E., Figlio, R. M., & Sellin, T. (1972). *Delinquency in a birth cohort.* Chicago: University of Chicago Press.

6

In-Home Programs for Juvenile Delinquents

Jeffrey A. Butts and William H. Barton

This chapter examines the potential role of in-home programs for juvenile delinquents. Such programs hold much unrealized potential for providing cost-effective supervision and rehabilitative services to many young people who are currently placed in more expensive residential programs. This potential should be tapped both at the front end of the juvenile justice system, as alternatives to secure pretrial detention and postadjudicatory incarceration, and at the back end, as an essential aftercare component of residential programs. The kinds of in-home programs to be discussed go beyond regular probation to include more intensive supervision and support services. As in all juvenile corrections, such programs must strive for a balance between protecting the public and rehabilitating juveniles. Such a balance is possible to attain with in-home programs.

We begin with a discussion of the current policy environment in juvenile corrections, one that seems to be returning to a greater reliance on incarceration for juveniles. We argue that such a trend is an ill-conceived "quick fix" that is not supported by the balance of the evidence concerning juvenile delinquency and correctional programs. Our review of this evidence turns up several models of successful community-based programs, many of them home-based. Following brief descriptions of promising in-home programs, we discuss ways in which in-home programs can be incorporated into a comprehensive system of delinquency interventions.

Present Policy Environment of Juvenile Corrections

Trends in juvenile justice appear to be cyclical. After a period of intense scrutiny in the 1960s and early 1970s, a number of reforms were initiated, including the removal of most juveniles from adult jails and prisons, the decriminalization of status offenses, and the reduced reliance by many states upon large training schools. "Community-based" diversion and alternative programs were developed, legal representation of juveniles in court was permitted and encouraged, and conditions in institutions were improved through the application of more stringent standards.

During the 1980s, the cycle began to turn back. The media presented numerous stories of violent or drug-related juvenile crime. Politicians were elected on "get-tough" platforms promising to arrest, convict, and incarcerate more criminals for longer periods of time. As a result, many states made huge expenditures for hundreds of additional institutional beds for juveniles, as well as adults. Did "community-based" alternatives fail, or were they simply not sufficiently evaluated or championed? We contend that the latter is the case. In this chapter, we first review the context of the institutionalization-versus-deinstitutionalization debate and then offer some evidence from the literature and from our own recent work suggesting that in-home programs can be effective for many juvenile offenders, including some of those for whom institutional placements are often recommended.

INSTITUTIONALIZATION VERSUS DEINSTITUTIONALIZATION

The institutionalization-versus-deinstitutionalization debate has raged in the United States for more than a century, at least since the reformers of the Progressive Era began to question the wisdom of placing poor and delinquent youth in the "houses of refuge" developed during the mid-nineteenth century. Social reformers of that period often sought to remove youthful offenders from these institutions by using forerunners of in-home supervision and probation (Empey, 1976; Platt, 1969; Schlossman, 1977). "Decarceration" movements, in fact, have been around almost as long as prisons themselves (Johnson, Hoelter, & Miller, 1981).

In the early part of this century, juvenile offenders were viewed quite differently from their adult counterparts. Children were seen as less responsible for their actions and more amenable to and deserving of rehabilitative opportunities. The juvenile court began as a relatively informal setting in which concerned judges and professionals made decisions in "the best interests of the child." As a result of efforts by advocates of due process protections for juveniles on the one hand and by those skeptical of the rehabilitative effectiveness of juvenile correctional programming on the other, this *parens patriae* model of the juvenile court has given way, at least somewhat, to a more adversarial model in which the protection of public safety competes with the due process rights of the child in determining decisions. Juvenile offenders are now viewed by many as more similar to, if not equal to, adult offenders and thus subject to the same range of correctional sanctions. Many states have made it easier, and in some circumstances mandatory, for the juvenile court to transfer jurisdiction of juvenile offenders to adult courts.[1]

Juvenile justice, like criminal justice (i.e., the adult system), is an area of public policy which is continually plagued by emotions, sensationalism, and fads. International relations, matters of science, and economic policy are thought to be complex and best left to trained professionals. Solutions to the crime problem, on the other hand, can be found in every living room and tavern. The public is barraged with crime images on a regular basis in the print and broadcast media. Every politician, whether running for the city council or the presidency of the United States, must offer a solution to crime. Discussions of how to reduce the impact of crime usually devolve to (1) warnings about the need to address the "root causes" of poverty and urban blight and (2) angry demands for getting "tough" on criminals by arresting them more, putting them in prison more often, and keeping them in prison for longer periods of time.

Most advocates of building and filling more institutions make one of the following three arguments:

1. *More institutions are needed because crime is increasing and getting worse.* Yet, official statistics suggest this is not true (Cook & Laub, 1986). The rate of most serious crimes held steady or even decreased during much of the 1980s and 1990s (Federal Bureau of Investigation, 1993). Even if the rates of some crimes are higher now than 10 or 20 years ago, it could be because the organizations that keep the official statistics (i.e., police departments, courts, the FBI) have vastly improved their methods for keeping records (Cicourel & Kitsuse, 1963; Galvin & Polk, 1982).
2. *More institutions are needed because the fear of being locked up keeps potential criminals from committing crimes.* Criminologists call this the "deterrence" argument, that the prospect of going to prison is the best way to "deter" someone from committing a crime. Researchers have been searching for the evidence to back this up for years. As yet, no one has found that

greater use of prisons reduces crime. If it did, the United States should have been experiencing drastic reductions in crime throughout the 1980s, as most states went on a prison "binge" during that time (Currie, 1985). Nor are boot camps and other shock incarceration programs likely to prove any more effective (Lipsey, 1989; Morash & Rucker, 1990; Parent, 1989).

3. *More institutions are needed because putting criminals away prevents them from committing any more crimes.* This is sometimes referred to as "incapacitation." In other words, as long as someone is behind bars, he or she is incapacitated and cannot commit more crimes against the community. Obviously, this is true. The question which must be asked, however, is does incapacitation make sense as a crime reduction strategy, or does it simply satisfy society's desire to punish? If the purpose of prison is just to punish, the denial of liberty is clearly punishment. Most people, however, want the government to do something about reducing and preventing crime, too. If crime reduction is the goal, prison appears to accomplish little in the long run (Currie, 1985; Scheingold, 1985).

On the other side, advocates of deinstitutionalization advance the following arguments:

1. *Institutional beds are expensive to build and operate.* Incarceration is obviously expensive. Current construction costs for juvenile correctional institutions are in the neighborhood of $50,000 per bed, and annual operating costs tend to fall between $25,000 and $35,000 per bed. Major increases in bed capacities can virtually bankrupt state budgets. In-home programs, in contrast, cost relatively little. A home detention program in Florida, for example, costs $10 per day per youth, or $3,650 per year per slot. Intensive probation programs in Detroit cost less than $10,000 per year per slot. The issue boils down to how much the public wants to pay to incapacitate how many youths for how long.

2. *Institutions do not rehabilitate—they are merely "schools for crime."* Youth in correctional institutions are clearly placed in an unnatural environment. Most of their peers are equally or more delinquent, and the negative influence of such peer societies and institutional culture has been well documented in the past (Bartollas, Miller, & Dinitz, 1976; Cloward, 1960; Lerner, 1986; Street, Vinter, & Perrow, 1966; Sykes, 1965). However, many institutional programs can and do promote positive changes. It may

be more difficult to run an effective program in an institutional context, but not impossible.

3. *Behavioral improvements from institutionalization are rarely sustained upon individuals' return to the community.* As discussed below, there is considerable evidence supporting this argument. Most incarcerated youth eventually return to their communities. Without comprehensive aftercare and reintegration programs (and such programs are rare), youth tend to revert to their former patterns of association and behavior.

4. *Institutionalization disrupts families.* This is undoubtedly true, and our society supposedly places considerable value on family preservation. On the other hand, many delinquent youth come from seriously distressed families. Should we remove youth from such families, or should we provide the families with sufficient support? Moreover, might there not be other alternatives besides institutions when continued placement with the family is impossible?

After the emotions are vented, either about the acts of criminals or the inequities of the social structure, the search for policy solutions inevitably raises the question, What works? (Martinson, 1974; Wilson, 1980). Should society spend more of its resources on imprisonment, or is this "throwing good money after bad?" In the midst of political pressures to build more and more costly institutions and the rhetoric on both sides of the issue, it behooves us to step back and seek rational, empirically based answers to questions regarding the distribution of scarce juvenile justice resources. This chapter is an attempt to contribute to the search for those answers.

What Works?

Some observers doubt whether anything can rehabilitate. The misperception that "nothing works" arose in the wake of several reviews of the literature in the 1970s, most notably that of Martinson (1974) and his colleagues (Lipton, Martinson, & Wilks, 1975).[2] These researchers did not actually say that "nothing works," only that sound evaluations were few and that aggregate rehabilitative effects were found to be small. In fact, nearly half of the studies reviewed by Lipton, Martinson, and Wilks reported some level of success (Sechrest, White, & Brown, 1979).

It would seem that the question to be asked, then, is not, "Does anything work?" but rather, "What works, for whom, under what conditions?"

Recent evidence suggests that quite a few programs work in the sense of demonstrating some reduction in delinquent behavior, but that residential program gains are difficult to sustain upon the youths' return to the community (Andrews et al., 1990; Catalano, Wells, Jenson, & Hawkins, 1989; Cavior & Schmidt, 1978; Garrett, 1985; Gendreau & Ross, 1987; Greenwood & Zimring, 1985; Jesness, 1971; Lipsey, 1989). Models for effective residential and nonresidential programs can be found in a number of states. Although there appears to be no "magic cure" for delinquency, there are various approaches that may change or control delinquent behavior.

Our review of the literature is presented in four sections: a summary of key studies of institutional versus community-based programs; descriptions of selected in-home program models; a summary of effective program components; and some cautionary remarks about the implementation of in-home programs.

KEY PROGRAM EVALUATION STUDIES

Although few in number, the evaluation projects that have explicitly compared the effectiveness of community-based alternatives with incarceration represent the best knowledge base for planning juvenile corrections innovations. The most well-known programs have, in fact, been imitated by other jurisdictions. Policymakers experimenting with alternative models in juvenile justice have often examined the outcomes of these studies for guidance in program development and implementation. All of them have some flaws, but together these studies represent the core of the evaluation literature on community-based alternatives.

Highfields Project

In many ways, the origins of evaluation research on non-institutional, correctional alternatives for juveniles can be traced to the evaluation of a delinquency intervention program in New Jersey known as the Highfields project.[3] The Highfields research is remembered as the first reasonably controlled "experiment" in correctional alternatives.

Highfields, however, was not a home-based program; some might argue whether it was even a community-based one (Coates, 1981). The program was located in a suburban area, and all the youth lived on-site. The evaluation examined the effect of assigning first-commitment male delinquents to the program at Highfields instead of incarcerating them in the New Jersey reformatory at Annandale. Over 200 boys assigned to Highfields were compared with a group of 116 youths sent to Annandale. The juvenile court judges were given criteria to use in deciding which youth were appropriate for assignment to Highfields. The researchers had no real control over which youth entered the program and which were sent to Annandale. Weeks (1958) found that the Highfields youth recidivated less than those in the comparison group. Recidivism was defined as any recommitment. Not surprisingly, the study was often cited as evidence of the effectiveness of the Highfields project. Although the methodology was rudimentary by today's standards, the study was advanced for its time just for including such features as a comparison group, known assignment procedures, and follow-up measures of recidivism.

Community Treatment Program

Another well-known program, this one sponsored and monitored by the California Youth Authority (CYA) during the 1960s, was known as the Community Treatment Program (CTP) (Lerman, 1975; Palmer, 1974). The CTP evaluation randomly assigned thousands of young offenders either to community-based, intensive probation programs or to juvenile correctional institutions operated by the CYA.

The researchers claimed success when the community treatment youth appeared to have significantly lower rates of recidivism than did the institutionalized youth. The study was later criticized, however, for measuring program outcomes by parole revocations, which were subject to the discretion of the program caseworkers and probation officers (Lerman, 1975). Despite these criticisms, the CTP is credited with stimulating a program of research that "substantially increased our understanding of the correctional process" (Krisberg, 1987, p. 46).

Provo and Silverlake Experiments

Two other important projects were coordinated by LaMar T. Empey and his colleagues. One of these studies, known as the Provo Experiment (Empey & Erickson, 1972), used a random-assignment design to compare the effectiveness of traditional probation versus an intensive supervision program for male repeat offenders in the state of Utah. The researchers had intended to compare both probation programs with another group of youth who would be randomly assigned to institutional care. However, they were unable to ensure randomization in commitments to the training school and used a comparison group instead. The findings of the Provo Experiment supported the effectiveness of the community-based programs, although the failure of the research design weakened the internal validity of the study and detracted from its ultimate impact in the literature.

In the Silverlake Experiment, however, Empey and Lubeck (1971) succeeded in using an experimental design to compare the recidivism of institutionalized youth with youth assigned to a specialized community-based group home. The findings, once again, supported the community alternative. Since the two groups of youth had comparable reductions in criminal charges after one year, the project was deemed a success.

Unified Delinquency Intervention Services

One of the most controversial studies of community-based alternatives evaluated the effect of programs coordinated by the Unified Delinquency Intervention Services (UDIS) in Cook County (Chicago), Illinois (Murray & Cox, 1979). The programs that served the UDIS youth represented five different levels of intensity. Level 1 programs, aimed at youth who remained in their own homes, provided services such as counseling, advocacy, and educational or vocational training. Most of the UDIS youth were served by these nonresidential programs. The other levels represented various residential settings (group homes, camps, etc.). Youth in the UDIS programs were compared with a sample of youth who were assigned to institutions run by the Illinois Department of Corrections.

Murray and Cox reported that both the UDIS programs and the institutions seemed to achieve significant reductions in the recidivism of their clientele. They added, provocatively, that incarceration was better at reducing subsequent arrests than the "less severe" alternatives of UDIS. Murray and Cox concluded that just about any level of correctional severity—beyond probation—would reduce recidivism. Murray and Cox proposed the term "suppression effect" to describe this reduction. Maltz and his colleagues (Maltz, Gordon, McDowall, & McCleary, 1980), among many others, called it a selection-regression artifact and criticized Murray and Cox for confusing a statistical artifact for the effect of the programs. The ensuing debate between Murray and Cox and their critics contributed greatly to the development of methodology in correctional program evaluation. Moreover, the marketing of the research had an enormous impact on policymakers who had grown tired of the pessimism and despair that they perceived among criminological researchers.

Wayne County Intensive Probation Study

In our recent study, the effectiveness of intensive probation for juveniles compared favorably to the impact of commitment and placement in state facilities (Barton & Butts, 1990). In 1983, the Wayne County (Detroit), Michigan, Juvenile Court responded to pressures for reducing its number of state commitments by initiating three in-home, intensive supervision programs to serve a portion of the juveniles normally committed to the state's Department of Social Services for placement.[4] Over the next five years, an evaluation study compared the recidivism and other outcomes of youth randomly assigned to the intensive supervision programs with those of a control group of state wards. Youth receiving their first commitment to the state, excluding violent offenders, were eligible for the programs. Most of the eligible youth were serious and chronic property offenders.[5]

The study followed more than 500 randomly assigned youth for two years and collected data from court, police, and program records as well as from interviews with youth and their parents. The results of the evaluation showed that the intensive supervision and control group youth did not differ significantly on measures of recidivism, either in terms of subsequent charges or self-reported delinquent behavior, at the time of follow-up.[6] Similar findings of no difference were observed for a variety of other outcome measures, including educational progress, family and peer relationships, and attitudes. The main factor differentiating the two groups was the cost of the interventions. State commitment per diem costs averaged about $80 per youth, while the comparable cost of the intensive supervision programs averaged about $25. The overall conclusion from the study was that a substantial proportion of youths normally committed to the state could be managed no less effectively in in-home programs at about one third the cost (Barton & Butts, 1990).

Statewide Deinstitutionalization Projects

Other major research efforts in juvenile correctional alternatives resulted from dramatic changes in two states that removed most of their delinquent youth from large institutions and initiated community-based networks of smaller facilities. In both Massachusetts and Utah, some attempt was made to evaluate the impact of introducing the alternatives to incarceration. Although their contributions to knowledge about correctional effectiveness were limited, these programs demonstrated the feasibility of reducing institutional populations by shifting resources to community-based alternatives.

Massachusetts, like most states in the 1970s, depended heavily on a few large residential facilities to handle juvenile offenders. One by one, over a period of slightly more than a year, the Department of Youth Services closed all of these facilities and instead developed a network of community-based, nonresidential programs. The evaluation of this change rested upon a comparison of two samples of youth. One group of youth was drawn from those in the community-based alternatives, while the other was composed of recent discharges from the training schools. The results showed that the youth in well-implemented community-based networks had lower levels of recidivism than the youth who had been incarcerated (Bakal & Polsky, 1979; Ohlin, Miller, & Coates, 1977). Today, Massachusetts operates some small, secure residential programs but continues to incarcerate relatively few youth. A more recent assessment suggested that the state's array of community-based programs is highly effective in protecting public safety in a cost-effective manner without widespread use of incarceration (Krisberg, Austin, & Steele, 1989).

In the mid-1970s, political leaders in Utah were also faced with a crisis concerning their one large, congregate training school, then known as the State Industrial School. An acknowledged problem with abusive conditions and poor results at the school was underscored by the filing of a lawsuit against the state in 1975. In search of alternative approaches, and encouraged by federal assistance, state officials closed the training school and reduced the number of secure beds from 350 to 60. Community-based programs and a limited number of 30-bed secure treatment units created 250 new "slots" for the supervision of juvenile offenders in the community.

The results of Utah's efforts were promising; during the 1980s Utah had one of the lowest rates of juvenile incarceration in the nation (Austin, Krisberg, & Joe, 1987). The National Council on Crime and Delinquency researchers who examined the Utah experience concluded that "Utah's policy of community-based corrections did not worsen public safety" and that "the recidivism data for Youth Corrections offenders strongly indicate that the imposition of appropriate community-based controls on highly active serious and chronic juvenile offenders does reduce the incidence of subsequent criminal behavior" (Austin et al., 1987, p. 137).

Since then, other states, notably Missouri and Maryland, have begun to explore reductions in the use of large residential institutions. Still other states, such as California, Nevada, Arizona, and Ohio, continue to be institution-oriented (U.S. Department of Justice, 1988). At the broad policy level, the evidence from Utah and Massachusetts suggests that the move away from institutions does not jeopardize public safety (Krisberg, Austin, & Steele, 1989; Loughran, 1987; Van Vleet, Rutherford, & Schwartz, 1987).

SELECTED COMMUNITY-BASED PROGRAMS

In this section we present examples of in-home programs used at three points in the juvenile justice system: pretrial detention, postadjudicatory placement, and aftercare following residential placement. These are not the only examples that could have been cited but are illustrative of the role that in-home programs can play in a comprehensive system.[7]

In-home programs for delinquents, as opposed to other client groups, are faced with the challenge of pursuing the multiple and often conflicting goals of protecting public safety by monitoring and controlling the youths' behavior and addressing the needs of youth by providing a variety of services to them and their families. The balance between these two orientations is slightly different in the three examples discussed below. At the detention stage, the emphasis is clearly on controlling risk rather than meeting needs. The youth has not yet been formally adjudicated, and "treatment" per se would be inappropriate. The legitimate purposes of pretrial detention are simply to ensure that the youth appears at court hearings and to protect the public from offenses that the youth might commit prior to the court hearing. Of course, even the provision of structured behavioral supervision may have some beneficial treatment effects, and referral to other sources of support is a legitimate function of a home detention program.

At the other two stages, placement and aftercare, both risk management and services to meet needs are critical. Most in-home programs are based on a case management model in which a worker has overall responsibility for a small caseload. This worker embodies the tension between supervision and treatment goals and must somehow combine the role of police or probation officer with that of trusted youth advocate.

Home Detention

Juvenile detention is an area that is becoming increasingly problematic in many jurisdictions. National data indicate that the detention populations are increasing and that many detention facilities are overcrowded, but, paradoxically, that only about half of the youth detained have been charged with major felony offenses (Jones & Krisberg, 1994; Steketee, Willis, & Schwartz, 1989). To some extent, detention centers have become the receptacles for logjams at other parts of the system. In any event, there does not appear to be a compelling need to hold so many youth in costly, secure facilities. Several jurisdictions have developed home detention programs to provide intensive supervision to youth who may not need to be securely detained but who cannot simply be released prior to their court hearings.

The first juvenile home detention program was started in St. Louis in the early 1970s (Keve & Zantek, 1972). Other notable programs were developed in Jefferson County (Louisville), Kentucky (Community Research Center, 1983), and Cuyahoga County (Cleveland), Ohio (Huff, 1986). In such programs, workers are assigned small caseloads (10 or fewer cases) and are expected to have one or more daily contacts with youth at irregular times, to be on call 24 hours a day for crisis intervention, and to have frequent contacts with parents, schools, and other agencies as needed. All of these programs have demonstrated laudatory success rates, with only 5% to 10% of their youth failing to appear at hearings and 10% to 20% acquiring additional charges prior to their court hearings.

To be fully effective, home detention programs should be supplemented with nonsecure residential alternatives (e.g., small group shelters or family foster homes) for youth ordinarily detained primarily because they lack a suitable home and with day programs (e.g., report centers combining educational and recreational activities) for youth who are not involved in school or work activities. A recent demonstration project in Broward County (Fort Lauderdale), Florida, found that the use of home detention with such supplementary programs helped reduce overcrowding in a severely overcrowded detention facility without jeopardizing public safety concerns (Schwartz, Barton, & Orlando, 1991).

Intensive Probation

The Wayne County study discussed earlier in this chapter examined three in-home, intensive supervision alternatives to state commitment for relatively serious adjudicated delinquents (Barton & Butts, 1990). One program was operated directly by the juvenile court's probation department; the other two were run by private agencies under contract to the court. The three programs did not differ significantly in outcomes, with all three successfully terminating about half of their cases. The average length of stay for the successful cases was about 13 months. Most of those who were successfully retained in the community remained out of trouble throughout the two-year study period.

All three programs utilized an intensive probation model with workers responsible for frequent and varied contacts with a relatively small caseload (8 to 10 youths per worker). One program emphasized family involvement and in-home visits, another emphasized on-site educational and other day programming, while the third relied more upon traditional probation methods of behavioral supervision supplemented by individual and group counseling and collateral contacts. Youth received an average of three to four contacts per week, which may not appear to be truly intensive but is a higher rate of contact than regular probation. Moreover, such averages obscure the fact that many cases received more frequent contacts while other cases received very few.

Participation in job-related program components and good worker-youth relationships were the program factors that appeared to be most closely associated with positive outcomes. Evaluation from clients indicated that youth and their parents appreciated the extension of services to include other family members and direct material assistance.

Aftercare

Many treatment approaches, in residential or nonresidential settings, *can* achieve some measurable behavioral change when implemented carefully and consistently. Gains from residential programs are difficult to sustain, however, once the youth have left the program and returned to the community. Thus, reintegration or aftercare is probably the most critical program component and the one too often overlooked (Altschuler, 1984; Greenwood, 1986a). Even with the most violent juvenile offenders in secure residential programs, intensive community supervision following release has been demonstrated to have a positive effect on reducing recidivism (Fagan & Hartstone, 1986). Aftercare should involve families or other significant persons in each youth's community, the identification of potential community resources including educational, vocational, health, and support opportunities, and a strategy for behavioral supervision during the transitional period. Aftercare should not be viewed as a separate component of the program but should be incorporated from the outset. Community outreach staff can become involved with youth and their families from the beginning, coordinating services, perhaps leading family group sessions, and beginning the collateral contacts with community agencies on behalf of the youth.

Relatively little research has been done on aftercare programs for juveniles returning to the community following residential placements (Jenson, Hawkins, & Catalano, 1986). Too often aftercare, if it exists at all, resembles typical probation or parole services where workers have enormous caseloads and little contact with clients. The most promising aftercare programs resemble the intensive, in-home programs already discussed and feature small caseloads, frequent contact, and a variety of service and advocacy activities.

For example, an experimental evaluation of an intensive, home-based aftercare program in Philadelphia showed promising results. When compared to a control group of youth released from a training school with regular aftercare, intensive aftercare youth received ten times as many contacts with their workers, were more likely to have firm work or school plans, were more cooperative with their workers, had fewer family and school problems, and showed lower rearrests, reconvictions, or reincarcerations (Sontheimer, Goodstein, & Kovacevic, 1990).

The Social Development Research Group at the University of Washington (Catalano et al., 1989; Haggerty, Wells, Jenson, Catalano, & Hawkins, 1989) developed Project ADAPT based on their social development model of delinquency intervention. There are two program phases in this aftercare program for delinquents released from state institutions. The first, reentry, occurs during the last 10 weeks prior to release from the institutions. During this phase, the aftercare case managers establish relationships with the youth, explain the orientation of the program, and work with the youth to develop their postrelease plans. Visits to schools, homes, and other community sites are included in this phase. The second phase, aftercare, consists of six months of intensive case management and skills-training services in the community. As in the intensive probation programs, case managers have small caseloads (six to eight cases) and combine frequent personal contacts with provision or coordination of a range of services including individual and family counseling, education, job training, health, and recreation.

In developing a prototype for intensive community-based aftercare, Altschuler and Armstrong (1991) stress the importance of assessment and classification for the development of individualized intervention plans, case management to ensure coordination and delivery of services, and sound evaluation practices. A key element of their model is a system of graduated incentives and consequences to reward positive behavior and sanction noncompliance *without* resorting to recommitment, except as a last resort. This model, currently undergoing field testing prior to more widespread replication, holds great promise.

Characteristics of Successful Programs

The evidence and examples reviewed above suggest that long-term, residential programming is neither helpful from a rehabilitative standpoint nor necessary from a public safety standpoint. Of course, there are other factors, mostly political, that encourage the use of secure, residential programs. Moreover, there will always be some youth for whom institutional placement is necessary. A reasonable policy goal would be to reserve secure settings for the most serious and chronic offenders, to develop a comprehensive array of alternative community-based programs, and to maximize the rehabilitative potential of all programs. What characteristics should these programs have?

INTERVENTIONS BASED ON RISK AND NEED

Programs that tailor their interventions to an individual's identified risks and needs appear to be more successful than those that try to impose a single strategy on all cases. Accordingly, an essential first step is a thorough assessment.

COORDINATION AND CONTINUITY

Someone must be responsible for seeing that appropriate interventions address the needs identified in the assessment. That responsibility does not end with the development of an intervention plan, but includes continuous monitoring to guarantee that quality services are provided as intended. All of the successful in-home programs reviewed used some model of case management.

FLEXIBILITY

Case managers must have sufficient flexibility to provide, seek, develop, or broker whatever services are needed. The enemies of such flexibility are overly bureaucratic procedures and fiscal policies that fund categorical programs. Small programs are often better able to avoid rigid bureaucratic constraints. Programs need to provide case managers with flexible resources and allow them to pursue creative strategies as long as accountability is maintained.

CONCRETE FOCUS

The literature suggests that cognitive, behavioral, and social learning approaches are more effective than psychodynamic approaches, and a focus on family intervention appears to be helpful (Catalano et al., 1989; Gottschalk, Davidson, Gersheimer, & Mayer, 1987; Greenwood, 1989; Greenwood & Zimring, 1985; Lipsey, 1989). Interventions focusing on concrete needs (educational, vocational, material, etc.) appear to be more effective than more abstract "therapy." (Andrews et al., 1990). Successful programs tend to expand the focus from the individual youth to the family and others in the community (Barton & Butts, 1988).

COMMUNITY LINKAGES

Community linkages (utilizing existing community resources, providing support to families, encouraging client-community contact, etc.) have been shown to be related to effectiveness (Altschuler, 1984; Barton & Butts, 1988; Coates, Miller, & Ohlin, 1978). In large part, these linkages are necessary to bridge the gap between residential placement and reintegration.

RELATIONSHIP SKILLS

There is much anecdotal evidence indicating that a key to program success lies in the ability of line staff to form close relationships with the youth (Barton & Butts, 1988; Huff, 1986). Such relationships are not sufficient in the absence of the other structural and resource variables mentioned above, but are probably necessary. Careful hiring, training, and supervision practices are obviously important.

Cautions

It is clear that in-home programs such as those discussed above can play a vital role in a comprehensive system of programs for delinquents. They hold the promise of equally effective and less costly management of a substantial portion of youth currently held in detention centers, training schools, and similar institutions. However, those seeking to introduce such programs in their own jurisdictions should be aware of several pitfalls that have accompanied such efforts in the past. Failure to do so would likely result in a system that continues to allocate resources unwisely.

First, such programs must clearly be developed and sustained as *alternatives* to out-of-home programs. That is, the youth whom they serve must clearly have been headed for secure detention centers, training schools, or similar institutions. Often, in-home programs end up serving less seriously delinquent youth than originally intended because of resistance on the part of in-home programs to accept more seriously delinquent youth or because of reluctance on the part of courts to refer such cases to in-home programs. As a result, the institutions remain full or overcrowded, the jurisdiction now has the additional expense of the in-home programs, and youth are still not being assigned to the least restrictive alternative consistent with the protection of public safety. To avoid such an unintended outcome, strict and objective intake criteria for in-home programs must be established and maintained.

Second, in-home program staff must have sanctioning mechanisms other than a return to the regular institutional system to deal with youth who may not be committing new crimes but who violate program rules or are generally uncooperative. Youth in such programs are naturally under much more intense scrutiny than the average teenager and subject to a variety of terms and conditions for program participation. Even minor infractions are likely to be detected. Program staff should resist the inclination to refer problem cases back to the court for removal from the program. Instead, programs should develop a system of graduated rewards and sanctions like those recommended by Altschuler and Armstrong (1991) in their aftercare prototype.

Third, in-home programs demand a great deal of their case managers. The intensity of involvement, long and irregular hours, and role ambiguities all make it difficult for staff to retain necessary levels of energy and commitment. Programs need to support line staff, provide them with sufficient, flexible resources, and plan for frequent but orderly staff turnover.

Finally, sound evaluations should accompany the introduction of in-home programs at any point in the system. These evaluations should focus not only on individual case outcomes but also on documenting program activities and on assessing the programs' impact on the broader juvenile justice system. Sound evaluations of such programs require sufficient time for follow-up of a substantial number of individual cases—at least a year beyond program completion—in order to conduct meaningful analyses of outcomes.

Conclusion

Beyond the rhetoric, what have we learned about what works in juvenile corrections? First, we have learned that placement in secure residential programs is not a necessary condition for successful intervention with all or even most delinquents. The balance of the research has shown little measurable difference in effectiveness between institutional and community-based programs. Control can be effectively maintained by staff supervision in community-based residential or in-home programs, and the rehabilitative potential of such settings is perhaps greater. The most effective programs seem to rely on a multimodal approach that combines behavioral supervision with a focus on skill development, family support and involvement, attitudinal and motivational change, advocacy, and service brokerage in the community delivered by a motivated staff with good relationship skills. This flexible, individualized package can be provided in community-based residential settings or in nonresidential programs. The evidence shows that such programs can be cost-effective alternatives to incarceration for even relatively serious delinquent youth.

The "null" finding, that correctional programs differ very little in their effect on recidivism, has become quite common in research literature (Barton & Butts, 1990; Empey, 1978; Farrington, Ohlin, & Wilson, 1986; Sechrest et al., 1979; Wilson, 1980). It is important to remember, however, that community-based programs should be assessed as an *alternative* to traditional methods for handling delinquent youth. There is no absolute standard for judging whether programs "work" or not. The task of the evaluator is to determine how they compare with what is already being done. In this sense, a "null" finding could be taken as evidence of success, since the community-based programs are able to reduce delinquency just as much as incarceration and at far lower cost.

Policymakers must recognize the implications of such a finding. Unless the public is willing to pay the potentially enormous cost of long-term incapacitation, most incarcerated juvenile offenses will eventually be released. The social "costs" of delinquent behavior are at best delayed by incarceration, not eliminated. While the available research cannot (and probably never will) guarantee the effectiveness of a particular correctional approach, it does underscore the limitations of incarceration. When compared to community-based programs, correctional institutions do not seem to be significantly more effective at deterring subsequent offenses by youth. Pending the development of a better knowledge base, it would seem that community-based alternatives are an option worth pursuing for all but the most serious delinquent offenders.

Program effectiveness is clearly not the only criterion in policymaking. Juvenile justice policy in particular can sometimes seem to be based more on political and ideological considerations than on sound programmatic knowledge and the demonstrated effectiveness of various alternatives (Sarri, 1981). There are short-term benefits to the community of removing certain youth for some period of time. The public's retributive desire—at least as perceived by policymakers—for "tough" measures to deal with delinquency and crime also plays a part. Prisons and training schools offer the public tangible, if largely symbolic, evidence of a government's efforts to reduce crime. Community programs, on the other hand, may seem vague, extremely variable, and may appear to the public to be "soft" on young criminals.

There will always be some youth who will need to be placed out of the home. Most of these, however, will eventually return home. The literature has stressed the importance of aftercare in maintaining any positive gains from residential placements. Here, too, is an opportunity for in-home programs to make a vital contribution.

Whether employed as front-end alternatives to incarceration or as an aftercare component to a residential program, in-home programs perhaps hold the key to successful treatment of juvenile offenders. Only by acquiring and maintaining constructive skills and behaviors in the community environment can youth develop productive and lasting roles in society. The specific programs highlighted in this chapter are not panaceas to be replicated blindly. Rather, they provide evidence that such approaches can work, and they suggest some of the important characteristics that good programs should adapt to their own circumstances. As investments in the future, in-home programs hold out the promise of far better returns than incarceration for most youthful offenders.

Notes

1. The political motivation for facilitating such transfers is usually a desire to impose tougher sanctions, especially prison terms, on juvenile offenders. Whether such

changes have had the effect of sentencing substantial numbers of young offenders to significant time in prison remains unclear. In many cases, adult courts view these transferred juveniles as relatively nonserious in comparison to adult offenders, so transferred juveniles often receive lighter sanctions than they would have had they remained in the juvenile system. One study in Florida (Polivka, 1987) indicated that a large increase in transfers did not produce a drop in juvenile crime and that the recidivism rate of transferred youth was extremely high.

2. Other reviews with comparable conclusions include those of Logan (1972) and Wright and Dixon (1977).

3. There were earlier evaluations of delinquency interventions, but Highfields was the first project to examine differential impacts on individual delinquent offenders. The work of Shaw and McKay (1969), for example, focused on community prevention, while another predecessor of Highfields, the Cambridge-Somerville study (Powers & Witmer, 1951), tested the effectiveness of preventive counseling on a group of nondelinquents that had been identified as "at-risk" for future delinquency.

4. The large majority (about 80%) of youth committed to the Michigan Department of Social Services from Wayne County received out-of-home placements, mostly in large training schools or similar private institutions. In Michigan, the cost of state commitments is split between the county of origin and the rest of the state. Thus, the rest of the state resented subsidizing the disproportionately large number of commitments from Wayne County.

5. Youth in the study averaged three prior charges, most had been on regular probation previously, and most were currently charged with a felony offense.

6. Although program youth acquired more charges than control group youth, these differences disappeared when the study controlled for offense seriousness and time at large in the community. On the self-report measures, the program youth tended to show slight reductions in the level of offenses at follow-up, whereas control group youth reported slight increases. For violent offenses, this difference was significant, with the program youth reporting fewer offenses.

7. More extensive examples of community programs can be found in Greenwood (1986b); Krisberg, Bakke, Neuenfeldt, and Steele (1989); and Krisberg, Rodriguez, Bakke, Neuenfeldt, and Steele (1989).

References

Altschuler, D. M. (1984). Community reintegration. In R. A. Mathias, P. DeMuro, & R. S. Allinson (Eds.), *Violent juvenile offenders: An anthology.* San Francisco: National Council on Crime and Delinquency.

Altschuler, D. M., & Armstrong, T. L. (1991). *Intensive community-based aftercare prototype: Policies and procedures.* Baltimore: Johns Hopkins University, Institute for Policy Studies.

Andrews, D. A., Zinger, I., Hoge, R. D., Bonta, J., Gendreau, P., & Cullen, F. T. (1990). Does correctional treatment work? A clinically-relevant and psychologically-informed meta-analysis. *Criminology, 28,* 369–404.

Austin, J., Krisberg, B., & Joe, K. (1987). *The impact of juvenile court intervention* (Draft Report). San Francisco: National Council on Crime and Delinquency.

Bakal, Y., & Polsky, H. W. (1979). *Reforming corrections for juvenile offenders.* Lexington MA: Lexington Books.

Bartollas, C., Miller, S. J., & Dinitz, S. (1976). *Juvenile victimization: The institutional paradox.* New York: Halsted.

Barton, W. H., & Butts, J. A. (1988). *Intensive probation in Wayne County: An alternative to state commitment for juvenile delinquents* (Final Report). Ann Arbor: University of Michigan, Institute for Social Research.

Barton, W. H., & Butts, J. A. (1990). Viable options: Intensive supervision programs for juvenile delinquents. *Crime and Delinquency, 36,* 238–255.

Catalano, R. F., Wells, E. A., Jenson, J. M., & Hawkins, J. D. (1989). Aftercare services for drug using adjudicated youth in residential settings. *Social Services Review, 63,* 553–577.

Cavior, H. E., & Schmidt, A. A. (1978). Test of the effectiveness of a differential treatment strategy at the Robert F. Kennedy Center. *Criminal Justice and Behavior, 5,* 131–139.

Cicourel, A. V., & Kitsuse, J. I. (1963). A note on the use of official statistics. *Social Problems, 11,* 131–139.

Cloward, R. A. (1960). Social control in the prison. In R. A. Cloward (Ed.), *Theoretical studies in social organization of the prison.* New York: Social Science Research Council.

Coates, R. B. (1981). Community-based services for juvenile delinquents: Concept and implications for practice. *Journal of Social Issues, 37,* 87–101.

Coates, R. B., Miller, A. D., & Ohlin, L. E. (1978). *Diversity in a youth correctional system: Handling delinquents in Massachusetts.* Cambridge MA: Ballinger.

Community Research Center. (1983). *A community response to a crisis: The effective use of detention and alternatives to detention in Jefferson County, Kentucky.* Washington DC: U.S. Department of Justice, Office of Juvenile Justice and Delinquency Prevention.

Cook, P. J., & Laub, J. H. (1986). The (surprising) stability of youth crime rates. *Journal of Quantitative Criminology, 2,* 265–277.

Currie, E. (1985). *Confronting crime: An American challenge.* New York: Pantheon.

Empey, L. T. (1976). The social construction of childhood, delinquency and social reform. In M. W. Klein (Ed.), *The juvenile justice system.* Beverly Hills CA: Sage.

Empey, L. T. (1978). *American delinquency: Its meaning and construction.* Homewood IL: Dorsey Press.

Empey, L. T., & Erickson, M. L. (1972). *The Provo Experiment: Evaluating community control of delinquency.* Lexington MA: Lexington Books.

Empey, L. T., & Lubeck, S. G. (1971). *The Silverlake Experiment: Testing delinquency theory and community intervention.* Chicago: Aldine.

Fagan, J., & Hartstone, E. (1986). *Innovation and experimentation in juvenile corrections: Implementing a community reintegration model for violent juvenile offenders.* San Francisco: URSA Institute.

Farrington, D. P., Ohlin, L. E., & Wilson, J. Q. (1986). Understanding and controlling crime: Toward a new research strategy. In A. Blumstein & D. P. Farrington, (Eds.), *Research in criminology.* New York: Springer-Verlag.

Federal Bureau of Investigation. (1993). *Age-specific arrest rates and race-specific arrest rates for selected offenses, 1965–1992.* Washington DC: U.S. Government Printing Office.

Galvin, J., & Polk, K. (1982). Any truth you want: The use and abuse of crime and criminal justice statistics. *Journal of Research in Crime and Delinquency, 19,* 135–165.

Garrett, C. J. (1985). Effects of residential treatment on adjudicated delinquents: A meta-analysis. *Journal of Research in Crime and Delinquency, 4,* 287–308.

Gendreau, P., & Ross, R. R. (1987). Revivication of rehabilitation: Evidence from the 1980's. *Crime and Delinquency, 25,* 463–489.

Gottschalk, R., Davidson, W. S., II, Gersheimer, L. K., & Mayer, J. P. (1987). Community-based interventions. In H. C. Quey (Ed.), *Handbook of juvenile delinquency.* New York: Wiley.

Greenwood, P. W. (1986a). *Correctional supervision of juvenile offenders: Where do we go from here?* Santa Monica CA: RAND Corporation.

Greenwood, P. W. (1986b). Promising approaches for the rehabilitation or prevention of chronic juvenile offenders. In P. W. Greenwood (Ed.), *Intervention strategies for chronic juvenile offenders* (RAND Corporation, pp. 207–233). New York: Greenwood Press.

Greenwood, P. W. (1989, November). Overview of recent intervention research.

Paper presented at the annual meeting of the American Society of Criminology, Reno NV.

Greenwood, P. W., & Zimring, F. E. (1985). *One more chance: The pursuit of promising intervention strategies for chronic juvenile offenders.* Santa Monica CA: RAND Corporation.

Haggerty, K. P., Wells, E. A., Jenson, J. M., Catalano, R. F., & Hawkins, J. D. (1989). Delinquents and drug use: A model program for community reintegration. *Adolescence, 24,* 439–456.

Huff, C. R. (1986). *Home detention as a policy alternative for Ohio's juvenile courts.* Columbus: Ohio State University, Program for the Study of Crime and Delinquency.

Jenson, J. M., Hawkins, J. D., & Catalano, R. F. (1986). Social support in aftercare services for troubled youth. *Children and Youth Services in Review, 8,* 323–347.

Jesness, C. F. (1971). The Preston typology study: An experiment with differential treatment in an institution. *Crime and Delinquency, 8,* 38–52.

Johnson, R., Hoelter, H. J., & Miller, J. G. (1981). Juvenile decarceration: An exploratory study of correctional reform. In S. E. Zimmerman & H. D. Miller (Eds.), *Corrections at the crossroads: Designing policy.* Beverly Hills CA: Sage.

Jones, M. A., & Krisberg, B. (1994). Images and reality: Juvenile crime, youth violence and public policy. San Francisco: National Council on Crime and Delinquency.

Keve, P. W., & Zantek, C. S. (1972). *Final report and evaluation of the home detention program, St. Louis, Missouri, September 30, 1971, to July 2, 1972.* McLean VA: Research Analysis Corporation.

Krisberg, B. (1987). Preventing and controlling violent youth crime: The state of the art. In M. Wolfgang, D. S. Elliott, D. Huizinga, B. Morse, & B. Krisberg (Eds.), *Violent juvenile crime: What do we know about it and what can we do about it?* (pp. 35–55). Ann Arbor: University of Michigan, Center for the Study of Youth Policy.

Krisberg, B., Austin, J., & Steele, P. A. (1989). *Unlocking juvenile corrections: Evaluating the Massachusetts Department of Youth Services.* San Francisco: National Council on Crime and Delinquency.

Krisberg, B., Bakke, A., Neuenfeldt, D., & Steele, P. (1989). *Selected program summaries: Demonstration of post-adjudication non-residential intensive supervision programs.* San Francisco: National Council on Crime and Delinquency.

Krisberg, B., Rodriguez, O., Bakke, A., Neuenfeldt, D., & Steele, P. (1989). *Demon-*

stration of post-adjudication non-residential intensive supervision programs: Assessment report. San Francisco: National Council on Crime and Delinquency.

Lerman, P. (1975). *Community treatment and social control: A critical analysis of juvenile correctional policy.* Chicago: University of Chicago Press.

Lerner, S. (1986). *Bodily harm: The pattern of fear and violence at the California Youth Authority.* Bolinas CA: Common Knowledge Press.

Lipsey, M. W. (1989, November). The efficacy of intervention for juvenile delinquency. Paper presented at the annual meeting of the American Society of Criminology, Reno NV.

Lipton, D., Martinson, R., & Wilks, J. (1975). *The effectiveness of correctional treatment: A survey of treatment evaluation studies.* New York: Praeger.

Logan, C. (1972). Evaluation research in crime and delinquency: A reappraisal. *Journal of Criminal Law, Criminology, and Police Science, 63,* 378–387.

Loughran, E. J. (1987). Juvenile corrections: The Massachusetts experience. In *Reinvesting youth corrections resources: A tale of three states* (pp. 7–18). Ann Arbor: University of Michigan, Center for the Study of Youth Policy.

Maltz, M. D., Gordon, A. C., McDowall, D., & McCleary, R. (1980). An artifact in pretest-posttest designs—How it can mistakenly make delinquency programs look effective. *Evaluation Review, 4,* 225–240.

Martinson, R. (1974). What works? Questions and answers about prison reform. *Public Interest, 35,* 22–54.

Morash, M., & Rucker, L. (1990). A critical look at the idea of boot camp as a correctional reform. *Crime and Delinquency, 36,* 204–222.

Murray, C. A., & Cox, L. A., Jr. (1979). *Beyond probation: Juvenile corrections and the chronic delinquent.* Beverly Hills CA: Sage.

Ohlin, L. E., Miller, A. D., & Coates, R. B. (1977). *Juvenile correctional reform in Massachusetts.* Washington DC: U.S. Government Printing Office.

Palmer, T. (1974). The Youth Authority's community treatment project. *Federal Probation, 38,* 3–14.

Parent, D. G. (1989). *Shock incarceration: An overview of existing programs.* Washington DC: U.S. Department of Justice, National Institute of Justice.

Platt, A. M. (1969). *The child savers: The invention of delinquency.* Chicago: University of Chicago Press.

Polivka, L. (1987). *Juveniles in the adult corrections system: The Florida experience.* Tallahassee FL: Office of the Governor, Office of Planning and Budgeting.

Powers, E., & Witmer, H. (1951). *An experiment in the prevention of delinquency.* New York: Columbia University Press.

Sarri, R. (1981). The effectiveness paradox: Institutional vs. community placement of offenders. *Journal of Social Issues, 37*, 34–50.

Scheingold, S. A. (1985). *The politics of law and order: Street crime and public policy.* New York: Longman.

Schlossman, S. L. (1977). *Love and the American delinquent.* Chicago: University of Chicago Press.

Schwartz, I. M., Barton, W. H., & Orlando, F. (1991). Keeping kids out of secure detention: The misuse of juvenile detention has a profound impact on child welfare. *Public Welfare, 49*(2), 20–26, 46.

Sechrest, L., White, S. O., & Brown, E. D. (Eds.). (1979). *The rehabilitation of criminal offenders: Problems and prospects.* Washington DC: National Academy of Sciences.

Shaw, C. R., & McKay, H. D. (1969). *Juvenile delinquency and urban areas* (rev. ed.). Chicago: University of Chicago Press.

Sontheimer, H., Goodstein, L., & Kovacevic, M. (1990). *Philadelphia intensive aftercare probation evaluation project.* Harrisburg PA: Pennsylvania Juvenile Court Judges' Commission, Center for Juvenile Justice Training and Research.

Steketee, M. W., Willis, D. A., & Schwartz, I. M. (1989). *Juvenile justice trends: 1977–1987.* Ann Arbor: University of Michigan, Center for the Study of Youth Policy.

Street, D., Vinter, R., & Perrow, C. (1966). *Organization for treatment.* New York: Free Press.

Sykes, G. M. (1965). *The society of captives: A study of a maximum security prison.* New York: Atheneum.

U.S. Department of Justice, Office of Juvenile Justice and Delinquency Prevention. (1988). *Juvenile detention and correctional facility census, 1986–1987: Public facilities* [Computer file]. Washington DC: U.S. Department of Commerce, Bureau of the Census (Producer). Ann Arbor MI: Inter-University Consortium for Political and Social Research (Distributor).

Van Vleet, R., Rutherford, A., & Schwartz, I. M. (1987). Reinvesting youth corrections resources in Utah. In *Reinvesting youth corrections resources: A tale of three states* (pp. 19–32). Ann Arbor: University of Michigan, Center for the Study of Youth Policy.

Weeks, H. A. (1958). *Youthful offenders at Highfields: An evaluation of the effects of the short-term treatment of delinquent boys.* Ann Arbor: University of Michigan Press.

Wilson, J. Q. (1980). "What works?" revisited: New findings on criminal rehabilitation. *Public Interest, 61,* 3–17.

Wright, W. E., & Dixon, M. C. (1977). Community prevention and treatment of juvenile delinquency: A review of evaluation studies. *Journal of Research in Crime and Delinquency, 14,* 35–67.

7

The Systemic Impact of
Family Preservation Services:
A Case Study

Ira M. Schwartz

Family preservation services are sweeping the country. Child welfare administrators in every state are implementing home-based service strategies designed to strengthen families, prevent out-of-home placements, and reunite families. It is also hoped that these services will help officials control the skyrocketing costs of child welfare systems.

While family preservation services enjoy broad professional and political support, there are relatively few rigorous studies of such programs. Most of the studies, particularly those claiming great success in preventing placements, have significant methodological deficiencies (Rossi, 1991), while findings from studies with credible designs are far from compelling and raise serious questions that need to be addressed by policymakers and practitioners (Littell, Schuerman, & Rzepnicki, 1991; Rossi, 1991; Schuerman, Rzepnicki, Littell, & Chak, 1993). For example, the concept "imminent risk of placement" is proving to be extremely difficult to implement in practice. There are also some who question whether placement prevention should be the only or even the major criterion for measuring program success (Rossi, 1991; Schuerman, Rzepnicik, Littell, & Budde, 1992; Wald, 1988).

Another problem with research on family preservation services is that it has largely focused on measuring the outcomes of discrete programs and models of intervention (Rossi, 1991). There have been no careful studies exploring the systemic impact of such services.

This chapter examines systemic and policy issues regarding family preservation services. It draws upon information and data about the Families First program and child welfare system in Michigan.

The Organization of Social Services in Michigan

The Michigan Department of Social Services (MDSS) is responsible for management and delivery of social and economic support services to individuals and families. Although MDSS is a state agency, services are primarily delivered on a local level through county offices located throughout the state. In addition to providing services directly, MDSS contracts for services with numerous private providers.

MDSS has a Family Services Administration for Child and Family Services, which is responsible for providing state-level policy and program leadership in areas related to children and families. These include child welfare services (i.e., adoptions, child protective services, and foster care) and delinquency programs for youth committed to state custody. The Family Services Administration is also responsible for management and implementation of the Families First program.

The Michigan Families First Program

The Michigan Families First program is reported to be one of the largest intensive home-based services programs in the country (Michigan House Appropriations Subcommittee on Social Services, 1992, p. 2). The program is designed to work "with those families enduring the most extreme pressure—those in danger of losing their children, or those families who have children placed in institutional care. Families First is directed at keeping families together and safe by providing intensive therapeutic interventions to resolve major parenting problems and to assist families in learning to adequately care for their children" (Families First of Michigan, undated, p. 2). Families First also provides families with a variety of "hard" services (e.g., rent, child care, clothing). One of the major goals of the program is "to significantly reduce Michigan's out of home placements for high risk children" (*Federally Funded Child Welfare*, 1990). The program, patterned after the Homebuilders model, was initially targeted to serve cases of child abuse and neglect. It is now being expanded to include delinquency cases. All Families First services are delivered by private providers under contract with MDSS.

The Families First program is growing at an extraordinary rate. It started in FY 1988 as a $434,348 pilot program serving 17 Michigan counties (Michigan House Appropriations Subcommittee on Social Services, 1992). In FY 1994, Families First's projected budget is $20,331,700 for statewide coverage (Engler, 1992).

158

The expansion of Families First is, in large part, motivated by MDSS reports about the program's success in preventing placements and due to broad support from the public and private child welfare community and from elected public officials. For example, MDSS submitted data to the legislature in May 1991 indicating that 2,378 families had been served by Families First since its inception. MDSS claimed that placement into the child welfare system had been prevented in over 79% of the cases served, based upon one-year follow-up (Families First of Michigan). Testimony by MDSS staff before the U.S. Congress indicated that there was a "decrease in the foster care growth rate" in counties served by Families First (*Federally Funded Child Welfare*, 1990). In a special report on strengthening families, Michigan governor John Engler referred to Families First as "perhaps the best example of this concept" (Engler, 1992, p. 19). He also made a point to emphasize that "the good news is that it works!" and that "it has become a national model" (p. 19).

According to MDSS, "the only families eligible for this [Families First] service are families who are at imminent risk of having at least one child removed for reasons of abuse, neglect, or delinquency, or who have already had one child removed and are working toward reunifying the family" (Michigan House Appropriations Subcommittee on Social Services, 1992). Although services are supposed to be for both prevention and reunification, MDSS officials acknowledge that relatively little is done in the area of reunification and they are now in the process of developing services to address the issue.

Periodic MDSS informational bulletins about Families First, congressional testimony and presentations at state and national conferences, and meetings by MDSS staff suggest that the program is effective in preventing placements. Although these reports would have to be considered anecdotal, they offer important insights into the services delivered and placement outcomes with respect to individual families.

MDSS contracted for an evaluation of Families First. The findings suggested that "The Families First Program is effective in preserving families by enabling children to remain with their families, thus averting out-of-home placement" (Evaluation of Michigan's Families First Program Summary Report, 1992, p. 3). Based upon the assumptions in the study, MDSS claimed that Families First saved the state of Michigan approximately $80 million in child welfare costs (Kresnak, 1993).

These impressive study findings and reported cost savings are generating a lot of enthusiasm about Families First within MDSS, among Families First's supporters in the state, and within the broader child welfare community. Unfortunately, the excitement will probably be short-lived. Careful scrutiny of the evaluation, particularly the entire report as compared to just the summary, indicates that it suffers from some of the same methodological weaknesses (e.g., absence of a randomized design, lack of an appropriate comparison group, problems regarding the definition of "imminent risk of placement," questions about how the cost-benefits and savings were derived) that are characteristic of most other evaluations of family preservation programs. The evaluation provides some interesting information about the program and the families served. However, those hoping that it would provide the "proof" that Families First works (that it is effective in preventing out-of-home child welfare placement) are likely to be disappointed.

Collectively, the MDSS reports about Families First and the evaluation of the program contribute little toward the making of effective child welfare policy. MDSS is in the process of launching another study of Families First, one with a rigorous design. This study, if successfully implemented, should provide important information about this particular treatment intervention.

Evaluations and assessments that focus on outcomes at the family and individual levels are critical. However, a comprehensive evaluation of Families First, or any other placement prevention strategy, must also explore the impact that placement prevention efforts may have on the entire child welfare system. In addition, such an assessment should identify and discuss the broad policy and administrative factors that may influence the system, particularly those factors that might be quite independent and beyond the influence of a specific treatment program or intervention strategy.

A comprehensive approach is needed because the history of services to children and families is replete with examples of specific treatment interventions that have had little or no systemic impact. There are also treatments that have contributed to significant and unintended adverse consequences. For example, federal and state juvenile justice policies during the 1970s and 1980s emphasized diversion and deinstitutionalization. Massive amounts of federal, state, and local dollars went into programs designed to divert status offenders and youth accused of petty delinquent acts from the juvenile courts. In addition, many states invested in creating alternatives to incarceration.

The strategies to divert youth from the juvenile courts failed miserably.

As hundreds of diversion programs sprang up all over the country, they filled up with youth and increased the overall costs of the juvenile justice systems, but they did not curb referrals to the juvenile court (Schwartz and Prieser, 1992). In fact, there is evidence that such programs widened the net of social control (Blomberg, 1983; Ezell, 1992; Krisberg & Austin, 1981). Many state and local strategies targeted at developing community-based alternatives to training schools failed as well (Blackmore, Brown, & Krisberg, 1988; Krisberg, Schwartz, Litsky, & Austin, 1986; Schwartz, 1989). In most instances, admissions to training schools temporarily declined, or youth were institutionalized either in private youth corrections facilities instead of public institutions or in another child care and control system (child welfare or mental health) under a different label.

The diversion and deinstitutionalization efforts failed in part because of problems in defining the target population. The identifying criteria tended to be vague and allowed for considerable discretion on the part of police, prosecutors, juvenile court judges, and youth correction officials. These difficulties, coupled with the fact that there are almost infinite numbers of children whose behavior could bring them to the attention of juvenile justice authorities, undermined the hopes of reformers and the spirit and intent of the landmark federal Juvenile Justice and Delinquency Prevention Act of 1974.

Child abuse and neglect present even greater definitional problems. While state statutes and agency policies provide some guidance, the terms allow for considerable professional discretion and subjective decision making. They are so vague that an almost endless number of children and families could be brought into the grasp of a benevolent child welfare system.

Child Welfare System Placement Trends in Michigan

In May 1993, MDSS submitted a report on children's services to the legislature indicating that foster care case openings increased steadily between 1988 and 1991 and declined for the first time in 1992. There were 6,490 case openings in 1988, 8,299 in 1991, and 7,632 in 1992 (Michigan Department of Social Services, 1993; Michigan House Appropriations Subcommittee on Social Services, 1992).

This decline in foster care case openings is encouraging but certainly cannot be considered a trend. Moreover, there is no evidence directly linking the decline to the Families First program.

Table 7.1 Michigan Numbers and Rates of Children in Out-of-Home Placement for the First Time, Fiscal Years 1987–1991

	1987 rate per		1988 rate per		1989 rate per		1990 rate per		1991 rate per	
	n	1,000	n	1,000	n	1,000	n	1,000	n	1,000
Families First counties outside Wayne County	2,065	1.7	2,273	1.9	2,368	2.0	2,807	2.4	2,861	2.4
Wayne County	2,342	3.8	2,780	4.6	2,320	3.9	2,195	3.7	2,496	4.3
Total all Families First counties	4,407	2.5	5,053	2.8	4,688	2.6	5,002	2.8	5,357	3.1
Total non–Families First counties	1,193	1.6	1,285	1.7	1,439	1.9	1,770	2.4	1,667	2.2

Notes:
1. Families First counties are the 17 counties in which the program was initially implemented and has been in operation the longest.
2. Rates were calculated by CSYP staff based on Michigan Department of Management and Budget projections for youth aged 0–17 in each county.
3. Michigan's fiscal year runs from October 1 through September 30.
4. Out-of-home placement includes children in MDSS and private foster families, MDSS group homes, shelters, residential and private child care institutions, and relatives' homes. It does not include mental health or other placements, youth in adoptive homes, or youth who are AWOL.
Source: Michigan Department of Social Services CSMIS data.

The report submitted to the legislature by MDSS also indicated a large decline in the proportion of substantiated abuse and neglect reports beginning in the first quarter of 1993. MDSS speculated, "The reduction in [the] substantiation rate is likely the result of policy changes that provide clearer, more uniform definitions of child abuse and neglect, require workers to have credible evidence before substantiating a case and require notification of the perpetrator when his or her name is added to the central registry" (Michigan Department of Social Services, p. 20). The drop in substantiated abuse and neglect reports may contribute to a further decline in foster care case openings or may help maintain the decline experienced in 1992. This could make it even more difficult, if not impossible, to explore changes and fluctuations in the numbers and rates of placements and their relationship with the Families First program.

The Center for the Study of Youth Policy, which has been monitoring child welfare placement trends in Michigan for the past several years, has been particularly interested in placement trends for children placed out of their homes for the first time. These data (Table 7.1) are generally consistent with the case-opening data that MDSS submitted to the legislature. With the exception of FY 1989, the number and rates of children placed out of their homes for the first time in the counties in which Families First was initially implemented and had been in operation the longest increased steadily between FY 1987 and FY 1991. First-time placements also steadily increased in all other counties in Michigan as Families First was being implemented statewide. The only time such placements declined in the other counties was in FY 1991.

Families First does not concentrate on preventing the placement of children at risk of being removed from their homes for the first time. However, it is not unreasonable to expect to see declines in the numbers and rates of placement of these children. Theoretically, their cases should be somewhat less problematic than those with prior out-of-home placement histories.

Although not shown in the table, there are extraordinary variations in the rates of out-of-home placements between counties and within counties over time. This suggests that the policies and practices in individual counties need to be examined in order to understand what factors may be affecting the system.

Discussion and Policy Implications

As indicated earlier, one of the major goals of the Michigan Families First program is "To significantly reduce Michigan's out-of-home placements for high risk children" (Kelly, 1990, p. 3). The data presented in this chapter suggest that this goal has yet to be realized. In addition, there are no hard data directly linking the one-time statewide decline in foster care case openings in 1992 to the Families First program. Nor have the fluctuations in the numbers and rates of first-time placements in Michigan's counties been linked to the Families First program. One could argue that placement rates would be much higher were it not for Families First. This may be true, but, unfortunately, there is no hard evidence to support this assertion.

163

Child welfare systems are large and complex organizations. In order to fully comprehend and assess the impact of a program like Families First, one must take into account the broader political, social, policy, and administrative variables that may be influencing these systems. For example, examining the Michigan system in a broader context identifies many factors that might impact rates of placements, some of which are clearly beyond the influence of the Families First program.

There has been a sharp increase in the number of infants placed into Michigan's child welfare system, particularly in Wayne County. The growth in infant placements is being attributed to such factors as the crack epidemic, AIDS, large numbers of preteen and teenage girls bearing children, and the withdrawal of federal and state funding for abortions. There are also mixed reports about the extent to which Families First services are targeted and equipped to prevent the placement of these children.

Families First is a relatively small program with a projected 1994 budget of $20,331,700. It is expected that this program will reform or will at least have a major impact on Michigan's $220 million highly bureaucratic and entrenched child welfare system. The expectations appear to be quite unrealistic, given the comparatively modest amount of resources allocated to the program. There are also questions about the proportion of cases referred to Families First that were really at "imminent risk of placement." While this is a common problem experienced in other family preservation programs, it dilutes the impact of such an intervention strategy for curbing child welfare placements (Rossi, 1991; Schuerman et al., 1992).

MDSS is increasingly relying on placements with relatives. This, in part, reflects the department's desire to maintain a child's contacts with extended family members. Relatives can be paid as foster parents only if they meet state licensing and other requirements. While the policy of trying to maintain a child's contacts with extended family members may have merit, it is unclear whether such placements are always counted in MDSS statistics. If some relative placements are not included, it distorts the numbers of children placed out of their homes. This issue takes on added importance because of research suggesting that relative placements are being used to meet the growing demand for foster care (Wulczyn & Goerge, 1992). It also raises the question about whether Families First services are being, or should be, targeted to prevent relative placements.

Placing growing numbers of children with relatives also raises the concern that this practice may, in part, be driven by economic considerations. This could be an important issue in an economically depressed state like Michigan, where relatives are not entitled to foster care reimbursement unless they are licensed by the state. They may receive AFDC, but AFDC rates are lower than foster care rates.

In 1988, the Michigan legislature enacted a law requiring that juvenile courts transfer to MDSS those cases in which dependent and neglected children are placed in foster homes (Child Protection Law, 1988). The legislation, which went into effect in 1989, resulted in a one-time increase in the number of MDSS placements (Michigan House Appropriations Subcommittee on Social Services, 1992). The legislation had a differential impact in Michigan's counties. For example, Wayne County juvenile court and social services officials report that a small number of cases (less than 30) were transferred from the court to MDSS. In contrast, officials in other counties report that more cases were transferred from the juvenile courts to social services. Assessing the precise impact of the legislation would require the number of transferred cases in each jurisdiction. The relatively small number of transfers in Wayne County suggests that other factors need to be explored in order to determine the variables driving placements in that jurisdiction.

The recent large drop in substantiated abuse and neglect reports could also have a major impact on placements. Although the reasons for the drop are unclear, MDSS officials believe that the decline can be attributed to changes in policies.

Recently, MDSS officials announced their intentions to develop performance agreements with local county social services offices. The agreements will include fiscal incentives for counties to reduce foster family and residential treatment placements. While it is too early to tell what impact these policy thrusts will have, these initiatives will further cloud MDSS's ability to determine the precise impact of Families First. Conceivably, the implementation of performance agreements and fiscal incentives may prove to be far more effective in curbing placements than any type or array of treatment interventions.

Social researchers, public policy experts, and human service professionals are becoming increasingly sensitive to the interrelationships between the child welfare, juvenile justice, and mental health systems (Lerman, 1980; Schwartz, 1989; Schwartz, Jackson-Beeck, & Anderson, 1984). They are becoming aware that attempts to reduce placements into any one of these systems often result in increased numbers of placements in one or both of the other systems. Although this issue has not been examined to any great extent in Michigan, there is some evidence suggesting that delinquency placements have been increasing while MDSS has been trying to curb child welfare placements (Schwartz & Ortega, in press).

In 1982, prompted by severe budget cuts, MDSS management staff were forced to lay off employees. Because the layoffs resulted in foster care workers having to supervise excessive caseloads of children in placement, more than 800 foster care cases were reassigned to protective service workers. This decision triggered a union grievance which was won by the employees in 1984 (American Arbitration Association, 1984). The result was that the 800 plus cases had to be reassigned from protective service workers back to foster care workers. It appears that when these cases were reassigned back to the foster care workers, an unknown number may have been recorded as new admissions to foster care, which would artificially inflate the number of children recorded as first-time out-of-home placements in FY 1985.

While these events took place long before Families First was implemented, they illustrate the impact that internal administrative decisions, union activities, and fiscally driven decisions can have on a child welfare system. These are the kinds of events and activities of which researchers, policymakers, and child welfare professionals need to be cognizant in order to develop a complete picture of what may be going on in a system. One-time and periodic spikes and large dips in placements need to be closely scrutinized.

Many reports have documented the decline in the economic, physical, and social well-being of growing numbers of Michigan's children and families (Abbey & Schwartz, 1992; Abbey, Schwartz, & Vestevich, 1991; Center for the Study of Social Policy, 1992). Such factors as increasing numbers of families and children in poverty, high rates of unemployment, high rates of adult imprisonment, domestic violence, the widespread availability and use of illicit drugs, and shortages in affordable housing are also contributing to the need for substitute care for children in Michigan. Unfortunately, there is little reason to believe that these conditions are likely to improve in the near future. There is even less reason to believe that single programs such as Families First can surmount these social problems in order to achieve the desired goals.

Conclusion

Family preservation services are emerging as a primary strategy for preventing the out-of-home placement of children. While there is still much that needs to be known about these services, the research in the field is almost entirely focused on evaluating the effectiveness of particular models or methods of family preservation treatment interventions. Hardly any attention is being paid to the policy, administrative, and social factors that impact child welfare services, factors that can facilitate or impede the goals of interventions or make it impossible to assess their true impact.

The examination of policy, administrative, and social variables is complex and focuses on different kinds of questions than does intervention research. Yet the questions are interrelated with the intervention research questions. They are also questions that researchers and child welfare professionals cannot afford to overlook. To do so increases the probability that research on family preservation services outcomes will be incomplete and perhaps misleading.

For example, the best available data in Michigan suggest Families First is probably not having an appreciable impact on reducing the rates of out-of-home placement. The changes that may be occurring cannot be directly linked to Families First and appear to be largely influenced by other factors. This suggests that policymakers and child welfare professionals should be cautious about conveying such a rosy picture about the program's impact and its future potential.

Recently, MDSS officials have claimed that Families First, or the intensive home-based services, alone are probably not sufficient to substantially curb the rate of out-of-home placements. They feel Families First is an important component of what should be a broader overall strategy. This is a more realistic and appropriate observation in light of the state of our current knowledge.

In order to avoid these problems, a number of broader issues and questions should be explored when examining the impact of an intervention strategy:

1. Are there fiscal incentives and disincentives that may be affecting placements?
2. Are there agency policy thrusts that may influence rates of placements (e.g., more emphasis on relative placements, modifications in adoptions

practices, internal pressures to curb placements, raising the standards for placements, changes in the definitions of abuse and neglect)?

3. Are there legislative changes that may be affecting the system?

4. What role might other institutions such as the juvenile court be playing with respect to placements?

5. Are there changes in the health and social service delivery system that may affect placements (e.g., prenatal and postnatal care, maternal and infant support services, substance abuse treatment programs)?

6. Are there conditions or factors within the community that may affect out-of-home placements?

Intensive home-based services may help to provide services that many families need but that may otherwise be unavailable. They may even help generate better information leading to more informed decision making about whether to remove a child from his or her home. However, unless more information is known, policymakers and child welfare professionals would be ill-advised to expect these types of programs to have a major impact on curbing placements into the child welfare systems and on controlling child welfare system costs.

References

Abbey, J. M., & Schwartz, I. M. (1992). *Raising Michigan's children.* Ann Arbor: University of Michigan, Center for the Study of Youth Policy.

Abbey, J. M., Schwartz, I. M., & Vestevich, A. (1991). *Michigan's children went missing.* Ann Arbor: University of Michigan, Center for the Study of Youth Policy.

American Arbitration Association, Case Number A. A. No. 54 39 1521 83, In the matter of arbitration between Michigan State Employees Association and Department of Social Services (1984). Arbitrator: Jerome Gross.

Berlin, G. (1991, March 19). Testimony before the Subcommittee on Human Resources, State of the Nation's Child Welfare System.

Blackmore, J., Brown, M., & Krisberg, B. (1988). *Juvenile justice reform: The bellwether states.* Ann Arbor: University of Michigan, Center for the Study of Youth Policy.

Blomberg, T. G. (1983). Diversion and accelerated social control. *Journal of Criminal Law and Criminology, 68,* 274–282.

Center for the Study of Social Policy. (1992). *1992 kids count data book: State profiles of child well-being.* Washington DC: Author.

Center for the Study of Youth Policy. (1993). *Distribution of relative placements*. Ann Arbor: University of Michigan, Author.

Child Protection Law (1988). Public and local acts of the legislature of the State of Michigan, P.A. 223, 224, 225 (1989).

Engler, J. (1992, June 2) *To strengthen Michigan families: A special message to the people of Michigan*. Lansing: Michigan Department of Management and Budget.

Evaluation of Michigan's Families First program summary report. (March 1992). Lansing MI: University Associates.

Ezell, M. (1992). Juvenile diversion: The ongoing search for alternatives. In I. M. Schwartz (Ed.), *Juvenile justice and public policy: Toward a national agenda*. Lexington MA: Lexington Books.

Families First of Michigan (undated). *A nationally recognized program of the Michigan Department of Social Services*. Lansing MI: Office of Children and Youth Services.

Families First staff survey: Summary of results. (1991). Lansing MI: Michigan Department of Social Services, Family Preservation Unit.

Federally funded child welfare, foster care, and adoption assistance programs: Hearings before the Subcommittee on Human Resources of the Committee on Ways and Means, House of Representatives, 101st Cong., 2d Sess. 46 (1990) (testimony of Susan A. Kelly).

Kerbs, J. J., Ortega, R. M., & Schwartz, I. M. (1993). *Family preservation services: Research methodology and the future*. Unpublished manuscript.

Knitzer, J., & Yelton, S. (1990, Spring). Collaborations between child welfare and mental health. *Public Welfare*, pp. 24–46.

Kresnak, J. (1993, March 11). Foster care alternative saves money. *Detroit Free Press*, pp. 1B-3B.

Krisberg, B., & Austin, J. (1981). Wider, stronger and different nets: The dialectics of criminal justice reform. *Journal of Research on Crime and Delinquency, 18*, 165–196.

Krisberg, B., Schwartz, I. M., Litsky, P., & Austin, J. (1986). The watershed of juvenile justice reform. *Crime and Delinquency, 32*, 5–38.

Lerman, P. (1980). Trends and issues in the deinstitutionalization of youths in trouble. *Crime and Delinquency, 26*, 281–298.

Littell, J. H., Schuerman, J. R., & Rzepnicki, T. L. (1991). *Preliminary results from the Illinois Family First experiment*. Chicago: University of Chicago, Chapin Hall Center for Children.

Michigan Department of Social Services. (1992, October). *Management Information Report for Child Welfare*. Lansing: Author.

Michigan Department of Social Services (MDSS). (1993, April). *To strengthen Michigan families preliminary status report.* Lansing. MDSS Family Preservation Unit.

Michigan House Appropriations Subcommittee on Social Services (1992). *Children's Services* (February 25, 1992). Lansing: Author.

Ortega, R. M., & Guo, S. (1993, January 21). Memorandum to Ira M. Schwartz. (These data were given to the Michigan Department of Social Services and the Skillman Foundation.)

Pecora, P. J., Phrase, M. W., & Haapala, D. A. (1991). Client outcomes and issues for program design. In K. Wells & D. E. Biegel (Eds.), *Family preservation services: Research and evaluation* (pp. 3–32). Newbury Park CA: Sage Publications.

Rossi, P. H. (1991, August). *Evaluating family preservation programs: A report to the Edna McConnell Clark Foundation.* Amherst: University of Massachusetts.

Schneider, G. (1993, January 12). Personal correspondence to David Berns, Director, Office of Children's Services, Michigan Department of Social Services.

Schuerman, J. R., Rzepnicki, T. L., Littell, J. H., & Budde, S. (1992). Implementation issues. *Children and Youth Services Review, 14,* 193–206.

Schuerman, J. R., Rzepnicki, T. L., Littell, J. H., Chak, A. (1993, June). *Evaluation of the Illinois Family First placement prevention program: Final report.* Chicago: University of Chicago, Chapin Hall Center for Children.

Schwartz, I. M. (1989). *(In)Justice for juveniles: Rethinking the best interest of the child.* Lexington MA: Lexington Books.

Schwartz, I. M., Jackson-Beeck, M., & Anderson, R. (1984). The "hidden" system of control. *Crime and Delinquency, 30,* 371–385.

Schwartz, I. M., & Ortega, R. M. (In press). Michigan's child welfare system: A dynamic perspective. In G. Melton (Ed.), *Toward a child-centered, neighborhood-based child protection system.*

Schwartz, I. M., Ortega, R. M., Guo, S., & Fishman, G. (1994). Infants in nonpermanent placement. *Social Service Review, 68,* 405–416.

Schwartz, I. M., & Preiser, L. P. (1992). Diversion and juvenile justice: Can we ever get it right? In H. Messmer & H. U. Otto (Eds.), *Restorative justice on trial* (Chapter 16, pp. 279–290). The Netherlands: Kluwer Academic Publishers.

Spaid, W. M., & Phrase, M. (1991). The correlates of success/failure in brief and intensive family treatment: Implications for family preservation services. *Children and Youth Services Review, 13,* p. 77–99.

Wald, M. S. (1988, Summer). Family preservation: Are we moving too fast? *Public Welfare,* pp. 33–38.

Wells, K., & Biegel, D. E. (1991). *Family preservation services: Research and evaluation*. Newbury Park CA: Sage.

Wulczyn, F. H., & Goerge, R. M. (1990a). *Foster care placement with relatives*. Unpublished manuscript. New York: Department of Social Services.

Wulczyn, F. H., & Goerge, R. M. (1992). Foster care in New York and Illinois: The challenge of rapid change. *Social Service Review, 66,* 278–294.

Wulczyn, F. H., & Goerge, R. M. (1990b). *Public policy and the dynamics of foster care: A multi-state study of placement histories (New York, Illinois, and Michigan)* (Research Report). Washington DC: U.S. Department of Health and Human Services, Office of Assistant Secretary for Planning and Evaluation.

8

Issues in Government Purchase of
Family-Based Services

Sandra O'Donnell and Ronald D. Davidson

Family-based services, like other social services, can be either provided directly by government agencies or purchased from the private sector. In longer-standing fields of service, we have witnessed a clear trend in the past two decades toward increased use of purchase of service (Hansmann, 1980; Kettner & Martin, 1987; Kramer, 1982; Kramer, 1985; R. S. Smith, 1989). This trend is the product of funding programs such as Title XX and other policies that encourage purchase of service and that are based on a philosophy of "privatization." Because most family-based services have originated since the enactment of Title XX, we do not know if there is a trend in the field toward public purchase and away from public provision of service. Nor do we know of any evidence to support ideological statements that family-based services delivered in one sector are superior to those delivered in another, or if services delivered by private for-profit agencies are more or less effective than those delivered by nonprofit agencies.

We *do* know that many family-based services *are* provided by the private nonprofit sector through purchase of services with government agencies (National Resource Center on Family Based Services, 1987; K. Nelson, Landsman, & Deutelbaum, 1990; Pecora, Kinney, Mitchell, & Tolley, 1980; Stehno, 1987), particularly in state-administered systems (Tyler, 1990). Accordingly, how we purchase family-based services and how well these methods promote effective, efficient services to families are important issues in government implementation of family-based service systems. Little attention has been given to them, in part because the family-based field has focused on more basic issues, such as securing political support and designing programs, and in part because the primitiveness of contract technology in human services has given us little knowledge to impart to the family-based field (Kramer, 1985). This chapter is an admittedly modest effort to begin to fill this void.

Why Purchase Services?

The issue of whether to purchase or directly provide human services is a complex topic under review at all levels of government. Since the late 1960s, there has been growing use of government contracts with private agencies for the provision of child welfare services (R. S. Smith, 1989). The trend toward increased purchasing of services in all fields is apparent throughout the nation, fueled in part by the Reagan administration's emphasis on privatization (Moe, 1987; Pecora et al., 1990; R. S. Smith, 1989). However, organized labor and its supporters continue to aggressively oppose privatization, which they consider to be an erosion of public service employment. The debates often deteriorate into a diatribe of clichés.

Proponents of purchasing will argue that the private sector is more efficient (i.e., less wasteful than government). Proponents of public provision of services counter with the charge that the private sector's focus on profit inevitably leads to a reduced quality of care. The discussion is further complicated when the private sector includes both for-profit and not-for-profit service providers.

Whether the focus is mail delivery, satellite launching, or family-based services, the issues are identical. Regrettably, the decision to purchase or provide is usually not made on the basis of a dispassionate review of the facts. Political bias, policy intransigence, and superficial cost analysis ultimately tend to sway decision making. Regardless of whether the reader can make the decision to provide or purchase family-based services, we believe that it is important to understand the basis for reaching this decision rationally (Kramer, 1982; Pecora et al., 1980).

ADVANTAGES OF PURCHASE OF SERVICE

Cost

Cost savings is the most frequently cited reason for purchasing services. Although the cost analysis is often shallow, there is evidence to support this contention (Pecora et al., 1980). Private agencies are generally able to avoid the restrictive work rules, higher salary costs, and political influence prevalent in most public organizations. Many are able to focus on a specific task and avoid the general malaise and deleterious bureaucratic requirements so common in government. Not-for-profit agencies are often willing to accept government reimbursement rates significantly below their actual costs. Although such willingness artificially deflates the "true" cost of family-based services, such efficiency claims—and the "public/private partnership" that makes them possible—have sometimes been key in gaining policy support for family-based services.

Flexibility

Because the private sector is often able to avoid government's cumbersome purchasing rules, intractable budget appropriations, and arcane work rules, private agencies are able to implement new programs more quickly (Pecora et al., 1980). This advantage is of great importance when political leaders are required to demonstrate fast action and is also important in responding rapidly to fluctuations in client demand for services, which, in turn, keeps unit costs down.

Private agencies have a particular advantage because they are generally not bound by the personnel rules and union agreements usually found in the public sector. Private agencies have more freedom in personnel matters. For home-based services, this advantage is key to the success of the program, permitting the selection of uniquely skilled staff and implementation of flexible work schedules (Pecora et al., 1980).

Political Support

By adding the private sector as a partner in the provision of government-supported services, the political support for those services is automatically enhanced. The private sector, both proprietary and not-for-profit, often has sophisticated and effective lobbying efforts at all levels of government (Pecora et al., 1980). This support can be used to foster expansion of new programs while protecting existing programs in periods of retrenchment. For example, in Illinois there was widespread interest in family-based services among public officials and child welfare advocates. However, the passage of landmark legislation, the Family Preservation Act of 1987, was largely the product of political mobilization by private agencies.

Community Acceptance and Support

When private agencies have a visible existence within a community, they greatly increase the community's acceptance and support of the new programs. While NIMBY ("not in my backyard") is common everywhere, it is more easily overcome by local residents than by public employees. Community support for family-based services is vital because this field of service is constantly at risk of losing policy support due to public outcry when children served in their parents' homes are hurt.

Creativity and Diversity

The private sector brings a creativity and rich diversity to service delivery. This is apparent in both the competition among the providers for government contracts and in the variety of service options available. Such variety allows experimentation with many approaches to determine the most effective models, while the competition will ultimately increase the quality and efficiency of family-based services. The development of a variety of service options enhances the probability that the services will be responsive to local needs and minority clients. It is virtually impossible for governments to display the same creativity and variety of service models for programs under their direct supervision.

Focused Services

The private sector can isolate a particular program and protect it from intrusion by other tasks. In contrast, public agencies are often called upon to expand their services or broaden their focus without a commensurate increase in resources.

DISADVANTAGES OF PURCHASE OF SERVICE

Loss of Control

The very act of contracting with the private sector to provide services leads to the inevitable loss of some control over procedures for client intake and discharge, over kinds of services provided, and over the use of funds (R. S. Smith, 1989). On the other hand, in an age of rigid work rules and widespread unionization among public employees, it is unclear that public officials have any more control over their own employees than they do over contractors.

The loss of control over program implementation can also result from the ability of private sector lobbyists to change or reprioritize the purpose of the service or its components while the government agency watches impotently.

Reduced Accountability

Private agencies vary greatly in their commitment to accountability (R. S. Smith, 1989). Although many take the responsibility seriously, others try to minimize it or even refuse to acknowledge that they are accountable for use of government funds.

Inappropriate Political Intervention

The advantages of political and community support gained through purchase of service also have an inherent disadvantage. Political support for a program can be viewed as unwarranted (and unwanted) intervention when public officials attempt to reduce or eliminate programs. The political influence of certain agencies, rather than the merits of their programs, may force public officials to contract with them. The political necessity of responding to diverse local demands may impede the design of a coherent service delivery system.

Funding Mechanisms

Once the decision to purchase rather than provide services is made, a beginning step in designing the system is the selection of the funding mechanism. As described below, what the funding mechanism pays for and how it is implemented will greatly influence the shape of the service delivery system. The funding mechanism selected also influences the service processes and outcomes that will be rewarded financially, producing both intended and unintended consequences. Therefore, the choice of the funding mechanism should be based on a careful examination of service system goals and priorities.

GRANTS

Grants are typically paid out in total or in partial payments with few strings attached. The assumptions with this funding mechanism are that the expertise is held by the provider and not the grant maker, that the grant maker is assured of the professional integrity of the provider, and that the best service will be generated with minimal involvement of the grant maker. This kind of funding mechanism is typically used to start new, experimental kinds of programs. It is more often used by private philanthropies than by state and local governments, which seem to be backing away from grants-in-aid systems in the wake of criticisms that such systems lack accountability (Kettner & Martin, 1987; Wedel & Colston, 1988). When governments do elect to use a grants system, they typically impose monitoring requirements concerning staff levels, service responses, quantity and quality of client service, and the like. Homebuilders of Tacoma, Washington, is funded through such a grants system (Stehno, 1987).

PER DIEM PAYMENTS

Family Strength, a family-based service in New Hampshire, bills the state $32 per day per family in service. Reimbursement is the same whether families receive more or less support on a given day or week, and whether some families require more service support than others. Philadelphia County's Services to Children in their Own Homes (scoH) purchases at three different per diem rates based on differing requirements of kinds and amounts of service support needed (Stehno, 1987). The logic of per diem reimbursement for family-based services is the importance of being available on a 24-hour, 7-day basis to families in need, as in residential care. Although per diem payments provide more accountability than a straight grant, they raise the unintended consequence of overutilization. Governments must thus establish some utilization review system to assure that the services delivered and billed were necessary.

HOURLY PAYMENTS

The states of Iowa and Illinois purchase many family-based services on an hourly basis. The state defines which services are "billable" and pays for them upon proof that they have in fact been delivered. The logic of hourly contracts is that family-based services are in some ways similar to psychotherapy, other outpatient counseling services, and homemaking services— all services that historically have been purchased through hourly billing. Hourly payments have a direct relationship to the quantity of services. This approach maximizes output and process (see the discussion of outputs and processes later in this chapter) efficiency because it only rewards the delivery of billable units of service. On the other hand, quantities of service do not necessarily produce effective outcomes. Further, the focus on billable units of service inhibits flexibility of service delivery. Finally, hourly payments for services exacerbate the potential problem of overutilization discussed above.

PERFORMANCE-BASED CONTRACTS

Increasingly, government purchasers of service are turning to funding mechanisms that tie payments to mutually agreed-upon results. Performance-based contracts go beyond traditional monitoring systems in that payment can actually be withheld for failure to meet performance goals, and in some cases, incentive payments are made for exceeding performance goals. Although there is increasing interest in tying payments to *client outcomes*, more often *program performance* measures (staff levels, intake response times, amount of service) are used instead (Wedel & Colston, 1988). There are major problems in implementing outcome-based performance contracts in the family-based service field. Performance contracting raises the possibility of incentives for goal displacement (keeping children in unsafe homes). It also risks holding providers responsible for environmental conditions over which they have no control, and which place children at risk of placement, such as burnouts and losses of extended family support. Further, the lack of agreement concerning clinical measures of improved family functioning makes definition of family functioning outcomes difficult, if not impossible. Nevertheless, some experts are urging contractors to tie payment to the achievement of aggregate performance standards. They urge focusing on placement prevention, because it is readily measurable, and setting realistic standards in order to minimize goal displacement, such as a 75% rather than a 90–95% goal (Center for the Study of Social Policy, 1989).

CAPITATION SYSTEMS

Capitation mechanisms seek to contain the costs of service delivery by capping the amount that can be spent on specific services or on the service system itself. Several states are experimenting with capitation systems to fund family-based services. There are striking similarities between the goals of family-based services and other service systems that are using such mechanisms. One form of capitation is the *social health maintenance organization* (SHMO), which, similar to a health maintenance organization, focuses on early identification and the provision of preventive services in order to avoid unnecessary acute care services later. SHMO experiments include ones that seek to maintain infirm older people in their homes (and thus avoid nursing home costs) and that target people at risk of mental illness for community-based services in an attempt to avert psychiatric hospitalization (Stehno,

178

1987). An agency might receive a fixed sum of money to provide appropriate home-based services to all of the community's families at risk of child abuse and neglect, with the service goal being to minimize the unnecessary use of out-of-home placements. At the implementation level, the funding for experimental SHMO programs appears similar to a grant.

Another form of capitation more frequently being discussed with respect to family-based services is *case weighting,* which is similar in concept to Diagnostic Related Groupings (DRGs) that specify what amounts will be paid for specific treatments for specific diagnoses (Hutchinson & Nelson, 1985; Smits, 1984). The logic, of course, is that families with more difficult problems will require more expensive services to avert foster care placement. The major concern about adapting DRGs to family-based services is that the basic assumptions that make DRGs possible—a specific initial diagnosis that calls for a specific treatment, with both diagnosis and treatment being empirically validated—simply do not hold true for family-based services. Nevertheless, some modifications of the system seem both possible and promising.

What Is to Be Purchased?

Purchasers of family-based services face important choices about what services they will fund. These decisions will help them select the most appropriate funding mechanism to achieve their service goals and will shape the service delivery system itself. Purchasers should consider the following questions:

1. *Who should be eligible to receive the purchased services?* Some systems target families that are at imminent risk of foster care placement. Others cast a wider net in hopes of providing early intervention services and preventing child abuse or neglect from occurring or worsening. Other systems target families with children already in placement.
2. *Who should be eligible to provide purchased services?* Some purchasers prohibit or discourage for-profit agencies. Others discourage for-profit providers with little experience in providing child abuse treatment services, while some *encourage* such providers, seeking new ideas and a diversity of locally defined service models. Other choices include "traditional" versus "nontraditional" (such as minority) child welfare service providers, in-state or out-of-state agencies, and neighborhood versus citywide or countryside catchment areas. There is little empirical evidence to guide

purchasers in making provider eligibility decisions (Frankel, 1988). The issue of encouraging or discouraging community-based agencies is further complicated by the lack of definitional consensus regarding the term *community-based*. Some jurisdictions focus on criteria such as referral catchment area, knowledge of community resources, and cultural sensitivity of staff. Others focus more on the organization itself, such as the number of board and staff members who live in the community. Lacking an empirical basis for such criteria selection, purchasers must turn instead to service system goals, target population needs, the importance of local political support, and other relevant considerations to make provider eligibility decisions.

3. *What kinds of programs are to be purchased?* A basic decision is whether to purchase a *system of services* (such as homemaker, day care, drop-in, or parent education services) or a *specific kind of program* (such as short-term or in-home programs). Jurisdictions in which few support services of any kind exist may need to consider the option of purchasing a variety of services. One possible pitfall of this approach is that inappropriate "net widening" may occur—the purchased services might serve many families not targeted for service support. On the other hand, targeting on brief, crisis services, as is currently the trend, risks slighting the support for services that might have averted the crises from occurring or recurring.

A similar but different decision is whether to select *one program model or many*. Advocates of the "one model" approach argue that (1) there are programs that have demonstrated effectiveness with diverse populations, so there is no need to "reinvent the wheel," and (2) these programs are capable of simple explanation and defense in the policy advocacy arena (Farrow & Duva, 1987). Conversely, proponents of the "multiple model" approach argue that (1) the evidence of these programs' effectiveness is thin (Frankel, 1988), (2) more program experimentation is needed to determine what works best, and with whom, and (3) a variety of programs are needed to meet a variety of service needs. The stimulation of locally defined program models must be considered when community ownership and minority perspectives are major system goals.

4. *What kinds of services are to be supported?* Some definitional attention needs to be given to the kinds of services to be supported and the amounts of services to be purchased. Among the dimensions to consider are direct

and collateral services (done on behalf of the client, such as referral and monitoring), "hard" (emergency cash and goods) and "soft" (counseling and teaching) services, and the amounts and duration of services. For example, some purchasers place limits on the number of billable units of collateral services, some cap the amounts of cash that can be given directly to families, and some focus on the length of the purchased intervention. Issues in determining appropriate definitions are tied, of course, to the purpose of the funding program, the availability of community-based services to families supported by other funds, and the projected service needs of the target population. An especially important consideration related to the boundary decisions is that of defining service *success*. Is success the resolution of the immediate crisis? Then, clearly, very short-term boundaries can be drawn. If *success* also encompasses demonstrating significant improvements in family functioning or welfare, then very short-term boundaries may be inappropriate.

5. *What program development activities will be supported?* In addition to client services, governments may choose to support some of the following activities that must be undertaken to make the services available and get them delivered:

☐ Capacity building: efforts to help community agencies gain the administrative, governance, and service expertise to provide family-based services well. Capacity building is especially important in jurisdictions where there is a dearth of providers. It may be supported by grants or by technical assistance.

☐ Program start-up: especially staff recruitment, training, and coverage in the beginning stage of the program when referrals are few. Supporting start-up costs is especially important when family-based services are a distinctly new and different agency service and already trained staff cannot simply move into the program on moment's notice.

☐ Case management: especially client outreach, client service planning, liaison with community resources, and follow-up monitoring. The case management function is often oversimplified in the human services; in fact, it is multifarious, extremely time-consuming, and a shared responsibility between the private sector and the public sector.

☐ Program evaluation: a vital need in this field, but a procedure that few purchase systems have prioritized. Choices include supporting primarily external evaluation (although the private agency will still typically bear the burden of much data collection), internal evaluation (including quality assurance systems), or a combination of both.

6. *To what performance measures will payments be tied?* Service contractors can tie payments to any or all of the following (Kettner and Martin, 1987):

□ Inputs: the resources deployed to deliver the program, such as staff, consultants, and facilities. Some funding attention to inputs is especially important if staff credentials, 24-hour staff coverage, and caseload size are important to effective service delivery.

□ Processes: the ways in which people enter the program, receive services, and leave the program. Process issues of particular importance to the purchase of family-based services are rapid intake, referral criteria (some purchasers may choose to require acceptance on a "no decline" basis), length of intervention (does the purchaser want to limit this?), and discharge planning.

□ Outputs: the units of services provided, kinds of services, number of clients served, and other measures of what the program "did." Frequently, grants and contracts focus on outputs as a basis for accountability, in part because outputs are easier to measure than outcomes, and in part because quantity is easier to measure than quality.

□ Outcomes: the results to clients of delivering the program. The logic of focusing primarily on outcomes is somewhat analogous to contracting for goods such as pencils. The purchaser wants a certain number of good-quality pencils, and if they are delivered on time, issues such as how the pencils were made and by whom are of little interest. Because we cannot define outcomes very well yet in human services, we would be leaping too quickly if we chose to tie payments exclusively to the achievement of client outcomes. (Consider, for example, experiences with the Jobs Training Partnership Act, with endemic client "creaming" and examples of goal displacement that occurred, such as graduating word processors who were unable to read.) But efforts to define acceptable levels of success in achieving placement prevention as well as improved family functioning might be encouraged in the purchasing process.

The art of designing an effective system of purchased services is often one of trying to anticipate otherwise unanticipated consequences. Surely this is true of the inputs-processes-outputs-outcomes balance of payment incentives. Too heavy an emphasis on inputs could generate incentives to hire therapists who had advanced degrees but who were untalented. Too heavy an emphasis on outputs could generate incentives to provide a lot of billable services with little discernible effect on the clients' welfare. Too heavy an emphasis on outcomes could generate incentives for goal displacement, such as keeping children in their homes when such homes are not safe.

How to Purchase

Having considered why we would want to purchase and what we would want to purchase, we next face the question of *how* to implement the purchase decision. Thankfully, this issue has been given attention in the human service field (Kettner & Martin 1987; Kramer & Grossman, 1987). Although this is a complex issue deserving of a full text in its own right, the major components are identified below.

SELECTION OF A PROVIDER

The process of selecting a provider, also known as the procurement process, is the first step in implementing the purchasing process. The procurement process for family-based services is particularly difficult because of our relative inexperience and general inability to identify the most effective intervention methods. The two general types of procurement processes are competitive bidding and sole source contracting.

Competitive Bidding

Competitive bidding applies the long accepted business practice of encouraging competing organizations to submit proposals. In the human service field, this approach is generally known as a request for proposals (RFPs). The competitive bidding process in human services must rely both on relatively objective cost measures and on painfully subjective measures of agency expertise, program design, staff qualifications, and expected outcomes. The definitive manuscript on this topic is Harry Hatry and Eugene Durman's *Issues in Competitive Contracting for Social Services* (1984).

The competitive bidding process is typically lengthy and complex because it depends on a detailed description of the problem, a detailed written proposal, and a formal proposal review. The length of time for completing the entire process can exceed six months. A variation of the RFP process designed to reduce complexity without sacrificing the benefits of competitive bidding is the concept paper. Under this option, potential applicants are requested to submit a brief paper describing their conception of the services to be offered, the model to be used, and other relevant information. The funding agency can then negotiate with the most responsive applicants to select the programs to be funded.

Sole Source Contracting

Sole source contracting accommodates the selection of one or more service providers without the more open process of competitive bidding. It is used when there is a dearth of qualified providers, when one provider is demonstrably superior to all others, or when there is inadequate time for full competition. Sole source contracting is being used frequently in the family-based field to establish Homebuilders-type demonstrations. Those choosing this route argue that the model has demonstrated cost-effectiveness and that its reputation can help leverage greater support for family-centered policies. On the other hand, critics of this approach argue that "importing" the model impedes the development of community support, constituent support, pluralism of models, locally defined and locally responsive models, and more rigorous evaluation (Frankel, 1988; Wald, 1988).

There are a variety of other purchasing alternatives that employ characteristics of both competitive bidding and sole source contracting. Although competitive bidding can be a cumbersome, time-consuming, and expensive process, all other approaches expose government purchasers to allegations of favoritism. In selecting service providers, the public agency must be sensitive to assure appropriate minority participation. A related factor is the need to choose service providers with a demonstrated relatedness to the community where the service will be delivered.

CONTRACT CONTENT

The contract is the legally binding document that sets forth the conditions and responsibilities of both the government purchaser and the service provider. In its most useful form, the contract clearly defines the service and is clearly understood by both parties. In practice, it often becomes a "Christmas tree" from which to hang unnecessary or inappropriate ornaments. External forces often dictate the inclusion of extraneous requirements that clutter the contracts. The inevitable reliance on legalese and inclusion of irrelevant requirements can blur the original purpose of the contract. The ultimate result may be a cumbersome document irrelevant to service delivery.

Both public and private officials must remain constantly vigilant to the intrusion of stifling bureaucratic requirements on the contract process. There is a tendency by government to impose internal requirements onto private agencies. Requirements imposed under the banner of accountability have the effect of stripping private agencies of their flexibility and creativity. One example for family-based services is the availability of "flexible cash" for emergency dispersal to clients. Although flexible cash is programmatically desirable, it is almost impossible to implement within the constraints of governmental accounting controls.

REFERRAL PROCESS

Defining the client referral process is one of the major issues in developing contracts for family-based services and is discussed in the following section.

Target Population

The referral process becomes the focal point for implementing the decision about the recipients of these services. Some choices for family-based programs would be families with children in placement, families at imminent risk of placement, families "founded" for abuse and neglect, families "at risk" of abuse and neglect, families with troubled youth, or families with disabled children. In the original conceptualization of a family-based service initiative, the government funder will have designated who is to receive the service. With the definition of the client population, the governmental agency, as the referral agency, normally reviews individual client eligibility. The definition of the client population and screening of individual clients are of critical importance both to assure adherence to program design and also to aid program evaluation (Feldman, 1988). Although the primary responsibility for screening cases rests with the public agency, both the public and private workers must fully understand how the process will be conducted. Also, it is vitally important that the private agency worker have the ability to request a reevaluation of the appropriateness of a referral to further assure that the program is accepting families eligible for and amenable to services. Contracts with "no decline" clauses must allow flexibility to reconsider the appropriateness of clients referred to the program.

Referring for Services

In addition to defining the target population and screening individual clients, the governmental agency must consider how the referral process will be implemented. This implementation is of critical importance to family-based services because it must occur quickly, while the family is in crisis, in order to assure the protection of the children. There are several approaches.

GEOGRAPHIC FRANCHISE

The most common approach for processing referrals is for public agencies to assign full-service responsibility to a private agency for a specific geographic area. This approach provides ease of administration for the public agency and improved prediction of utilization for the private service provider. Although the actual referral process is made simple, the determination of the geographic area and choice of service provider can be complicated. Special care must be taken in defining the geographic area of service. Considerations include political boundaries, demographics, and existing patterns of service delivery.

LAISSEZ FAIRE

The other extreme approach is an open competition for referrals among approved service providers. In this approach, the referral worker assumes the role of a purchasing agent. The decision to refer to a particular provider is ideally based on the provider's performance (i.e., cost efficiency, responsiveness, effectiveness). However, in the absence of specific criteria, the referral process can deteriorate into an exercise of inappropriate influence. The authors would discourage the use of a laissez faire referral process for family-based services. This approach places unnecessary pressure on the referral worker and can subvert goals of securing the most appropriate services for each eligible family.

ROTATING REFERRAL

When there are multiple service providers within a geographic area, the pressure on the referral agent can be reduced by mandating the systematic referral of clients on a rotating basis. Under this approach, a well-defined process is implemented to assure that each service provider receives an equal number of referrals. In the most "mechanized" process, the referral is automatically made to the next service provider "in line." The referral is made regardless of whether there is a good match between the service provider and the client. A less ritualistic approach provides some discretion to the referral agent, with the assurance that each provider receives the same number of referrals during a month. Regardless of the approach chosen, the rotating referral process reduces the competition among service providers and alleviates much of the pressure on referral workers, but it also limits their ability to choose the "best" provider.

CLIENT CHOICE

Throughout most fields of human services, there is increasing policy attention to the inclusion of the client in the choice of a service provider. Client choice is thought to foster personal dignity and make real the concept of "empowering families." Certainly these are desirable objectives. However, it is doubtful that resistive families in the midst of a serious crisis can act as informed consumers. This may not be a realistic alternative referral mechanism for family-based services.

MONITORING

The final stage in the contracting process is monitoring, which provides the feedback loop regarding how the contractors are performing. The primary purpose of monitoring is contract compliance—that is, did the service provider do what was intended? The focus of monitoring is typically "process" and "output" program characteristics.

Monitoring is different from but related to program evaluation, which addresses the questions of program effectiveness—did the program work, with whom, why, and with what policy implications? Monitoring more modestly provides the immediate feedback on "how the program is doing"—is the program being implemented according to plan? It provides valuable information that may reveal the need to make changes in the program. It also provides data useful in evaluation. Ideally, family-based services purchased from the private sector would be subject to both monitoring and evaluation. More of both are critically needed to build the empirical base of support for family-based services.

Monitoring most typically includes periodic review of the following performance measures:

☐ Staffing: staff qualifications, agency retention or turnover.

☐ Quantity of services: the number of clients served, units of services provided, length of the service.

☐ Workload measures: client-staff ratios, percentage of direct service workers' time actually used in direct contacts with clients.

☐ Actual versus budgeted program costs: most often displayed as comparison between these two costs. Cost analysis requires a sophisticated understanding of the performance of private agencies (Yuan, 1988) and must be sensitive to unexpected variations caused by start-up and implementation problems.

☐ Unit cost: a derivative of costs and units of services. Unit cost analysis allows comparison between actual and budgeted costs as well as comparison among various contractors. Since both the units of service statistic and the cost per unit statistic are subject to error, the composite unit cost statistic must be subjected to thorough examination.

☐ Case costs: a derivate of cost and total cases served. Case costs (both budgeted and actual) are a popular statistic for family-based services, with the costs of such services comparing favorably with the costs of out-of-home placement.

☐ Miscellaneous: a variety of compliance issues, such as licensing and zoning requirements, affirmative action planning, and auditing and accounting requirements of other state agencies and the Internal Revenue Service. Although these miscellaneous compliance issues do not directly relate to service delivery, noncompliance can threaten the continuation of the program.

Monitoring, by its very nature, highlights the deviations between what was expected and what actually occurred. These deviations provide vital information regarding the program design and performance. Both the government funder and the private sector service provider must be prepared to determine the underlying cause of deviations in order to determine if corrective action is needed. Deviations between the planned and actual can be short-term anomalies or can reveal a systemic problem. They can be caused by overperformance or underperformance by the service provider or can result from an unrealistic service expectation. The contracting process must allow sufficient flexibility to accommodate ongoing modifications based on the results of monitoring.

Monitoring is usually conducted by external forces (i.e., the government funder monitoring a private agency). However, internal monitoring is a valuable resource for private agency administrators. The structured review of performance indicators by the private agency can lead to program improvements and can ease the stress caused by externally imposed monitoring.

Although monitoring is of vital importance, excessive monitoring can detract from service delivery, and excessive documentation requirements can stifle creativity. In the extreme, excessive attention to monitoring can undermine the purpose of family-based services. When monitors attribute all deviations from the plan to poor performance by the contractor, the focus of the service system will change to satisfying the monitor rather than provision of effective services.

Finance

A major advantage in purchasing family-based services is their affordability: family-based services have lower case costs than placement services, and purchased services tend to have lower costs than services provided directly. Nevertheless, despite past promises that family-based services could be "self-financing" (supported through avoided foster care costs) if targeted correctly (D. Nelson, 1988), and despite the hopes of Reaganomics that the private sector would finance services that historically had been government's responsibility (Kimmich, Gutowski, & Salamon, 1985), finding funds for family-based services remains a major problem in implementing service systems.

Before examination of current state and county strategies to secure adequate funding support for family-based service systems, examination of the limits of these two seemingly promising ideas is warranted.

SELF-FINANCING

This idea is based on one fact and one premise—that the case cost of family-based services, a national average of about $2,500 (S. Smith, 1990b; Tyler, 1990), is lower than the case cost of placement services, and that family-based services can target children who would otherwise have been placed outside the home but who can be effectively protected with this new service (D. Nelson, 1988). The targeting premise is the product of research on the placement-prevention success rates of family-based services (K. Nelson, Landsman, & Deutelbaum, 1990); namely, that a high percentage of families considered to be at imminent risk of child placement remain intact one or more years after receiving family-based services.

When subjected to experimental design, however, family-based services have not demonstrated lower child placement rates than the control condition after one year (Feldman, 1990; McDonald & Associates, 1990; Mitchell, Tovar, & Knitzer, 1989; Schuerman, Rzepnicki, & Littell, 1990). In fact, in all but one of these studies, the placement rates of experimental and control groups were roughly equivalent during and immediately after the service period. The New Jersey study (Feldman, 1990) found differences up to nine months following the completion of services.

These studies raise several possibilities that have implications for self-financing claims. The first is that the program studies are not vigilantly targeting families who would actually otherwise face child placement. To the extent that this is true, it would also likely be true of the programs whose high "success" rates fueled policy interest in the field in the first place. In other words, it is possible that family-based services have never served large proportions of families who otherwise would have had child placements. Improved targeting by program planners would likely yield lower success rates and lower foster care cost savings projections.

But the second possibility raised by the experimental design studies is that proponents of the Adoption Assistance and Child Welfare Act of 1980 were inaccurate when they determined that there was a large pool of families whose children were "unnecessarily" placed in foster care for lack of stronger systems of family-based services. If this is true, workers may be taking liberties with the concepts of "imminent risk" and "widening the net" in order to keep family-based services programs operating at full capacity (Schuerman et al., 1990). The implications for "self-financing" are the same, although the reasons are different; in this case, the dearth of unnecessary foster care placements makes the potential for avoiding foster care costs extremely limited.

The New Jersey study (Feldman, 1990) suggests that continued, or at least episodic, service support for families who have completed intensive family-based services might reduce subsequent placement rates. Of course, such continuing support has a price tag that would reduce—or even eliminate—the difference in case costs between family-based services and placement services.

Finally, initial case cost estimates and cost-avoidance projections came from sites that served low proportions of substance-abusing, homeless, or ghetto-dwelling poor families. Our projections of estimated costs and benefits of providing family-based services, rather than placing children, clearly need to better differentiate the service needs of the target populations. For some difficult service problems, family-based services might well be at least as costly as placement services but may still be the preferred treatment option. We caution against centering the policy "case" for family-based services on the self-financing promise.

PRIVATE FINANCING

We know of no systematic study of private sector support for the operations of family-based services. A recent survey by the National Conference of State Legislatures found minimal private sector support for family preservation services (brief, intensive, crisis intervention); private funds that were available were typically earmarked for program start-up (S. Smith, 1991). Family First providers in Illinois supplement Department of Children and Family Services contractual dollars with private funds, such as those received from the United Way and individual contributions, and with in-kind contributions of food and clothing. Foundations and corporations in Illinois, and likely in the rest of the country as well, tend not to support core program operations; they see their role more in terms of strengthening public policy support or in supporting innovation. Certainly private sector resources can provide supplemental funding of some private agency activities; emergency food, clothing, and shelter are typically supported by private sector donations in Illinois programs. But the private sector just as certainly cannot be relied upon as a major source of funds for cash-strapped state departments seeking creative financing strategies to support family-based services (Kimmich et al., 1985).

CURRENT FINANCE STRATEGIES

Most states are currently financing family-based services largely with state general revenue funds (Beck, 1990; S. Smith, 1990a). Efforts to strengthen or expand services focus on one or more of the following three options: reallocating existing child welfare resources, increasing general revenue support, and increasing federal government support. We should emphasize that data on finance and on the outcomes of different finance strategies are severely lacking in the family-based service field and that the following information is largely gleaned from expert opinion.

REALLOCATION STRATEGIES

Georgia, Iowa, Kentucky, New York, Tennessee, Texas, and West Virginia have passed legislation authorizing the financing of family preservation services initially from foster care dollars (S. Smith, 1990b). Minnesota, Pennsylvania, Colorado, and California have developed policy incentives in state funding of county-delivered service systems to expand family-based services and limit placement services. The incentives include carrots, such as dollars for family-based services, and sticks, such as requiring counties to put up the match for federal Title IV-E funds. In most states, foster care placements have risen along with the increased availability of family-based services. The projected additional increase in foster placements had the family-based services *not* been funded is the basis of the argument for continuing public investment in these services. Iowa and Michigan have successfully used trend analysis to secure funds for family preservation services (S. Smith, 1991).

Iowa, with technical assistance from the Center for Social Policy and the National Conference of State Legislatures, is experimenting with decategorizing child welfare funds as a means of getting services delivered more flexibly and efficiently, and as a means of expanding family preservation services. The experiment is too young to determine how well these objectives are being achieved.

INCREASED GENERAL REVENUE FUNDING

This is presently the most commonly used financing mechanism (Beck, 1990; S. Smith, 1990a, 1990b). Some states, among them Iowa, Maryland, Michigan, and Vermont, have secured general revenue funds to start up family-based service systems on the strength of arguments that the system would limit growth rates in foster care. States have been aided by new statutes that have provided for family-based service systems and by new appropriations for family-based services (S. Smith, 1990b).

INCREASED FEDERAL FUNDING

With many states experiencing severe financial crises, attention is increasingly turning to strategies to tap federal program support to finance family-based services. The following strategies are among the options available to states:

1. *Increase Title IV-E Foster Care Maintenance claims, and use the state money freed up from foster care maintenance to support family-based services.* This is the strategy Illinois used to begin funding its Families First program. The major limitation of the strategy is that some state child welfare agencies are not able to reinvest IV-E receipts because they are returned directly to the state's general revenue fund. If this obstacle can be overcome, the next limitation is that other pressing needs—such as needs for more caseworkers or for emergency shelter services—compete with family-based services for the use of the funds.

2. *Request Title IV-E administrative reimbursement for certain family-based services, such as case management, delivered to eligible families.* Kentucky and Tennessee are expanding funds for family-based services through this source (Allen, 1990).

3. *Use Title IV-B funds to support family-based services.* This is currently a strategy of limited use because of the small size of the program, even though states may elect to transfer unexpended Title IV-E funds to their Title IV-B programs. Several bills were introduced in Congress in 1990 to expand the Title IV-B program and to give states more flexibility in their use of IV-E and IV-B funds (Allen, 1990). Such efforts culminated in legislation providing for the Family Preservation and Support Services Initiative in 1993 (see number 6 below).

4. *Capture additional Medicaid funds for family-based services through the Early Periodic Screening, Diagnosis and Treatment (EPSDT) program.* 1990 Omnibus Budget Reconciliation Act (OBRA) amendments broadened eligibility for this program and required the delivery of any services, including parenting and mental health services, indicated through an EPSDT evaluation. The major barrier to child welfare agencies' accessing funds through this program is, of course, the ability of the state—and the willingness of the state agency that administers EPSDT—to contribute the state's share of Medicaid costs. In Illinois, for instance, the fierce and competing demands for the state's investment in Medicaid make this an unlikely new source of support for child welfare services.

5. *Capture more Medicaid funds through the Medicaid Clinic Option (MCO).* The MCO provides options for states to certify outpatient clinics and non-physicians to claim Medicaid reimbursement. The MCO is presently used by few states to fund family-based services, and those that do use the

193

option are providing family-based services through the mental health, not the child welfare, system (Beck, 1990). In Illinois, MCO is a more promising finance strategy than EPSDT, because the Department of Mental Health has shown unusual flexibility in certifying child welfare agencies and professionals.

6. Use funds made available through the Family Preservation and Support Services Initiative. This legislation, contained in the Omnibus Budget Reconciliation Act of 1993, provides major federal support for preventive services to support families, and also for family preservation services for at-risk families (U.S. Department of Health & Human Services, 1994, pp. 4–5). Direct support to states and Indian tribes increases from $60 million in federal fiscal year 1994 to $225 million in fiscal year 1998 (P.L. 103-66). This legislation in part attempts to remedy a paradox in the Adoption Assistance and Child Welfare Act of 1980: although that law sought to encourage family preservation and reunification, its federal funding was directed almost entirely toward reimbursement of the cost of foster care.

Family Preservation and Support Services Initiative funds are largely reserved for direct services, but planning is a significant priority. States must complete a comprehensive, inclusive planning process to access direct service funds under the Initiative; they may use up to $1 million in Initiative funds to undertake that process.

While providing much needed support for family-centered services, the Initiative is also a harbinger of further reforms in federal programs. There are three discernible themes:

□ consolidation of funding initiatives
□ coordination among federal programs
□ increased expectations for comprehensive planning

Evaluation

The list of good reasons not to fund an external evaluation (i.e., performed by neither the purchasing nor providing agency) is a long one. Evaluation is expensive. Professional researchers often do not understand the realities of the practice arena. Professional researchers are often more interested in methodological rigor than they are in the usefulness of their findings to the service delivery field. Practitioners find the time required to participate in formal evaluation as burdensome. Dollars and hours spent on evaluation could otherwise be invested in direct services to clients. And so on.

Nevertheless, we strongly urge readers to include external evaluation in their purchase of family-based service systems. Although there is accumulating evidence that family-based services can effectively keep many families together, that evidence is still, nevertheless, quite thin (Feldman, 1990; Frankel, 1988; Mitchell et al., 1989; K. Nelson et al., 1990; McDonald & Associates, 1990). We need to learn much, much more about which family-based services seem to work best, with whom, under what circumstances, and in which community and service system contexts. For purchasers, providers, and policymakers alike, evaluations of program implementation and program outcome are essential to refine practice, design service delivery systems, and secure political support for family-based services.

Like direct services, external evaluators can be selected through competitive bidding or through modified competitive bidding processes such as concept paper submission. Like purchase of direct services, the criteria for selection of an evaluator should be based on service system goals; that is, who can best give the evaluative information that would help implement, expand, and improve the system of services? We thus emphasize that responsibility for framing the research questions is largely that of the purchaser, aided, of course, by the service providers. The abrogation of this responsibility to the researcher is, we believe, one reason for expensive, rigorous studies that collect dust because they do not address implementation realities. In addition to framing the research questions, the purchaser can assure a practical, useful evaluation product by requesting process-focused as well as outcome-focused research, by requiring the evaluator to work closely with government and private agency representatives, and by selecting an evaluator who has practice-based research experience.

Conclusions

How can we make providers of family-based services more accountable without restricting the flexibility that they must have in order to provide the kinds and amounts of service appropriate to each family's needs?

This question is often at the heart of the decision whether to purchase family-based services or provide them directly (Kramer, 1985). In the main, purchasing services has the relative advantage when flexibility concerns are paramount, and providing services directly has the advantage of accountability. However, purchase systems can be accountable, and public provision systems, especially when bureaucracies are decentralized and unions are cooperative or absent, can support flexible service provision. We have urged readers, whenever possible, to make the purchase-versus-provide decision on the basis of careful examination of the relative importance of various service system goals. More typically, this choice has been made on the basis of ideology (the unsubstantiated belief that one system is inherently better than the other) or history (our state is a "private agency" or a "public agency" state).

The question of flexibility versus accountability is also at the heart of decisions about how to purchase family-based services, once the decision to purchase rather than provide has been made. At one extreme, grants-in-aid funds come with few strings attached and thus promote flexibility. However, in an era of great concern for efficiency and for conservation of increasingly scarce human service dollars, this system is rapidly becoming an anachronism. At the other extreme, purchase of "billable" units of family-based services maintains tight accountability for kinds and amounts of services, but it has so severely restricted provider flexibility in some jurisdictions that home-based services have not been able to survive. The inherent limitations in both of these systems have generated interest in exploring the potential of other funding mechanisms such as performance-based contracting (especially where the performance measures focus on outcomes) and capitation systems (agreed upon, capped amounts allotted to achieve service or service system goals). There are several major issues that these emerging systems must resolve:

1. Can funding incentives be focused on the achievement of service outcomes and, at the same time, foster the achievement of high service standards with respect to inputs, processes, and outputs?
2. If funding incentives are based on the successful achievement of outcomes, how can creaming (accepting only families deemed amenable to treatment) and goal displacement (keeping children in unsafe homes) be prevented?
3. Can contracting mechanisms be designed that assure that families will receive the quantity and quality of services appropriate to their needs? In other words, how do we promote efficient use of scarce dollars and not provide incentives that are too "cheap"?
4. Can funding interest in supporting "tried and true" programs be balanced

with the need to stimulate new program development (including paying start-up costs) among new—especially minority—program providers?

The limitations of traditional purchase of service mechanisms in supporting systems of family-based services are pressing us to explore new options. As we argue in this chapter, decisions that we make about how to purchase family-based services will influence the shape of the service delivery system itself. Because family-based services are delivered in life-threatening circumstances, our decisions about how to purchase them must be carefully made. A systematic examination of the effectiveness of different options for the purchase of service is thus paramount.

References

Adoption Assistance and Child Welfare Act of 1980, 42 U.S.C. § 670.

Allen, M. L. (1990). Personal communication with Sandra O'Donnell, 17 December 1990. (Allen is the director of child welfare programs at the Children's Defense Fund, Washington DC.)

Beck, D. (1990). Personal communication with Sandra O'Donnell, December 1990. (Beck is with the child welfare division of the Center for the Study of Social Policy, Washington DC.)

Center for the Study of Social Policy. (1989, June). *Purchasing family preservation: Methods of payment that encourage high quality programs* (Working paper series). Washington DC: Author.

Family Preservation Act of 1987 (Ill. Rev. Stat., 23, Sect 2057, 4).

Farrow, F., & Duva, J. (1987). Personal communication (10/26/87).

Feldman, L. (1988). Target population definition. In Y. Y. Yuan and M. Rivest (Eds.), *Evaluation resources for family preservation services*. Alexandria VA: Center for the Support of Children.

Feldman, L. (1990). *Evaluating the impact of family preservation services in New Jersey.* Trenton: New Jersey Division of Youth and Family Services.

Frankel, H. (1988). Family-centered, home-based services in child protection: A review of the research. *Social Service Review, 62*(1), 137–157.

Hansmann, H. (1980). The role of non-profit enterprise. *Yale Law Journal, 89*(5), 835–901.

Hatry, H. P., & Durman, E. (1984). *Issues in competitive contracting for social services* (Executive Summary). Washington DC: Urban Institute.

Hutchinson, J., & Nelson, K. (1985, Summer). A topology of service needs for family-centered services. *Prevention Report*. Iowa City: University of Iowa, National Resource Center on Family Based Services.

Kettner, P. M., & Martin, L. L. (1987). *Purchase of service contracting*. Newbury Park CA: Sage Publications.

Kimmich, M., Gutowski, M., & Salamon, L. (1985). *Child serving nonprofit organizations in an era of government retrenchment*. Washington DC: Urban Institute.

Kramer, R. M. (1982). From volunteerism to vendorism: An organizational perspective on contracting (PONPO Working Paper No. 54). New Haven: Yale University, Institute for Social and Policy Studies.

Kramer, R. M. (1985). The voluntary agency in a mixed economy: Dilemmas at entrepreneurialism and vendorism (PONPO Working Paper No. 85). New Haven: Yale University, Institute for Social and Policy Studies.

Kramer, R. M., & Grossman, B. (1987). Contracting for social services: Process management and resource dependencies. *Social Service Review, 61*(1), 32–55.

McDonald, W. R., & Associates. (1990). *Evaluation of AB 1562 In-Home Care Demonstration Projects* (2 vols.). (Available from Author, Sacramento CA.)

Mitchell, C., Tovar, P., & Knitzer, J. (1989). *The Bronx Homebuilders Program: An evaluation of the first 45 families*. New York: Bank Street College of Education.

Moe, R. C. (1987). Exploring the limits of privatization. *Public Administration Review, 47*, 453–459.

National Resource Center on Family Based Services. (1987). *Annotated directory of selected family-based service programs*. Iowa City: University of Iowa, Author.

Nelson, D. (1988). *Recognizing and realizing the potential of "family preservation."* Unpublished manuscript. Washington DC: Center for the Study of Social Policy.

Nelson, K., Landsman, M., & Deutelbaum, W. (1990). Three models of family-centered placement prevention services. *Child Welfare, 69*(1), 3–21.

Omnibus Budget Reconciliation Act of 1993, P.L. 103-66; 45 C.F.R. 92.

Pecora, P., Kinney, J., Mitchell, L., & Tolley, G. (1980). Selecting an agency auspice for family preservation services. *Social Service Review, 64*(2), 288–307.

Schuerman, J., Rzepnicki, T., & Littell, J. (1990, November). *Evaluation of the Illinois Department of Children and Family Services' Family First Initiative: Progress report*. Chicago: University of Chicago, Chapin Hall Center for Children.

Smith, R. S. (1989). The changing politics of child welfare services: New roles for the government and the nonprofit sectors. *Child Welfare, 68*(3), 289–299.

Smith, S. (1990a). Personal communication with Sandra O'Donnell, 24 December

1990. (Smith is manager of the Children, Youth and Families program at the National Conference of State Legislatures, Denver CO.)

Smith, S. (1990b). *Family preservation services: State legislators' initiatives.* Washington DC: National Conference of State Legislatures.

Smith, S. (1991). Personal communication with Sandra O'Donnell, 11 January 1991.

Smits, H. L. (1984). Incentives in case-mix measures for long-term care. *Health Care Financing Review, 6*(2), 53–59.

Social Security Act Title XX, 42 U.S.C.A. § 1397; 45 C.F.R. 96.

Stehno, S. M. (1987). [Purchase of Family Based Services]. Unpublished memo, draft paper, and interview data available from the author.

Tyler, M. (1990, Fall). State survey on placement prevention and family reunification programs. *Prevention Report, 7.*

U.S. Department of Health and Human Services, Administration on Children, Youth, and Families. (1994, January 1). *Program instructions.* Washington DC: Author.

Wald, M. (1988). Family preservation: Are we moving too fast? *Public Welfare, 46*(3), 33–46.

Wedel, K. R., & Colston, S. W. (1988). Performance contracting for human services: Issues & suggestions. *Administration in Social Work, 12*(1), 73–87.

Yuan, Y. Y. (1988). Cost analysis. In Y. Y. Yuan & M. Rivest (Eds.), *Evaluation resources for family preservation services.* Alexandria VA: Center for the Support of Children.

9

Concluding Remarks

Ira M. Schwartz

Although the concept of working with troubled and troubling children and families in their own homes is not a new idea (see chapter 1 by Wells), it is one that is gaining in popularity. In fact, home-based services are mushrooming throughout the country. With the recent enactment of the federal Omnibus Budget Reconciliation Act of 1993 and the availability of nearly $1 billion in federal funds for family preservation and family support services during the next few years, these programs will enjoy continued support well into the future.

Child welfare professionals, juvenile justice officials, mental health professionals, child advocates, and elected public officials at the local, state, and national levels have been advocating more preventive-oriented services for decades. Their voices have finally been heard.

In enacting the Omnibus Budget Reconciliation Act of 1993, Congress wisely mandated the Secretary of the Department of Health and Human Services to take steps ensuring that family preservation and family support programs are carefully evaluated (Omnibus Budget Reconciliation Act of 1993). Despite the broad support these programs enjoy from professionals and child advocates, the early claims of success in preventing placements, particularly in cases of child abuse and neglect, were based upon studies that were flawed or information that was largely anecdotal. More recent studies with rigorous designs suggest that we should be more cautious and lower our expectations until we learn more about the potential of these programs. They may help provide services families desperately need, but they may not be as effective with respect to preventing placements as many would hope and that some have claimed.

There is some evidence that delinquent youth, including youth who have committed serious offenses and may be repeaters, can be worked with and managed in their own homes without compromising public safety (see chapter 5 by Henggeler and Bourduin and chapter 6 by Butts and Barton). This is encouraging, especially when there are growing concerns about the juvenile crime problem. While more needs to be known about how to increase our effectiveness in working with juvenile offenders in their own homes, there is a foundation upon which to build and reason for optimism. Further experimentation and research in this area could lead to more informed public policy and a better use of local, state, and federal juvenile crime-fighting dollars.

There is also reason to believe that intensive home-based services may be effective in preventing costly residential placements, particularly in inpatient psychiatric settings and for treatment in group homes and residential treatment centers (AuClaire & Schwartz, 1987; Schwartz & Wernert, in press). Inpatient psychiatric care and residential treatment for children and adolescents are costly services. While some children and adolescents need such services, many, if not most, do not. Inpatient treatment and other forms of residential care represent a prime target for policymakers and professionals interested in providing more cost-effective services and in redirecting financial resources.

The biggest push for intensive home-based services is in the child welfare arena involving cases of child abuse and neglect. Ironically, this is the area where the findings from studies with rigorous designs are raising the most serious questions about their impact and potential (see chapter 7 by Schwartz). In addition, questions about the appropriateness of family preservation services are beginning to surface in the media and within the child advocacy community itself (Charen, Howard, & Kresnak, 1993; Murphy, 1993).

One of the basic issues that is beginning to emerge centers on the question of the primary mission of the child welfare system. Is the child welfare system's primary mission to protect children, to preserve families, or both? Patrick Murphy, the Public Guardian in Chicago and respected child advocate, maintains that family preservation services are often used to try to preserve families at the expense of children. Murphy even suggests that such programs reward families with services for committing what are essentially criminal acts against their children (Murphy, 1993). There are also serious questions about the capability of the child welfare system to provide the full array of services needed to keep families intact and about the wisdom of saddling the child welfare system with the responsibility of preserving families when the large and growing number of lawsuits against public child welfare agencies suggests that they are failing in their fundamental mission to protect and properly care for the children placed in their custody.

The prognosis for intensive home-based services is good, at least in the short term. The support for family preservation services on the part of the federal government ensures that these services will expand significantly throughout the rest of this decade. It is hoped that the federal government's emphasis on encouraging careful studies of such services will generate the policy-relevant data that are so desperately needed. In fact, the long-term survival of family preservation services may very well hinge on the quality of research that is done and findings that are credible.

References

AuClaire, P., & Schwartz, I. (1987). *Home-based services as an alternative to placement for adolescents and their families: A follow-up study of placement utilization.* Minneapolis: University of Minnesota, Center for the Study of Youth Policy, Hubert H. Humphrey Institute of Public Affairs.

Charen, M., Howard, B., & Kresnak, J. (1993, May). *Detroit Free Press.*

Murphy, P. T. (1993, June 19). Letter to George Bush.

Omnibus Budget Reconciliation Act of 1993, P.L. 103-66; 45 C.F.R. 92.

Schwartz, I. M., & Wernert, T. (1993). Reducing psychiatric hospitalization for children and adolescents in Toledo, Ohio. *Community Alternatives, 5*(2), 71–79.

The Contributors

Philip AuClaire (Ph.D., Bryn Mawr), formerly a faculty member of the University of Minnesota School of Social Work, is currently a senior planner and project director with the Hennepin County (Minnesota) Children and Family Services Department, where he directs a child abuse prevention research and demonstration project and a demonstration project serving chronically neglectful child protective service clients. Dr. AuClaire is a member of the Editorial Board of *Social Work*.

William H. Barton is an associate professor in the School of Social Work at Indiana University, Indianapolis. He received his doctorate in Social Work and Psychology from the University of Michigan in 1985. For nearly twenty years he has conducted survey research, program evaluation, policy analysis, and training in juvenile justice. He directed an evaluation of juvenile intensive probation programs in Detroit, and, as a research associate with the Center for the Study of Youth Policy at the University of Michigan from 1988 to 1992, he was involved in several projects with juvenile justice agencies in several states. Current projects include an evaluation of youth assistance programs in Michigan, the development of objective dispositional guidelines for juveniles in New Hampshire, and a study of the feasibility of computer-assisted interviewing for child victims of sexual abuse. He has published extensively and presented papers at numerous conferences.

Charles M. Borduin is a professor of Psychology at the University of Missouri–Columbia and director of the Missouri Delinquency Project. He received his doctorate in clinical psychology from Memphis State University and interned at Rutgers Medical School. His research interests include adolescent sexual offending, family violence, and the development and refinement of a multisystemic treatment approach for serious juvenile offenders. Dr. Borduin has published extensively in the areas of juvenile delinquency and adolescent psychopathology, and he has served as a consultant to numerous state and federal agencies on the reform of children's mental health services.

Bro. Francis Boylan, C.S.C., began working at Boysville of Michigan, Inc., in 1967. In 1975 he assumed the position of Executive Director. He joined the Brothers of the Congregation of the Holy Cross in 1962; received a Bachelor's degree from St. Edward's University in Austin, Texas, in 1966; and completed his master's degree in Social Work at the University of Michigan in Ann Arbor in 1972. Annually, Boysville cares for over 1,000 youth and families, with an operation budget of $26 million. The agency operates three residential treatment centers in Michigan and one in Ohio; eight group homes in Michigan; a number of non-secure and staff-secure detention and assessment centers throughout Michigan; and nonresidential programs including Specialized Foster Care, Supervised Independent Living, Day Treatment, In-home Family Treatment, and Family Preservation programs.

Jeffrey A. Butts is a senior research associate at the National Center for Juvenile Justice (NCJJ) in Pittsburgh, Pennsylvania, where he directs the Delays in Juvenile Justice Sanctions project and manages the National Juvenile Court Data Archive, both funded by the Office of Juvenile Justice and Delinquency Prevention within the U.S. Department of Justice. Prior to joining NCJJ in 1991, Dr. Butts was a research assistant at the University of Michigan's Center for the Study of Youth Policy. He has worked in the field of youth services for fifteen years, including service delivery positions with a local juvenile court and a state child welfare agency. He holds a Ph.D. in Social Work and Sociology from the University of Michigan and an M.S.W. in Social Planning and Administration from Portland State University in Oregon.

Ronald D. Davidson is the administrator of the Office of Planning and Training. Prior to appointment to his current position in 1991, Mr. Davidson served in a variety of policy and management positions within DCFS, including deputy director of the Division of Policy and Plans, private agency liaison, and associate deputy director in the Division of Management and Budget. Before joining DCFS in 1981, Mr. Davidson worked in policy development and administrative positions in the Department of Mental Health and Developmental Disabilities. He earned his bachelor's degree from Arizona State University and a master's degree from the University of Chicago. Throughout his career, Mr. Davidson has been deeply involved in the policy development, program design, and financial management of public agency funding of services in the private sector.

Kelly L. Dittmar received a bachelor's degree from Whitman College in 1982 and a master's degree from the University of Washington in 1985, where she was selected as an M. L. Schwartz Scholar in the Department of History. With a background in liberal arts and work-related experience in communications, editing, and grant-writing, Ms. Dittmar pursues writing and editing projects in a variety of fields including history and social services. Published articles related to this volume include "Family Preservation: The Homebuilders Model" in the *Children Youth and Family Services Quarterly* (1991) and "Keeping Families Together: The Homebuilders Model" in *Children Today* (1990).

Robert Halpern is a professor at the Erikson Institute for Advanced Study of Child Development. His research and writing focus on the effects of poverty on children and families, the role of supportive human services in poor children's and families' lives, and characteristics of effective welfare work approaches. He is author (with Mary Larner and Oscar Harkavy) of *Fair Start for Children: Lessons from Seven Demonstration Projects*, published by Yale University Press, and he has just finished a book on the history of neighborhood-based initiatives to address poverty in the United States, to be published by Columbia University Press.

Scott W. Henggeler is a professor of Psychiatry and Behavioral Sciences and director of the Family Services Research Center at the Medical University of South Carolina. He has published several books and more than 125 journal articles and book chapters. Much of Dr. Henggeler's research concerns serious antisocial behavior in adolescents and the development of family-based treatments that are clinically effective and cost-effective. Currently, Dr. Henggeler is conducting a NIDA-funded evaluation of the effectiveness of multisystemic therapy with substance-abusing delinquents, as well as a multisite study of violent and chronic delinquents and an evaluation of a family-based alternative to psychiatric hospitalization of youth in crisis, both funded by NIMH.

Dr. Jill Kinney is a cofounder of the internationally recognized Homebuilders model of family preservation, and a cofounder and former executive director of Homebuilders' parent organization, Behavioral Sciences Institute. Since 1990, Dr. Kinney has concentrated on helping drug-affected families and has headed a team effort dedicated to developing training and models for blending drug and alcohol treatment with family preservation services. She has written and cowritten numerous books and articles, including *Keeping Families Together* and *Reaching High-Risk Families*. Dr. Kinney has a B.S. with Honors from the University of Washington, and received M.S. and Ph.D. degrees in Psychology from Stanford University. She is currently director of Home Safe in Tacoma, Washington.

Paul Neitman has worked with Boysville for eighteen years. Beginning as a child care worker, he has also held positions at Boysville's Clinton Campus as an assistant residential coordinator, program manager, and clinical supervisor for group treatment services. For over two years he served as regional director for Boysville's Family and Community Support Region, which includes the agency's home-based services. He has been director of Program Development since November 1991, with responsibility for the agency's program design, development, and evaluation activities. Mr. Neitman received a bachelor's degree in Psychology from Miami University in Ohio and an M.S.W. from the University of Michigan. He is a board member and training cochair for the Michigan Home-Based Family Services Association.

Sandra O'Donnell is an associate professor of Public Administration at Roosevelt University in Chicago, where she coordinates the nonprofit management program and teaches nonprofit and research methods courses. Dr. O'Donnell also consults with local nonprofits in the areas of program design and evaluation. Her research interests focus on the effectiveness of grassroots community organizations in strengthening family life and policy. Dr. O'Donnell has nearly twenty years' experience in juvenile justice and child welfare. She earned her master's degree and doctorate from the University of Chicago's School of Social Services Administration.

Edward Overstreet is Boysville's codirector. He has been with the agency since 1967. He received a bachelor's degree from St. Edward's University in Austin, Texas, a master's degree in Education from Siena Heights College in Adrian, Michigan, and an M.S.W. from the University of Michigan–Ann Arbor. Mr. Overstreet is twice past president of both the Michigan Association of Children's Alliances and the Michigan Federation of Private Child and Family Agencies. He is active with a number of professional groups, including the Child Welfare League of America, the National Association of Homes for Children, and the Michigan Federation. He is also interested in public policy, particularly those areas that directly affect children and families.

Ira M. Schwartz is dean of the School of Social Work and director of the Center for the Study of Youth Policy (CSYP), University of Pennsylvania. He was professor and director of the CSYP at the University of Michigan's School of Social Work from 1987 until 1993. Between 1981 and 1986, Professor Schwartz was a senior fellow at the University of Minnesota's Hubert H. Humphrey Institute of Public Affairs. Professor Schwartz served as the administrator of the Office of Juvenile Justice and Delinquency Prevention, U.S. Department of Justice, between 1979 and 1981. Prior to that time, he directed criminal and juvenile justice agencies in the states of Illinois and Washington and worked extensively in both the public and private sectors.

Professor Schwartz has authored numerous articles on juvenile justice as well as *(In)Justice for Juveniles: Rethinking the Best Interest of the Child* and *Juvenile Justice and Public Policy: Toward a National Agenda.*

Elizabeth M. Tracy, Ph.D., LSW, is an associate professor of Social Work, teaching courses in direct social work practice methods and coordinating the school's concentration in children, youth, and families and the school social work certification program. Dr. Tracy is interested in social work models that support families and make use of natural helping networks. As a social worker, she has developed programs to strengthen community support systems and preserve families. She is a consultant on family preservation services and family-centered child welfare practice, providing training in social support assessment and intervention. She has served on the Executive Committee of the Ohio Association of Family Based Services and has facilitated the work of a National Family Preservation Working Group in developing a source book on family preservation teaching. Dr. Tracy also participated as an alcohol fellow under an NIAAA grant awarded to the school, pursuing clinical and research interests with local family-based programs around substance abuse issues in child welfare. She has published and presented workshops on child welfare and substance abuse.

Kathleen Wells (Ph.D., University of Colorado) is a social psychologist and an associate professor of Social Work at the Mandel School of Applied Social Sciences, Case Western Reserve University. Dr. Wells teaches research and mental health courses in the school's doctoral and master's degree programs. She is codirector of the Cuyahoga County Community Mental Health Research Institute and has developed a research program focusing on child mental health services within that framework. She has published papers concerned with mental health and welfare services for children and youths and the development of clinical research programs within agencies. In the area of family preservation, she coedited *Family Preservation Services: Research and Evaluation* and has published several papers.

James K. Whittaker is a professor of social work at the University of Washington and a member of the National Research Advisory Committee, Boysville of Michigan. Dr. Whittaker's research interests lie in the full continuum of child and family service from prevention through out-of-home care. A frequent contributor to the professional literature, he is author, coauthor, or coeditor of seven books and over seventy-five articles on child, youth, and family service, including *The Child Welfare Challenge: Policy Practice and Research* (1992, with Pecora, Maluccio, Barth, and Plotnick), *Reaching High Risk Families: Intensive Family Preservation in Human Services* (1990, with Kinney, Tracy, and Booth), *Social Treatment*, 2d ed. (1989, with Tracy), and *Social Support Networks: Informal Helping in Human Services* (1983, with Garbarino and Associates). Dr. Whittaker's work has been translated into German, Dutch, Danish, Korean, and Japanese. His present research includes developmental testing of social support assessment and intervention for primary caregivers in high-risk families.

Author Index

Subject Index

In the Child, Youth, and Family Services series

Big World, Small Screen:
The Role of Television in American Society
By Aletha C. Huston, Edward Donnerstein, Halford Fairchild,
Norma D. Feshbach, Phyllis A. Katz, John P. Murray,
Eli A. Rubinstein, Brian L. Wilcox, and Diana Zuckerman

Home-Based Services for Troubled Children
Edited by Ira M. Schwartz and Philip AuClaire

Preventing Child Sexual Abuse: Sharing the Responsibility
By Sandy K. Wurtele and Cindy L. Miller-Perrin